U.S. Trade Policy and Agricultural Exports

U.S. Trade Policy

Iowa State University Center
for Agricultural and Rural Development

and Agricultural Exports

THE IOWA STATE UNIVERSITY PRESS

Ames, Iowa

1973

Organizational Committee: EARL O. HEADY, ROGER W. HEXEM, LEO V. MAYER, KEITH ROGERS, AND W. G. STUCKY

Volume Editor: ELIZABETH S. FERGUSON

Other publications of the Center for Agricultural and Rural Development are available from the Iowa State University Press as follows:

Future Farm Programs, 1972
Sociological Perspectives of Domestic Development, 1971
Benefits and Burdens of Rural Development: Some Public Policy Viewpoints, 1970
A North American Common Market, 1969
Food Goals, Future Structural Changes and Agricultural Policy: A National Basebook, 1969
Alternatives for Balancing World Food Production Needs, 1967
Roots of the Farm Problem, 1965
Economic Development of Agriculture, 1965
Family Mobility in Our Dynamic Society, 1965
Farmers in the Market Economy, 1964
Our Changing Rural Society: Perspectives and Trends (Developed by the Rural Sociological Society under editorship of James H. Copp), 1964
Farm Goals in Conflict: Family Farm, Income, Freedom, Security, 1963
Adjustments in Agriculture—A National Basebook, 1961

Composed and printed by
The Iowa State University Press

First edition, 1973

Library of Congress Cataloging in Publication Data

Main entry under title.

U. S. trade policy and agricultural exports.

At head of title: Iowa State University, Center for Agricultural and Rural Development.

Papers developed by persons participating in the U. S. Trade Policy and Agricultural Exports Conference sponsored by the Iowa State University Center for Agricultural and Rural Development.

Includes bibliographical references.

1. United States—Commercial policy—Congresses. 2. Produce trade—United States —Congresses.

I. Iowa. State University of Science and Technology, Ames. Center for Agricultural and Rural Development.

HF1455.U55   382'.0973   72-2786
ISBN 0-8138-1655-6

382.0973
458t

CONTENTS

117094

v

FOREWORD

WORLD TRADE has become one of the most important components of demand for U.S. farm products. Exports employ one of each five acres of the nation's cropland and one of each eight workers in the farm sector. The demand of domestic consumers is a somewhat "fixed component" of total demand and income of U.S. agriculture. Aside from rather "fixed variables" represented in domestic demand, the major variables affecting the welfare and income of America's commercial farmers are those of domestic farm policies and exports.

Trade in food products is, of course, important in the welfare and health of people. New technologies suggest that balance can be brought between world food supplies and demands over the next few decades. Whether this balance is attained rests in the hands of politicians and government administrators in countries of large populations and high birthrates. If these leaders default in the world responsibility which is clearly theirs, new farm technologies can only forestall disaster a few more decades. But supposing politicians and administrators of the countries involved are wise, responsible, and effective in constraining population growth, trade will still be an important element of balancing world food supplies and world food demands.

The focus of this volume is not on potential crises and solutions of world food problems. These facets of food supply and demand are under intense reevaluation in other studies and by other experts. Instead, this book evaluates U.S. trade and food exports in terms of their meaning to the nation's farm sector and food consumers. It evaluates the prospects broadly: the era of trade from which we have just emerged; the protectionism apparently emerging; and income distribution and curtailment of monopoly forces. It evaluates export and income potentials for different commodity groups under the potentials of various trade barriers and export potentials, and it allows a hearing of commodity groups whose prospects are dimmed under ongoing import magnitudes and trade restrictions of other countries.

Over the past three decades the United States and the rest of the world have moved nearer to widely expressed goals of broader and freer trade. However, the emergence of regional market entities with relaxed internal barriers but greater barriers for nonmember countries, and the unwillingness of some countries to reciprocate the relaxation of barriers afforded by others, threaten to bend earlier trade trends of the postwar period back in the direction of the 1920s. Patchwork policies of many countries to solve their balance of payments problems through direct and indirect constraints on imports provide further strength in these directions. Obviously these trends and prospects have important implications for the American farm sector.

The U.S. Trade Policy and Agricultural Exports Conference was organized accordingly—to review the present status of American agriculture with respect to export markets and to evaluate new international developments which affect trade. The important papers making up this book have been developed by persons participating in this conference sponsored by the Center for Agricultural and Rural Development of Iowa State University.

EARL O. HEADY

Director, Center for Agricultural and Rural Development

U.S. Trade Policy and Agricultural Exports

Fundamental Issues in Trade of Farm Commodities

Earl O. Heady

IMPORTANT SEGMENTS of farming and their representatives have come to recognize the economic importance of international trade in their income and welfare. And well they should, since most recent data show that exports consumed the product of one of each four crop-acres, represented 15 percent of total farm marketings, and employed one of each eight farm workers.

Domestic markets have highly restrained expansion possibilities. Income elasticities of demand are so low in the United States that further progress in per capita incomes promises little more food consumption per person. On the average, incomes are so high that further increments per capita will go almost entirely into nonfood goods and services, marketing services incorporated with food, and in shifts representing, to the consumer, quality upgrading of food intake. True, a fairly high proportion of low income families and ethnic groups can use a nutritionally upgraded diet. But this process cannot begin to absorb the large, immobilized, or potential capacity of American agriculture. Malnutrition in low income groups of the United States is more a function of vitamin deficiency and proportions of protein and carbohydrates than of weight or bulk of food intake. Correcting prevailing malnutrition would do little to absorb the underemployed land and labor of American agriculture.[1]

RESTRAINTS IN DOMESTIC MARKETS. Low income elasticities of demand for food mean that aggregate demand for the farm-produced portion can grow only at approximately the rate of the nation's population and export markets. In the absence of rapidly expanding markets

EARL O. HEADY is Distinguished Professor and Director, Center for Agricultural and Rural Development, Iowa State University.

in the form of government stockpiles and storage or exports, the low price elasticity of demand and the large underemployed production potential promise depressed prices and income each time the tempo of expansion in farm output exceeds the combined restraint of domestic population growth and exports. And this outlook will not soon change unless unexpected occurrences or policy changes take place. Such occurrences or changes could be the opening of large and continuous markets in China and Eastern Europe, or extreme environmental clamps on agriculture eliminating most modern inputs such as chemical fertilizers and pesticides, along with a diversion of irrigation water to almost entirely municipal and industrial alternatives.

Aside from a combination of unexpected events, recent projections indicate that U.S. farm supply capacity will still be large relative to domestic demand in another two and three decades. With a population of 300 million by the year 2000 and a continuation of trends in per capita food demand and farm productivity, the nation could still divert large chunks of its land and water resources from agriculture even though it doubled its farm exports and made no substantial substitution of simulated products for meat.[2]

REALISTIC EXPECTATIONS. Of course farmers and their leaders realistically expect these conditions to prevail over the next decade. But it has been only a half-dozen years since they were led to believe otherwise. Senior government administrators then in office but now out, and those then out but now in, made major pronouncements leading the agricultural sector to believe that the distress of world hunger and limited farm productivity would almost immediately and certainly in the next decade burden the U.S. farm industry with magnitude of demand rather than with size of supply. (Both "then" and "now" secretaries of agriculture made eloquent speeches indicating the imminence of a world food crisis and a need to step up production. As an indication of how suddenly and how far the pendulum can swing, one needs only to read recent literature on the subject.)[3] These notions were communicated by agricultural leaders, input suppliers, and trade interests perhaps more effectively than any other major expectations for agriculture to this time. However, the failure of this instant demand to appear, in combination with greater supplies forthcoming as USDA administrators with belief in their own speeches relaxed supply controls, brought the farm world back to reality in the late 1960s.

Farmers and their representatives in the 1970s have taken a more realistic view of the world market. For many of them, especially producers of feed grains and wheat, concern over trade has come to rest in resisting immediate and apparent export obstacles. They opposed the prolonged strike by dock workers in 1971–72 as a restraint on moving grain shipments into world markets. They favored and promoted direct government negotiations with Russia as a means to increase grain exports and reduce burdensome supplies resulting from heavily weighted expectations of corn blight and the relaxing of restraints on 1971 planting by the USDA. They opposed the surtax on exports which was included in the package of temporary economic measures preliminary to devaluation of the dollar in late 1971. They pressed for improved transportation facilities and for reduced inland rates so that farm commodities could move to ports more rapidly and at lower costs for a stronger competition in world markets. These actions and pressures by farmers and their representatives suggest broader and more sophisticated economic knowledge for a large sector of the farm public as they look to the future.

AGRICULTURAL IMPROVEMENT AND PROSPECTS. This view is more realistic than that communicated broadly to farmers by personnel of the public and private sector in the 1960s as they projected exhaustion of food production potential and pending starvation in developing countries. The food crisis could become reality in the long run, or at some time extending beyond the year 2000, but it is not imminent up to this time. And it need never be so if government administrators and politicians in the heavily populated developing countries lead their people to do something about population management. The leaders of developed countries really have very little control over the occurrence of this long-run prospect. Nor is it really their responsibility after they have, through food aid and investment in technical advance, bought a bit of time for leaders in developing countries to get themselves informed of the consequences of currently unconstrained trends in population growth and agricultural productivity.

The problems of world nutrition will never be solved through trade and exports developed on a foundation of persistently hungry people in less developed countries. It is increasingly obvious that the less developed countries do not plan it this way. Even if they have yet to come to grips with the population variable, they are making important progress in investments to stimulate more vigorous growth in food supplies. The momentum of agricultural improvement can be much more rapid than historically supposed even in developing countries. These possibilities are indicated in Table 1.1, which shows the high speed (at least relative to the rate of adoption of important innovations such as hybrid corn in Western countries) with which improved technologies and food supply might be augmented in the future.

While the overall rate of adoption of high yielding cereal varieties has greatly exceeded parallel varietal improvement in Western countries over the past fifty years, the potentials are not yet exhausted. For the countries included in Table 1.1 less than a third of their total wheat acreage had been planted to new varieties by the 1970–71 crop year, and

TABLE 1.1. Numbers of Acres Planted to High Yielding Varieties over a Six-Year Period

Crop Year	Wheat	Rice
1965/66	22,900	17,700
1966/67	1,542,200	2,505,200
1967/68	10,189,000	6,487,100
1968/69	19,815,400	11,620,300
1969/70	21,550,550	19,104,300
1970/71	25,255,500	25,293,500

SOURCE: Dana G. Dalrymple, *Imports and Plantings of High Yielding Varieties of Wheat and Rice in the Less Developed Nations*, USDA FEDR–14. Washington, 1972.
NOTE: Includes Afghanistan, India, Nepal, Pakistan, Iran, Iraq, Jordan, Lebanon, Syria, Turkey, Algeria, Morrocco, and Tunisia for wheat. Includes Ceylon, India, Nepal, Pakistan, Burma, Indonesia, Korea, Laos, Malaysia, Philippines, Thailand, and Vietnam for rice.

new varieties of rice used only about 10 percent of the total rice area. Even then, a landmark may have been attained in 1970–71 as India approached domestic self-sufficiency in cereals production, the Philippines extended exports, West Pakistan began looking for world wheat markets, and the combination of food aid from developed countries and enlarging food supplies of less developed countries began placing pressure on export markets and prices for third countries such as Thailand.

While failure of present leaders to inform their publics and implement population control could, even though unnecessarily, cause very long-run pressures of population on world food supplies, this is not the prospect for the majority of current farm operators in the United States. Their expectations are better geared to a market situation wherein supply will be large relative to demand, in terms of prices they consider acceptable. Any price and income improvement they can expect, aside from the interaction of supply and demand in the domestic market, will continue to come from national supply control programs and greater exports. This is certainly the outlook for more than the next two decades. Increasing the reliance on exports must come from commercial markets.

EXPECTATIONS IN COMMERCIAL EXPORTS. Through exports the greatest hope for current farm operators is in the commercial market. True, farm product exports through U.S. food aid programs created relief for domestic marketings, public storage costs, and the upper bounds on production for over a decade. The importance of these programs is indicated by the fact that publicly assisted exports during the 1960s rose to as much as 44 percent of the wheat crop, 22 percent of cotton, and 40 percent of rice. But the need and reality for less dependence on this publicly created and assisted market is indicated by the fact that these percentages had dropped to 25 percent for wheat, 10 percent for cotton, and 37 percent for rice by 1971. Another forewarning is the potential of convergence of annual cereals production at the levels of recent disappearance, with some possibility of domestic increments to buffer stocks or growing exports in some of the less developed countries.

With the potential in sight and a few success stories already in from the Green Revolution, the theme of less developed countries will be improvement of their agriculture toward a goal of self-sufficiency in supplies over the next decade as a means of eliminating the need for food aid. At least the elimination of food aid is becoming a goal pursued with increasing intensity because of national pride, the desire to be freed from political and economic dependencies, and even the long-standing human orientation to be free from dole. Finally, even the recommendations of U.S. experts and government officials to recreate the Agency for International Development (AID) wherein its economic functions are implemented as long-term loans through a bank mechanism suggests this general vision for the future.

Given the very large relative production capacity of American agriculture for the next two decades, a domestic demand tightly bounded by population growth rates, a dwindling demand for food aid in its conventional forms, an updraft in concern over environmental effects through agriculture, and exports already with a dominant marginal role in U.S. farm markets, any vigor in economic expansion (or even retention of the present position) of the farm sector is a function of the structure of trade policies.

From the one side, concern over restraints on the international market for U.S. farm commodities grows out of the economic concern for themselves by agricultural producers in other countries. The recent large increases in levies for grain entering the European Economic Community (EEC) is such a case. But all U.S. agricultural producers do not think the same about the direction of their interests in trade and its obstacles. The interest of feed grain, soybean, wheat, rice, cotton, and tobacco producers has been to sweep away the obstacles wherever in the world they exist and to extend the flow of commodities outward. Conversely, the interest of sugar, beef, and dairy product producers has been to extend the height and complexity of the trade obstacles and blunt the inward flow of commodities. Summing these opposite direct payoffs from trade and its obstacles, the net effect to U.S. farm producers still has been great gain in freer and extended exchange through international markets over recent decades.

For these reasons, the recent outbreak of domestic protectionism rash is not favorable in net for U.S. agriculture. The large payoff agriculture received in the 1960s began with the turnaround in U.S. trade policies in the 1930s after the depressing contraction of markets resulting from Smoot-Hawley and related trade legislation in the 1920s. Recent times and the suggestion or implementation of import quotas for steel and textiles, tax credits only for capital equipment produced domestically, and import surcharges provided the expectation of a return to the 1920s protectionism—a pessimistic net effect for U.S. agriculture which exports the product from one of four crop-acres and one of eight farm workers. Directly here then farmers have a fundamental stake in problems of balance of payments, since certainly, at least the temporary trade restraints and quotas enacted in the early 1970s (especially 1971) arose as a reaction to the nation's negative trade balance. But for farmers, the economic interest should transcend even the more nearly symptomatic nature of unfavorable trade balances, to focus on the more basic cause represented by international monetary policies. While the level of domestic price supports for farm commodities has had periods of prolonged and hard public beatings, these levels and values were minor deviations from competitive market values as compared to the extent the nation has supported the level of the dollar above its equilibrium price in international markets. Dollar devaluation and the reduction in its international exchange value favors greater grain exports and can at least partially compensate for other types of international barriers thrown up against U.S. farm exports. Policy at these levels and reaches in international markets and finance looms important for the extent of U.S. farm product markets and prosperity over the next two decades.

CONFLICTING PRODUCER INTERESTS. The resolution of conflicting trade goals by various economic interests and sectors of the United States is not simple. If it were, different segments of agriculture would not simultaneously press for tighter domestic import quotas of beef and sugar and for removal or restraint on levies in other countries of wheat and feed grains. As in the case of beef producers, workers also sell a product—their own labor embodied in commodities—and must compete with imports.

It can, of course, be proven mathematically and logically that in long-run, competitive markets the national product and community welfare can be maximized under free trade which conforms with international comparative advantage. Aside from compensation for short-run and abrupt shifts from one condition of markets to another for domestic producers of commodities and labor services, these equilibrium and optimization conditions never deal with the distribution of sacrifices and benefits among different producer groups, as a shift is made from a mix of markets different from that implied in a free, competitive international market geared precisely to patterns of international comparative advantage. In the real world of the moment, no nation is characterized internally by the institutional conformance with free trade in an international market geared to comparative advantage. To move suddenly from where they are, in a market pattern attained through a piecemeal institution of import protection over many decades, to the optimum defined by a free trade-international comparative advantage model, would reduce income and cause capital losses for some producers and consumers, while similar benefits accrue to others.

Trade theory has dealt only scantily with this problem in welfare and distribution, other than to imply that "foolish people should never have, even if long ago, allowed such inefficient institutions and market patterns to be created in the first place." But however foolish were those producers and legislators who brought their initial enactment, they are seldom the same persons who now own the assets involved and have an income stream which capitalizes the gains from protected markets based on legislation passed at a much earlier time. In the important cases where these conditions prevail, the facts of life need to be recognized and some form of compensation offered accordingly. Otherwise, selected producer groups may be burdened with heavy costs in income reduction and capital losses so that others may benefit as their product flows into an expanded international market made possible through lifting the restraints from the first group to improve the exchange position of other countries who then can better buy the products of the second group. At the minimum these changes can be phased, as was recognized particularly in international trade agreements in the early 1960s, so that they do not dump the costs of trade realignment too rapidly on producer groups who sacrifice. Without appropriate compensation under conditions where reduction of trade barriers causes drastic redistributions of income and capital values, we have no mathematical or practical basis to prove that short-run welfare is improved as trade patterns are made to approach or conform with free-trade—comparative-advantage, long-run conditions.

Unfortunately, given the facts that institutions do exist as trade obstacles and that often they were established long ago, the analysis of benefits from trade has been couched too largely in terms of the community losses posed in moving away from the optimizing conditions of a free-trade—comparative-advantage model in the long run and too little in the complexities and transfer problems in moving from the current status to such equilibrium conditions. In Chapter 3 Johnson shows that in countries where measurements have been made, the social costs of some major trade restrictions are small. Perhaps in many countries these social costs are now insignificant amounts relative to the sacrifices or costs engendered by insufficient and poorly allocated resources in education, human mobility, and vocational guidance. They probably sum to less in most countries than the effects of a small proportion of domestic policies which, due to the political advantage of some factory owners and bureaucrats, cause misallocations of resources or inappropriate income transfer policies which become manifested in resource prices.

STRUCTURAL AND LOW INCOME PROBLEMS. On the other hand, even if the real cost of prevailing trade restrictions is relatively small for advanced countries with large national products and resource endowments, compounding trade restrictions has little or no promise of solving long-run structural imbalances and low incomes in a sector such as agriculture. Improvement of farm prices can accomplish little in saving small farms from the competition of large-scale commercial units enjoying scale economies under current capital technologies. Under large supply capacity as in the United States these means can do little in solving low resource returns over the long run. Just as price support or deficiency payment programs become capitalized into land values because of low labor mobility, capitalization of income increments from trade barriers into asset values simply means that the next purchaser can buy fewer acres with the same funds. And at the same discount rates, over the long run he will pay the same price for a dollar of income under trade restrictions, as he paid in their absence. Although current owners may gain, the next generation does not, and continuance of the barriers brings gain to no one but is simply a price paid by consumers to hold land values at bolstered levels (though for the United States the capital value involved is much smaller than that due to domestic price and income programs). Perhaps this effect, continuous costs to consumers simply to maintain land values, overshadows the gain to the initially benefiting asset owners. Elimination of restrictions would cause capital losses to the generation of owners after prices have been increased under trade restrictions. But this is where the means of compensation outlined earlier has promise.

In general and as Johnson indicates, trade restrictions have little promise in solving the basic problems of low income farmers. Like conventional domestic price support programs in the United States, their main benefits go to large-scale operators with the capital to enlarge under higher prices, as theory would suggest they might. Certainly in the less developed countries they are a meaningless tool for income improvement for the mass of subsistence and near-subsistence farmers.

MARGINAL DIFFERENCES AND CHANGES. Johnson (Chap. 3) implies that the gain from trade may well have been overestimated, particularly in a time of large domestic markets and advanced technology which tends to erase part of the differential comparative advantage that long rested on natural endowments and primary products. But perhaps we have also overdone the fear for some producers of primary products through the classical presentation of the potential gains from trade and the consequent inter-country production patterns. The classical representation of comparative advantage and trade gains was long that shown in Figure 1.1 for two commodities, I and II, produced in countries A and B.

The presentation proposed that the production possibility curve for commodities I and II in both countries is linear. With the slope $\Delta / \Delta II$ less for country A than for country B, country A has a comparative ad-

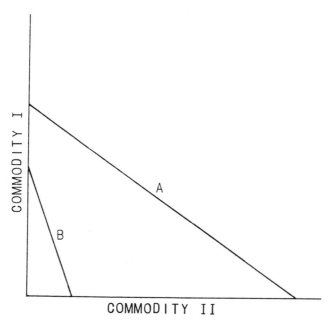

FIG. 1.1. Advantage for extreme specialization.

vantage in commodity II while country *B* has a comparative advantage in commodity I. With each specializing accordingly under conditions of sufficient demand, country *B* can be expected to produce only commodity I while country *A* produces only commodity II. Producers of commodity I in country *A* could be expected to be run out of business. For large countries with diverse soil and climatic resources, for production of primary commodities, however, production possibilities will certainly be of a general nature (Fig. 1.2).

The national production possibilities will not be linear (constant marginal rates of substitution will not prevail) and each country can have comparative advantage over some portion of its national opportunity curve. For example, the slope of production possibility curve *B* at its intersection by the vector *b* is equal to the slope of curve *A* at its intersection by vector *a*. Hence, above ray *b*, country *B* has a comparative advantage for commodity II as compared to country *A* over the portion of the latter's opportunity curve falling below ray *a*, even though in an overall sense country *A* has a comparative advantage lower (average slope of the opportunity curve) for commodity II. But Figure 1.2 is an oversimplification, even if the opportunity lines are considered to be isocost curves. More nearly each commodity in each subregion making up the major producing regions of a country will have a vector of resource requirements, A_{jk}, as in (1) where

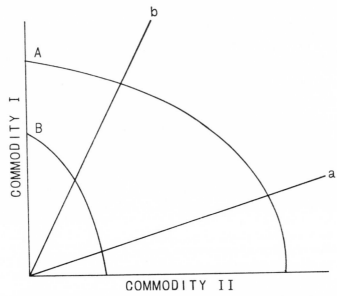

FIG. 1.2.   Relative comparative advantage.

$$A'_{jk} = (a_{1jk}a_{2jk} \ldots a_{ijk} \ldots a_{njk}) \tag{1}$$

a_{ijk} is the requirement of the jth commodity for the ith resource in the kth subregion. Then if the ratio $a_{1j1}/a_{1j2} > a_{2j1}/a_{2j2}$, subregion 2 will have a comparative advantage over subregion 1 in the use of the first resource for commodity j, but subregion 1 will have a relative advantage over subregion 2 in the use of the second resource for the jth commodity. Arraying these vectors over subregions and comparing the total possibilities of one country against those of another, the implications of trade differ considerably from those implied in the classical comparative advantage presentation posed in Figure 1.1, or even the more realistic modification presented in Figure 1.2. Trade will mean a greater degree of specialization than will a complex set of trade restrictions, but it need not mean complete specialization and a wiping out of one set of producers as implied in classical discussions of trade and comparative advantage. Just as Johnson illustrates that the gain in welfare from trade may be relatively small in some countries, the presentation above emphasizes that trade generally may not cause the revolutionary adjustments in production implied in the classical presentation of comparative advantage, production specialization, and trade—particularly for primary commodities whose production rests on technology, soil, and climatic resources which vary greatly within and among countries of large markets.

For this reason as Sorenson points out in Chapter 12 removal of import restrictions on dairy products would not wipe out the entire dairy industry. The market for fluid milk and cream largely would remain for domestic producers but domestically manufactured dairy products would have difficulty in competing with imports. With recapitalization of land values, the supply of domestically produced beef would be reduced relatively little with the relaxation of import restrictions. Over the long run also, with mobility of resources to the extent that they move into and out of agriculture until returns are equated with opportunities in other sectors, income to future producers would be approximately the same in the presence or absence of import restrictions (but the real income of consumers could be considerably different). However, those who live in the present and earn their living from resources whose prices include the capitalized benefits of import restrictions bear the costs of relaxations in trade restrictions. Future generations do not organize and form pressure groups on behalf of trade or its restrictions. The present generation does, and once it passes restrictions along to the future, the next generation of asset owners is also faced with losses from reduction of trade restrictions.

Potentially, the means to break this chain is compensation to present producers phased to allow them to shift use of their resources without burdensome costs and income sacrifices. Potential funds for compensation are not scarce in the United States. With farm programs to restrain supply and bolster prices running at $5 billion annually, the sum grows large in a few years. To the extent that the world affairs mentioned later and reduction of world trade restrictions can eliminate the need for supply control for major grains, a good-sized fund could be freed to compensate those farmers who would directly and greatly sacrifice from a freer trade policy.

With means to handle problems of short-run losses in income and asset values by producers currently benefitting from protection, the real long-run, sum-total prospect for American agriculture is gain from relaxation in restrictions and greater world trade. This point has already been emphasized in the proportion of agricultural resources engaged in exports—one of each four crop-acres and one of each eight workers. These opportunities in trade, of course, can be best augmented through more rapid development in the low income countries.

The ongoing Green Revolution, as indicated by Cochrane in Chapter 13, does have prospects of increasing food supplies more rapidly in these countries. Carried forward on a continuous basis, this spurt in world food production should have the short-run effects of (1) reducing the need and prospects of international food aid from major surplus countries, (2) causing increased competition in the international cereals market, and (3) increasing the certainty and lowering the real cost of food in the less developed countries. But agriculture is only one facet of economic development in these countries. The need is to speed economic development of other sectors as rapidly as the improvement in wheat production in parts of India, Pakistan, and other Asian countries. To do so with the mammoth world population growth still in prospect would increase greatly the demand for food from the surplus-producing countries. The hope, of course, is to move per capita income sharply upward from the sixty and one hundred dollars that prevail in many densely populated countries. Income elasticities of demand for food are sufficiently large that income improvement can still cause a tremendous increase in demand for grains and cereals for a majority of the world's population. The positive prospect is in an increase in demand because the incomes of low income people increase and add enjoyment to life accordingly, rather than that food imports increase to maintain growing populations at subsistence levels and a disutility of life.

At best, successful control of population growth is a generation away for most less developed countries. If this increment in the world's population can be paralleled by a rapid growth in per capita incomes, the prospects, especially for cereals producers in exporting countries, are indeed bright. These possibilities are emphasized by Mackie's data on destination of U.S. grain exports in Chapter 4. The large demand has developed in countries with high per capita incomes. The importance of Japan in this context is particularly significant. The large increase in per capita incomes and changes in dietary patterns accordingly in Japan has created a rapid increase in demand for grains to be used as livestock feeds.

To lift incomes from the typical sixty- and one-hundred-dollar per capita levels in densely populated countries to only modest levels of five hundred dollars would do more to vitalize the flow of grains in international markets than either (1) an erasure of all existing trade barriers, or (2) continued population increases with relatively stable and low incomes in developing countries. The hope of producers in developed countries is not that, as posed during the late 1960s, of burgeoning population growth which exhausts the capability of resources in less developed countries and opens the export doors for developed countries in order that starving masses over the world simply can be kept alive.

TRADE vs. AID. Food aid may not be much more costly, as Mayer indicates in Chapter 11, than other bail-out policies of countries which have the capacity to produce surpluses but only incapacity when it comes to providing domestic solutions to their farm problems. But this is an "ersatz export market" with little potential for the future. Once they have begun to pull together their economic sinews and bring order to the initial endowment of economic stagnation following national independence, few if any countries will long accept a continued diet of food aid. There are many known reasons. Among them are the abhorrence of apparent international dole, the intense need for domestic agricultural development even to absorb large underemployed labor forces, and the urge for national security. Even where it might prove economic to accept food aid on a loan basis with required repayments later, less developed countries are increasingly reticent to enter into such agreements as they bring their own agriculture out of its technological stalemate. It seems much less rational to borrow money for food now, eat the food, and pay for it forty years later, than to enter similarly into international loans for steel mills and transportation networks with extended spans of life and income generation. Certainly, the planners and administrators of developing countries understand the concept of import substitution, but they view it with a purpose different from food aid now with repayment later.

In the short run we can expect, as Cochrane points out in Chapter 13, a real potential for further rapid expansion in food supplies in the developing countries. Further, we can expect an increasing proportion of the increment to move into the export market. But the amount that moves may correspond only somewhat to the world population growth. It is unlikely to prove a drastic substitute for the major grain exports of developed countries, which move largely to other developed regions. It will more likely cause disruptions for other less developed countries emphasizing improvement and export sales of the same commodities, such as rice in Southeast Asia where Thailand suffers somewhat from the growing export capacity of other countries in the region (on top of U.S. food aid exports).

For the United States, apart from food aid, commercial sales are likely to follow their recent trend in the short run. Growing production and export capacity of developing countries can be absorbed largely by population and economic growth. The restrictions to trade by regional market structures such as the EEC may serve as more of a restraint on export realizations than the competing food supplies of developing countries. In the long run large and sustained economic growth in the developing countries is the main hope and potential for producers in surplus-grain-producing countries; food aid and population growth under economic stagnation are not.

AFFAIRS OF THE WORLD. Other affairs of the world are also important in this context. Economic growth and freer and broader trade of East Europe with the West could greatly increase the market for grain-exporting nations. While important improvements and increases can be made in grain production in East Europe, the limited soils and climatic regimes for grain production plus the latent demand for livestock products pose the possibility of very large grain imports for the future of trade, which provides appropriate foreign exchange.

The affairs of the world promise to be most important in the long run relative to export potentials, particularly for feed grains which absorb most U.S. farm export capacity. These "affairs" relate especially to trade arrangements with the East and the success or failure of more rapid economic growth and population management in the developing countries. The potential effects of these affairs overshadow domestic trade restrictions of the current nature and magnitude as forces determining future exports for U.S. farm commodities.

It is not likely, of course, that the long run is soon to be upon us. During the interim period it is important, especially to grain producers, that trade restrictions are not intensified. Given the fixity of grain-producing capacity and the per capita demand for food in the United States, the three important variables in the future prosperity of this farming sector are the magnitude of the U.S. population (zero population growth or not), the nature and magnitude of domestic farm programs, and how the affairs of the world are resolved.

We have just completed four decades of earnest attempt to relax trade restrictions. As a supplement in improving the welfare of mankind, we also invested very heavily for three decades in aid to international development. But as the 1970s begin, we have shown signs of turning back to economic isolationism and the course of events leading to our 1920s marginal line of trade restriction. Surely other judgment will prevail as the decade progresses and we will find our course again. As Johnson implies, to do otherwise is not likely to turn us back to a 1920s standard of living, or even to lower our affluence by any great degree. But only by doing so are we likely to participate in shaping the affairs of the world which have most meaning not only to agriculture's main export sector but also to those populations less well endowed than ourselves with resources and technology.

NOTES

1. John M. Wetmore et al., "Policies for Expanding the Demand for Farm Food Products in the U.S.," *Minnesota Agricultural Experiment Station Technical Bulletin 231*, pt. 1, History and Potentials (Minneapolis: Univ. of Minnesota, April 1959).

2. Earl O. Heady et al., "Future Water and Land Use: Effects of Selected Public Agricultural and Irrigation Policies on Water Demand and Land Use," report of the Center for Agricultural and Rural Development, Iowa State Univ., prepared for the National Water Commission, Springfield, Va.: National Technical Information Service, Report P.B. 206-790 NWC-EES-71-003), 1972; Earl O. Heady et al., "Agricultural and Water Policies and the Environment: An Analysis of National Alternatives in Natural Resource Use, Food Capacity and Environmental Quality" (Ames: Iowa State Univ., Center for Agricultural and Rural Development, CARD Report no. 40T, 1972).

3. Lester R. Brown, *Seeds of Change: The Green Revolution and Developments in the 1970s* (New York: Praeger, 1970); Willard W. Cochrane, *The World Food Problem: A Guardedly Optimistic View* (New York: Thomas Y. Crowell, 1969); Leroy L. Blakeslee, Earl O. Heady, and Charles F. Framingham, *World Food Production, Demand, and Trade* (Ames: Iowa State Univ. Press, 1973).

[2]

U.S. Trade Policy:
Background and Historical Trends

Robert L. Tontz

U NITED STATES trade policy has a long history going back to the establishment of the principle and practice of a common market among the states in 1789. The common external tariff that evolved over time which significantly affected trade policy evidenced divergent trends but was often characterized by relatively high protection.

The present trade policy of the United States largely reflects developments that have taken place over the past half century. This chapter presents a review of these developments and their background to gain a perspective for dealing with trade problems and opportunities in the context of the increasingly complex conditions of trade as they exist today and will likely exist in the future.

In the years following World War I, the trade policy of the United States represented a continuation of most of the predominant policy of the prewar period of undue protection of domestic production against foreign competition. An exception to the predominant prewar policy occurred with the passage of the Underwood-Simmons Tariff on the eve of World War I (1913) when tariffs were reduced significantly and several items were added to the free list.

With the discrediting of this policy by a strong foreign reaction of trade restriction resulting in a significant decline in U.S. exports, a major shift in U.S. trade policy took place in the 1930s. The shift was brought about with the inauguration of a policy of trade expansion

ROBERT L. TONTZ is Supervisory Agricultural Economist, Foreign Demand and Competition Division, Economic Research Service, United States Department of Agriculture. This chapter was prepared in June 1971, when Tontz was Head, Agricultural Markets Division, Organization for Economic Cooperation and Development, Paris. Grateful acknowledgement is extended to I. E. Lemon, Robert B. Brungart, and Harry Henderson for their helpful suggestions and assistance. The views expressed are the author's and do not necessarily reflect those of the OECD or others.

through encouragement of two-way trade under the auspices of the reciprocal trade agreements program. The trade expansion policy was
continued in the post-World War II period with a series of General
Agreement on Tariffs and Trade (GATT) negotiations and reached its
highest achievement of the series with the conclusion of the Kennedy
Round in 1967. Although progress was made toward implementing a
freer trade policy, domestic and foreign policy conflicts arose and trade-
inhibiting measures were at the same time introduced and are receiving
increasing attention.

POST-WORLD WAR I PERIOD: PROTECTIONISM. The sudden
collapse of farm prices in the early twenties and the resulting farm depression brought about by an overexpanded agriculture, deflation, and
loss of significant foreign markets posed a severe hardship on American
farmers.

With faith in the benefits of tariff protection based on the experience of growth and prosperity in the tariff-protective prewar decades,
agitation rose in agriculture for increased tariffs as the way to alleviate
the farm problem. Unfortunately, neither agriculture nor industry
recognized that the ability of the United States to carry on a policy of
protection in the prewar period without serious repercussions on the
economy resulted from the fact that the United States was then a large
debtor to Europe, exporting mainly unprocessed products and servicing
its foreign debts from its export earnings. Further, little consideration
was given to the possibility that Europe's reactions to U.S. tariff increases
in the post-World War I period would be different from those in the prewar decades. Being a heavy debtor to the United States and struggling
with serious reconstruction difficulties, Europe faced a much different
situation in the postwar period.[1]

This then was the setting when Congress passed the Emergency
Tariff of 1921 which imposed heavy import duties on agricultural products. Despite this measure, the benefit to farmers was negligible, and
low farm prices persisted, aggravated by the European reaction of increased tariff protection.

Like agriculture in the early twenties, industry requested similar increases in tariff protection. It received them through the Fordney-
McCumber Act of 1922 which raised duties, and gave the president authority to raise or lower duties by 50 percent to "equalize production
costs." This authority was used thirty-seven times—thirty-two times to
raise duties. Few complained of the unconstitutionality of the president's
power to raise or lower duties.[2]

EQUALITY FOR AGRICULTURE UNDER THE TARIFF. Despite the apparent
teaming up of agriculture and industry to seek tariff protection, there
were those in agriculture who argued that protection benefitted industry
to the detriment of agriculture, maintaining that the farmer sold on a

competitive world market and bought on a protected domestic market.

Although "tariff protection" continued to be basic to the thinking of the time, in agricultural demands it took the form of proposals to secure "equality for agriculture," that is, parity by making the tariff effective for agriculture. The origin of this approach reaches back to the Peek-Johnson remedy for agriculture's problem as presented in their first edition of *Equality for Agriculture*.[3] The proposed remedy for the ills of agriculture consisted of revising the doctrine of protection to insure agriculture a fair exchange value, that is, price equality or parity on the domestic market and the world price on the exportable surplus. The remedy unrealistically assumed that the already overburdened and increasingly protective world market could take the surplus.

The fair exchange value idea was incorporated in the McNary-Haugen two-price plans in the late twenties. The bills were twice passed by Congress and twice vetoed by President Calvin Coolidge for being price-fixing, among other reasons.

Although not enacted at the time, the fair exchange value proposals served as the forerunner for the agricultural adjustment parity acts beginning in the early 1930s.[4]

With worsening farm conditions in 1929, President Herbert Hoover, three days after his inauguration, called Congress to meet in special session in April of that year to consider farm relief and limited changes in the tariff. During the session the Agricultural Marketing Act of 1929 was passed.

In the words of Senator Arthur A. Capper of Kansas, for many years one of the most influential Senate leaders in farm relief legislation, the act would achieve parity for the farmer by placing agriculture on a basis of economic equality with other industries. It was to do this by such measures as preventing and controlling agricultural surpluses through orderly production and marketing.

The Federal Farm Board, established to implement the policy of the Agricultural Marketing Act, failed in the early thirties principally because it had no authority to reduce production other than by voluntary means, and it lacked the necessary funds to carry out stabilization operations through as severe a depression as that which developed after 1929.

HAWLEY-SMOOT ACT. Besides demanding and securing a major farm relief measure, farmers sought new tariff increases in 1929 as farm prices declined further. Once more, industry followed with similar demands. Meanwhile, a sharp downward trend in both agricultural and industrial exports stimulated demands for increased tariff protection against any possible further deterioration of the domestic market. Imports were considered disturbances that should be eliminated. The essential two-way trade relationship between exports and imports was not fully understood.

Congress responded in 1930 to the demands of agriculture and in-

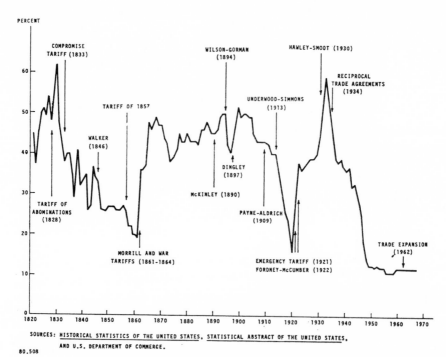

SOURCES: HISTORICAL STATISTICS OF THE UNITED STATES, STATISTICAL ABSTRACT OF THE UNITED STATES,
            AND U.S. DEPARTMENT OF COMMERCE.
80,508

FIG. 2.1.   Selected tariff acts and ratio (percent) of U.S. duties
on dutiable imports on and/or after passage.

dustry by passing the Hawley-Smoot tariff, one of the highest in U.S. history (Fig. 2.1).

The Hawley-Smoot tariff increase prompted many trading nations to increase their own levels of protection.[5] As a consequence of this and other developments, the volume of U.S. exports, industrial and agricultural, suffered catastrophic declines. During the Great Depression in 1932–33, U.S. industrial exports fell to an annual average of $0.8 billion, down 73 percent from their previous four-year average, while annual U.S. agricultural exports were only $0.6 billion, down 67 percent.

THE THIRTIES AND FORTIES: RECIPROCAL TRADE AGREEMENTS AND POLICY CONFLICTS. With the failure of the U.S. post-World War I policy of trade restriction, the demise of the Federal Farm Board, and the deepening of the Great Depression in the early thirties, it became clearly evident that emergency action was needed to improve the economic status of agriculture and industry.

In the area of trade policy, President Franklin D. Roosevelt, following the recommendation of Secretary of State Cordell Hull, requested that Congress authorize executive commercial agreements with foreign

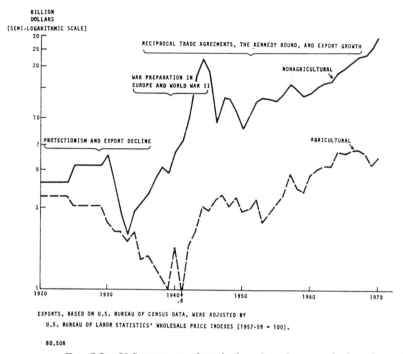

BILLION
DOLLARS
(SEMI-LOGARITHMIC SCALE)

RECIPROCAL TRADE AGREEMENTS, THE KENNEDY ROUND, AND EXPORT GROWTH

NONAGRICULTURAL

WAR PREPARATION IN
EUROPE AND WORLD WAR II

PROTECTIONISM AND EXPORT DECLINE

AGRICULTURAL

EXPORTS, BASED ON U.S. BUREAU OF CENSUS DATA, WERE ADJUSTED BY
U.S. BUREAU OF LABOR STATISTICS' WHOLESALE PRICE INDEXES (1957-59 = 100).

80.508

FIG. 2.2. U.S. exports of agricultural and nonagricultural products for years ending June 30.

nations within carefully guarded limits to modify the existing duties and import restrictions to benefit American agriculture and industry.

THE TRADE AGREEMENTS ACTS. Congress passed the Hull-inspired Reciprocal Trade Agreements Act of 1934 as an amendment to the Hawley-Smoot Tariff Act of 1930. The Trade Agreements Act was designed to attain a reduction in the excessive duties set in the 1930 act and thus expand foreign markets for U.S. products. This and consequent legislation was successful in contributing to a significant expansion of U.S. exports (Fig. 2.2).

The Trade Agreements Act was based on the premise that, to obtain and develop foreign markets for U.S. products, the United States must afford corresponding market opportunities in the United States to other countries.

Under the trade agreements legislation, the president was empowered for a period of three years to enter into reciprocal trade agreements with other countries through executive proclamation and without congressional approval. The act also provided that the unconditional most-favored-nation treatment (that is, equality of treatment to all nations) would be continued except in the case of nations discriminating against American commerce. Every trade agreement was subject to termination at the end of not more than three years after coming into effect if Congress failed to extend the authority. The president's tariff-reducing power was limited to 50 percent of duties existing on January 1, 1934. In previous tariff-adjusting, presidential authority had been dependent upon the findings of the Tariff Commission, whereas in the future there was to be no such inhibition on the new authority. Tariff rate adjustment was shifted from the Tariff Commission to the State Department.

Congress extended the authority to make trade agreements in 1937, 1940, and 1943 without significant amendments, and in 1945 it extended the authority and gave the president the further authority to lower rates by 50 percent of the existing duties as of January 1, 1945. Any item, reduced by 50 percent in the period from 1934 to 1945, was subject to another possible reduction of 50 percent—or a 75 percent reduction in all—for concessions from other countries. The year 1945 marked the legislative high point of the program. Since then, amendments tended to restrict rather than expand the power of the president.

In the period from 1934 to 1945, the United States concluded trade agreements with some thirty countries. However, in the years from 1844 to 1934—the ninety years preceding the Reciprocal Trade Agreements Act—the United States was able to negotiate and ratify only three reciprocity treaties under the general treaty-making power. During this same time there were at least eleven major failures in which treaties were either rejected by the Senate, were never submitted to the Senate, or on which the Senate failed to act. Clearly, it has only been under the delegation of power to the president that much success in trade reciprocity has been achieved.[6]

In making bilateral trade agreements, history shows that the two parties concentrated upon reducing duties on those items for which each tended to be the principal supplier for the other. The mutual tariff reductions agreed upon were then generalized to all traders with both parties.

This approach had both advantages and disadvantages. The main drawback was that, by extending the duty cuts to all countries, nonparticipants were able to increase their exports to the two countries without also opening up their economies to great imports. In view of the existence of widespread unemployment in most countries during this period, coupled with the notion of reciprocal concessions contained in the legislation, efforts were made to avoid this aspect of bilateral negotiations by confining the cuts between the two countries to a small number of items in which each was the other's main supplier. Items for which there was no single overwhelming supplier or countries that were not major suppliers of any item tended to be neglected.

Even between the two countries, where the principal-supplier trade was highly unbalanced, it was impossible to reduce one party's tariffs the same percentage as the other's and still achieve an acceptable balance of concessions for each. On the other hand the bilateral technique with its concentration upon principal supplier items permitted a movement toward freer trade without requiring the consent of all major trading nations.[7] During the thirties it would have been difficult to proceed on any other than this step-by-step basis, which was actually adopted.

To adjust for the unforeseen circumstances in which a tariff concession might bring on a larger volume of imports than had been anticipated and therefore lead to injury of domestic industry, the United States urged the adoption in later trade agreements of provisions allowing the contracting parties an escape clause to render inoperative that portion of an agreement causing injury to domestic industries. The trade agreement with Argentina in 1941 carried the forerunner of such an escape clause. This was developed into a standard clause which first appeared in the 1943 agreement with Mexico and appeared in all subsequent agreements.

Most of the trade agreements had been in effect for only a short time before war preparations, and the subsequent outbreak of war in Europe in 1939 significantly impeded trade development. The agreements were therefore hardly tested under peacetime conditions of trade.[8]

CONFLICT OF AGRICULTURAL AND TRADE POLICIES. To aid the increasingly hard-pressed American farmer during the Great Depression of the thirties, price supports were provided under the authority of the farm parity acts beginning with the Agricultural Adjustment Act of 1933. The programs implemented under these acts separated domestic prices of agricultural products from world prices.

The parity acts and the trade agreements legislation, although designed to help the farmer, were at cross-purposes. The policy of farm price support restricted the operation of market forces while the trade agreements policy sought to expand the operation of market forces in the international area.[9]

Of particular note in connection with price support policy in the thirties was the inauguration of benefit payments for sugar producers with the passage of the Sugar Act of 1934. This act significantly changed the domestic sugar producers to a system of import and production quotas in addition to benefit payments.

To make the high price supports effective even though world prices were depressed, export subsidies and import quotas and fees were used.

Subsidy payments were made under authority of Section 32 of the Agricultural Adjustment Act of 1935 which specified that 30 percent of all customs revenues were to be appropriated for financing surplus disposal. Payments were made to assist exports of such U.S. surplus commodities and products as wheat and cotton.

At the same time imports were limited by quotas or fees when protection provided by tariffs was not sufficient to prevent foreign sales in the United States under the benefit of U.S. price supports. Commodities affected were wheat and flour, cotton, and sugar for certain uses. Authority for imposing quotas or fees was provided by Section 22 of the Agricultural Adjustment Act of 1933.

Although the United States attempted to persuade other countries to eliminate quantitative restrictions and to insert rules preventing the use of such restrictions for bound tariff items in its trade agreements, it was necessary for the United States to add exceptions to this rule in order to protect the U.S. price support programs. Accordingly most U.S. trade agreements limited the use of such restrictions to products that were also restricted in production or marketing.[10]

The trade-impeding impact of price supports and the imposition of import quotas in the thirties was not of great significance at the time, because of the limitation of such supports, both in moderation of level and number of commodities involved.[11]

POST-WORLD WAR II PERIOD: GATT, EROSION OF TRADE NEGOTIATING AUTHORITY, AND POLICY CONFLICTS. During World War II it became quickly apparent that the extent of the destruction would exceed that of World War I. Hence it was soon recognized that to facilitate postwar reconstruction and development so essential to resumption of world trade, careful planning would be required to organize the postwar world economy. The United States and its allies did this. These plans, partially operational when the war ended, included the United Nations Relief and Rehabilitation Agency, the International Monetary Fund, the International Bank for Reconstruction and Development, the Food and Agriculture Organization, and the United Nations Economic and Social Council.

The official European Recovery Program, popularly known as the Marshall Plan, and the costly but helpful efforts that preceded it contributed significantly to facilitating recovery from the devastation of the war and in correcting basic postwar economic weaknesses. The European nations' Organization for European Economic Cooperation (OEEC) later evolved into the Organization for Economic Cooperation and Development (OECD) with U.S., Canadian, Japanese, Finnish, and Australian membership. The OECD provides a useful forum in which the developed countries can arrive at common understanding concerning trade problems and serves as a beneficial complement to the cause of the less developed countries in the United Nations Conference on Trade and Development (UNCTAD).

Besides these essential organizations, a further need for the postwar economy was an organization concerned with international trade. This was undertaken by the development of the principles for an International Trade Organization (ITO).

The ill-fated charter for the ITO drawn up at Havana in 1948 specified principles and rules for reduction of tariffs, elimination of quotas, and creation of conditions for expansion of multilateral trade on equal terms. It set up rules for international commodity agreements and government regulation of business practices that might restrain international trade. The charter recognized the need for governments to relate foreign trade policies to domestic measures, to assure stability and full employment, and it provided some of the elements of a code for private international investment.

President Harry S. Truman submitted the Havana charter for the ITO to Congress in April 1949. Although the House Foreign Affairs Committee held hearings in 1950, it did not go further.

The ITO did not materialize primarily because of changes on the world scene. The Korean War, the cold war, the North Atlantic Treaty Organization, and European reconstruction all made the ITO less urgent. In addition, few countries besides the United States were in an economic position to carry out any major broadening of their trade policies. Other obstacles included uncertainty about pledges to reduce trade barriers and guarantee equal treatment, difficulties caused by complexities involved in trying to achieve international understandings on raw materials and cartels, and the lack of safeguards to investors.[12]

GENERAL AGREEMENT ON TARIFFS AND TRADE. In recognition of the difficulties confronting them, most of the governments involved in the ITO negotiations subscribed to a more modest instrument, the General Agreement on Tariffs and Trade (GATT), which had earlier (1947) been drawn up in Geneva.

At the time that GATT was developed, eighteen governments negotiated an extensive series of tariff reductions. Though some of the bargaining was bilateral, all the results were made multilateral by extending the concessions to all members under a most-favored-nation clause, a central feature of the agreement. Its other major provisions largely paralleled those of the ITO charter, as far as trade policy proper was concerned, but nothing was said about full employment, commodity agreements, cartels, or investments. The charter and GATT also differed in that government obligations extended only to measures they could take by executive action without the passage of legislation.[13]

The governments that belong to GATT have developed working procedures and rules which have not only made possible effective tariff negotiations, but have also provided for adjustments, consultations, settlement of disputes, and accommodation of members' special problems without destroying the framework of general principles or setting in motion the process of trade retaliation. The price of this pragmatism and flexibility has been an inability to assure the full application of the principles at all times. Although departures from the rules have been tolerated, the processes of negotiation and cooperation have been continued.[14]

Of great significance to the United States in belonging to GATT has been the assurance of a multilateral framework for shaping U.S. international trade policies and those of other nations. Some of the basic principles embodied in the ITO have been preserved and put into practice to a large degree through GATT.

Besides establishing an organization through which periodic multilateral tariff negotiations designed to reduce duty levels could be undertaken, GATT set forth a code of commercial policy. The most-favored-nation principle is the cornerstone of GATT.

The first article of the agreement specified in detail that each nation shall grant nondiscriminatory treatment to the products of all other contracting nations with regard to import and export duties and subsidiary charges, rules, and formalities in connection with importation and exportation, internal taxes, and other internal regulations.

A second basic principle is the general prohibition of quantitative restrictions as a protective device. Except under special circumstances, only customs duties can be used for this purpose.[15]

NEGOTIATIONS UNDER TRADE AGREEMENTS AT GATT, 1947–61. American trade policy was implemented in the post-World War II period mainly under the authority of the Trade Agreements Act through GATT negotiations. With the 1945 increase of the president's power which allowed a maximum reduction of 50 percent in duties already reduced since the original passage of the act in 1934, there followed a number of successive extensions of the authority and legal restrictions on the president's power under the Trade Agreements Act. The formula established in 1945 was kept through five renewals between 1948 and 1954. In 1955, however, the president was restricted to a reduction of 5 percent a year. This restriction was continued for another four years in the 1958 renewal.

In 1947 under GATT arrangements twenty-two nations completed a multilateral tariff-cutting exercise that resulted in concessions on nearly two-thirds of total world trade. The United States negotiated under the additional 50 percent cutting power that Congress had granted the president in 1945.[16]

In 1948 the Trade Agreements Act came up for renewal. The one-year extension of the act carried several important amendments including the peril point clause which required the Tariff Commission to survey all commodities on which the president proposed to negotiate agreements and establish a peril point, that is, a specific rate of duty below which, in the commission's judgment, tariffs could not be lowered without damage to U.S. industry or business. If the president dropped rates below this point, he was required to send an official explanation to Congress. The 1948 extension of the Trade Agreements Act was repealed in 1949, the peril point amendment was eliminated, and the act extended retroactively from 1948 for a three-year period.[17]

The United States participated in two additional rounds of tariff negotiations within the GATT framework under the 50 percent tariff-cutting authority granted in 1945. One was held at Annecy, France, in 1949 at which ten more countries became contracting parties to the general agreement and another at Torquay, England, in 1950–51.[18]

The Trade Agreements Act was renewed for two years in 1951 and the peril point clause was restored. The president was directed to suspend tariff concessions to imports from the Soviet Union and any Communist-dominated countries, and the escape clause was made mandatory.[19]

The Trade Agreements Act in 1953 was extended for one year. At that time Congress also created the seventeen-member bipartisan Commission on Foreign Economic Policy (the Randall Commission) to study and report on international trade and its enlargement, consistent with a sound domestic economy, and on the trade aspects of U.S. national security.[20]

Basing his request on the Randall Commission's findings, President Dwight D. Eisenhower in 1954 asked for a three-year extension of the Trade Agreements Act. Congress extended the act for one year.[21]

Congress again extended the Trade Agreements Act in 1955 for three years, or until June 30, 1958. Although it gave the president additional tariff-cutting authority, it was considerably less than the authority given him in 1934 and 1945. The new authority permitted him to reduce duties by an additional 15 percent over the three-year period. With these powers the United States participated in the fourth round of GATT negotiations in 1956. The session at Geneva dealt also with the accession of Japan to the GATT.[22]

In 1958 Congress gave the president authority to reduce duties by another 20 percent on an item-by-item basis. The United States had authority to reduce the rates of U.S. duties existing on July 1, 1958, by 20 percent of the effective rate as, in the case of low rates, by 2 percent *ad valorem*. But use of this authority was highly limited by a number of protective clauses in the fifth GATT negotiating session held in Geneva in 1961–62 (the Dillion Round). A major practical limitation was the requirement that U.S. tariffs must not be reduced below certain peril points to be determined by the Tariff Commission.[23] Despite this limitation, of significance for agriculture were the free bindings negotiated with the European Economic Community (EEC) on soybeans, linseed, flaxseed, oilcakes, and cotton.

The fifth GATT session was the first negotiation held after the formation of the EEC. (In October 1972, current members were: France, West Germany, Italy, the Netherlands, Belgium, and Luxembourg.) The objective of the United States was to obtain a reduction in the common external tariff of the EEC in order to offset at least partially the trade diversion caused by reducing duties within the EEC toward zero.

The five rounds of negotiations under GATT between 1947 and 1960–61 represent a successful example of productive international cooperation. In general, tariffs among the industrial nations were reduced. Although not a part of the negotiations, the highly restrictive structure of quantitative controls erected for balance of payments purposes at the end of the war were also gradually dismantled.

CHANGES IN OTHER TRADE BARRIERS. Besides tariff changes, several changes in other import barriers were made in the postwar period.

In the interest of domestic oil and coal producers, crude oil imports were held down in the postwar years under the national security amendment of the Trade Agreements Act. "Buy American" legislation dating from the depression was liberalized during the postwar period but still required government agencies to give preference to domestic suppliers even when foreign goods could be had more cheaply.[24]

Starting in the mid-1950s, Japanese sales to the United States of a number of products—most importantly cotton textiles—were limited by export restrictions in Japan which, while nominally voluntary, were the result of negotiations with the United States. An agreement on cotton textiles extended the same kind of arrangement to other low cost producers of cloth and garments, notably Hong Kong, India, and Pakistan. The agreement provided for a 5 percent annual increase in imports, provided domestic markets were not disrupted, and gave some producers a better chance than they otherwise would have had to sell to continental Europe.[25]

PUBLIC LAW 480. With a significant decline of U.S. agricultural exports in 1952–53 (approximately 30 percent by volume and more by value), carry-over stocks of wheat, corn, and cotton, which had been relatively modest in 1952, rose rapidly.[26]

To remedy the situation the concept was developed to use U.S. surpluses to help countries unable to buy commercially all the food and fiber they needed; this was to be done primarily through sales for foreign currencies. The 83rd Congress approved this concept and incorporated it into the Agricultural Trade Development and Assistance Act (PL 480), adopted in 1954, which soon became an important instrument of U.S. foreign policy.[27] Food aid did not suffice as a means of disposal, and surpluses continued to increase, although it was possible to maintain higher domestic export prices than otherwise would have been the case.

Besides PL 480 sales mainly for foreign currency, subsidies derived from Section 32 funds under authority of the Agricultural Adjustment Act of 1935 continued to be used to dispose of U.S. surpluses abroad. After World War II export sales from Commodity Credit Corporation (CCC) inventories below costs were also made to dispose of surpluses.

Other agricultural exporting countries looked at PL 480 at the inception of the program with some apprehension because they feared that U.S. local currency sales might reduce their own commercial export opportunities despite the fact that normal commercial import requirements were included in the PL 480 agreements. This concern then subsided because foreign competitors became convinced that in the administration of Title I sales for foreign currencies the United States had no intention of taking their regular commercial markets. Foreign competitors continued, however, to be somewhat apprehensive about barter operations under PL 480 and competitive dollar sales by the CCC.[28]

The U.S. food aid programs, carried out mainly under PL 480, accounted for over one-third (as compared to 13 percent currently) of U.S. exports of agricultural products in the early years of the program—the mid-fifties.

RENEWED CONFLICT OF AGRICULTURAL AND TRADE POLICIES. During World War II farm price support levels were raised for the war period and two years following the end of the war to encourage production and to protect farmers against a postwar price decline. This was done by the Steagall Amendment which affected a number of major agricultural crops and dairy products.

Concern was felt, however, that with the possible postwar decline of agricultural prices in international trade, imports would be attracted to the United States by the higher price support levels.

Accordingly restrictions on the importation of agricultural products were enacted in 1948 under the provisions of Section 22 of the Agricultural Adjustment Act of 1933 as amended. This act authorized the president to restrict, through the use of quantitative limitations or fees, imports which tended to render ineffective or materially interfere with any price support or other program relating to agricultural commodities undertaken by the U.S. Department of Agriculture. It specifically provided that any trade agreement or other international agreement entered into at any time by the United States may not be applied in a manner inconsistent with the requirements of Section 22.[29]

The legal effect of Section 22 in 1948 was to limit the imposition of agricultural import quotas in general to products subject to restrictions on domestic production or marketing. Its political effect, however, was different because it seemed to offer opportunities for quota protection for any U.S. agricultural program, and indirectly for many U.S. farm products. When these seemingly wide opportunities were not realized, it came under attack.[30]

As a result another amendment of Section 22 occurred in 1951. The amendment made it mandatory to impose import quotas or fees whenever imports should threaten to render ineffective a domestic support program, and to do this even though the imposition of such quotas or fees would be inconsistent with the obligations of the United States under trade agreements. The policy conflict arising from this amendment was resolved by a GATT waiver for agricultural trade.[31]

A further conflict with U.S. GATT obligations occurred in 1951 when import restrictions on dairy and certain other products were made mandatory for national security reasons in connection with the Defense Production Bill designed to aid the Korean War effort.[32]

THE TRADE EXPANSION ACT OF 1962 AND THE KENNEDY ROUND. The formation of the EEC and the adoption of the principle of a common tariff along with the plan to abolish over time all tariffs and other trade barriers among the member countries brought the tariff to the forefront as one of the major barriers to trade in the early 1960s. This development along with the EEC offer to reduce its common external tariff by 20 percent across the board, that is, a "linear" reduction which the United States, because of its item-by-item method, was unable to match, presented a new challenge to U.S. trade policy in tariff negotiations held in 1960 in Geneva.

THE TRADE EXPANSION ACT OF 1962. To remedy the lack of U.S. negotiation authority which became apparent at the fifth round of GATT negotiations and in view of the more rapid removal of intra-EEC tariff and other trade barriers than was scheduled in the Rome Treaty establishing the EEC, President John F. Kennedy sought new tariff legislation in 1962.[33] The U.S. Congress responded and the Trade Expansion Act of 1962 became law.[34]

This act provided the president much more power than had been conferred by any single tariff law since the original Trade Agreements Act of 1934. The act sought to gain the benefits from allocative gains from trade by fostering changes in resource use, rather than renouncing those important gains by restricting foreign trade and subsidizing inefficient industries. [35]

From 1934 to 1963, responsibility for the administration of U.S. foreign trade policy was vested in an interdepartmental committee chaired by the Department of State. To give fuller weight to U.S. trade interests, the Trade Expansion Act of 1962 provided for the appointment of a Special Representative for Trade Negotiations (STR), reporting to the president.

In an executive order in 1963, President Kennedy established the office of STR as a separate agency within the executive office of the president. During the Kennedy Round, there were two deputy special representatives, both ambassadors—one in Washington and one in Geneva.

In Washington, policy for the Kennedy Round as well as for other trade matters was decided largely by the interagency committees chaired by STR. In Geneva the deputy was in charge of the day-to-day negotiations.

The 1962 Trade Expansion Act did not include many of the restrictive clauses of earlier trade legislation, particularly the peril point provisions. The act provided, however, that the Tariff Commission should advise the president as to the "probably economic effect" of modifications of duties or other import restrictions on the respective U.S. industries. The departments dealing with economic affairs (including the U.S. departments of State, Agriculture, Commerce, and Labor) were also to advise the president on these matters. Interested persons were afforded an opportunity to present their views at public hearings.

The act provided a major innovation with its adjustment assistance to firms and workers if, "as a result in major part" of U.S. trade agreement concessions, imports "cause, or threaten to cause, serious injury" to the firm. The philosophy underlying this was that the remedy for increased imports was to enable economic adjustment to new competitive conditions or a shift of resources to other activities in greater demand rather than to impose trade restrictions that would result in trade retaliation, loss of export markets, and higher consumer prices. Besides providing adjustment assistance, the act tightened the escape-clause criteria.

Some of the principal provisions of the act were as follows:

Negotiating Authority. The negotiating authority, granted for five years (until June 30, 1967), empowered the president to reduce most import duties by 50 percent of the rates in effect on July 1, 1961. Reductions up to 100 percent were allowed for duties not in excess of 5 percent *ad valorem* for products in whose case the United States and EEC together accounted for 80 percent or more of world trade; or agricultural commodities if before entering into such agreement the president determines that such agreement will tend to assure the maintenance or expansion of U.S. exports of the like article and, under certain conditions, for tropical products as well.

Limitations on Negotiating Authority. The tariff reductions made under the act could not be made effective more rapidly than in five equal annual portions. No concessions were to be made if the resulting duty reduction or elimination of import restrictions would threaten to impair national security; nor were concessions to be made where the president had ruled (e.g., in an escape-clause case) that import increases would create undue hardship to U.S. industry.

Linear-Cut Offers with Limited Exceptions. The broad new authority enabled the United States to shift from the previously used method of

32   CHAPTER TWO

offering selective concessions to offering 50 percent across-the-board reductions; only those items for which reasons of overriding national interest made it necessary to make a lesser offer or no offer were excluded
from this procedure.

MFN and Nonparticipating Countries. Except for products of communist countries, all U.S. offers were made on a most-favored nation (MFN)
basis. Therefore concessions made on the basis of these offers would also
benefit countries that were not members of GATT. Products for which
such countries, and not the group of countries participating in the
Kennedy Round, were the major suppliers were to be excluded from
the U.S. offers.

Foreign Nontariff Restrictions. Concerned about the continuing restriction by many countries of imports by nontariff barriers, Congress
enacted special provisions in Section 252 of the act, designed to limit
new concessions and possibly even withdraw or suspend previous concessions and impose new duties or restrictions on imports into the
United States if foreign import restrictions, including variable import
fees, "substantially burden U.S. commerce inconsistent with previous
trade agreements" and in certain similar cases.

This section of the act reflected congressional concern about possible adverse effects of the EEC's agricultural policy on U.S. agricultural
exports, particularly its import levies on grains and livestock products,
and its minimum import prices for horticultural products. In deciding
on action the president, with due regard for the international obligations of the United States, was to consider such objectives as stimulating
economic growth of the United States, maintaining and enlarging U.S.
foreign markets, and strengthening economic relations with foreign
countries.[36]

THE KENNEDY ROUND. The sixth in the series of GATT negotiations
beginning with the Trade Agreements Act of 1934 was referred to as
the Kennedy Round in recognition of the late president's leadership in
inaugurating the negotiations. When this round formally opened in
Geneva in May 1964, the major participants agreed as a working hypothesis to proceed on the basis of a 50 percent linear, or across-the-board,
reduction in tariffs. Exceptions (products not subject to any or to the
full linear cut) were to be limited to those necessitated by reasons of
overriding national interest. Other objectives of the negotiations were
to cover all classes of products; to provide acceptable conditions of access
to world markets for agricultural products; to include nontariff as well
as tariff barriers; and to reduce barriers to exports of less developed
countries, although these countries would not be expected to reciprocate
fully for benefits received.

It was decided to proceed first in 1964 with negotiations of industrial products. It was not then possible to start the negotiations on agricultural products because of lack of agreement on rules to govern such negotiations and because the EEC was not ready to negotiate on these products.

Agricultural negotiations got under way in September 1965 with an exchange of limited offers by principal importing and exporting countries concerning elements to be included in an international cereals arrangement.

A major indication of the effectiveness and impact of the Trade Expansion Act of 1962 as an instrument for U.S. trade policy may be obtained from a review of the four-year Kennedy Round negotiations.[37]

Tariff concessions covering about $40 billion worth of trade were exchanged by the participants. Tariff reductions of 50 percent were made on a broad range of nonagricultural products and smaller, but significant, reductions on many more. It is estimated that in terms of trade coverage roughly two-thirds of the duty reductions made by participants negotiating on a linear or across-the-board basis were uniform reductions of 50 percent or more.

Although the results of the Kennedy Round tariff negotiations are presented in terms of the value of trade covered by concessions and the depth of tariff reductions, numerous other factors were also considered in evaluating and arriving at the balance of concessions granted, such as the size of duties, characteristics of individual products, demand and supply elasticities, and size and nature of markets, including the reduction in the disadvantage to U.S. exports that might occur through reductions in the tariffs applied to the exports of the United States and other countries.

U.S. Concessions. Tariff concessions were granted by the United States on $8.5 billion of its imports. Of the $8.5 billion, almost $700 million was imported from developing countries that participated in the negotiations; about $500 million was imported from nonparticipants.

A concession represented a commitment in the Kennedy Round, usually with respect to the tariff treatment of imports of a given product. In such a case a concession could be a commitment (1) to make a specified reduction in the rate of duty on a product; or (2) that the rate of duty would not be increased or, if the product were duty free, that a duty would not be imposed on it. A concession of type (2) was termed a *binding.*

Tariff reductions were made by the United States on $7.9 billion or 64 percent of U.S. dutiable imports from all sources, including participants and nonparticipants in the negotiations.

Tariff reductions made by the United States under the Trade Expansion Act were in general to take effect in not less than five equal installments beginning for the most part on January 1, 1968. Most major participants agreed to stage their concessions in a similar manner. The final rates of duty were scheduled to take effect not later than January 1, 1972.

Concessions by Other Participants. The tariff concessions made by all participants other than the United States covered a total of about $32 billion of their imports, including $8.1 billion of imports from the United States. The other major participants made tariff concessions comparable in scope to those of the United States. The tariff concessions of all kinds made by these countries covered total trade of about $30 billion, including $7.6 billion of imports from the United States.

Nonagriculture. The United States obtained and made substantial concessions in the nonagricultural area.

Nonagricultural concessions by other participants covered slightly under $7.2 billion of their imports from the United States. The United States in return made tariff concessions on $7.4 billion of nonagricultural imports from participating countries, including about $550 million from developing countries.

The average percentage cut on nonagricultural tariffs by the linear countries, weighted by imports, was about 35 percent. The average duty reduction on U.S. dutiable imports from linear countries was 35 percent while the average reduction by other linear countries on imports from the United States was 34 percent.

Agriculture. Tariff concessions on a wide range of agricultural products, despite the difficulties encountered in negotiating, were made by major participants, although reductions were generally smaller than for industrial products. The United States obtained a wide range of concessions from its principal negotiating partners on soybeans, tallow, tobacco, poultry, and horticultural products, including citrus and canned fruit. The concessions obtained by the United States compared favorably with the concessions it made on foreign agricultural products. Agricultural concessions by other participants covered nearly $870 million of their imports from the United States. The United States for its part made tariff concessions on $610 million of agricultural imports from participating countries.

The essentials of a world grains arrangement were agreed upon during the conference, and provision was made for further negotiations, under the sponsorship of the International Wheat Council, to complete the agreement. The International Grains Arrangement later agreed upon provided an increased price range for wheat, which in practice was not fully realized, and established a program under which a number of countries would share in supplying food aid to developing countries.

The developing countries were permitted to participate in the negotiations without being required to make fully reciprocal tariff concessions. They also benefitted from the special efforts of developed countries to make concessions on products of particular interest to them through the food aid provision of the grains arrangement. The developing countries made tariff concessions which included about $200 million in imports from the United States.

In the area of *nontariff barriers*, the negotiations led to an antidumping code which reinforced the antidumping provisions of Article VI of GATT with agreed practices and procedures to be followed by the major trading countries. Modifications of certain other nontariff barriers were agreed upon in bilateral negotiations.

For chemical products the negotiations led to a two-part agreement. The first part consisted of an unconditional exchange of many U.S. and foreign tariff reductions in the main Kennedy Round. The second part was conditional upon elimination by the United States of the American selling price valuation system (price at which the imported article is sold or offered for sale in the United States) applied to benzenoid chemicals as well as to certain other products and its replacement by normal methods of valuation. Subject to this condition, not yet fulfilled, the second part provided for an additional exchange of concessions, including deeper tariff reductions on chemicals and removal of some European nontariff barriers.

Useful but limited progress was made on the problems concerned with steel, aluminum, pulp, paper, and textiles, including a three-year extension of the long-term cotton textile arrangement.

The Kennedy Round stands out as the one involving the deepest average tariff reductions as compared with previous GATT tariff-cutting exercises. It was the culmination of U.S. efforts since 1934 to promote expanding international commerce through negotiation of mutually advantageous agreements to reduce trade barriers.

President Lyndon B. Johnson, pursuant to Section 226 of the Trade Expansion Act of 1962, concluded in his report to Congress on the overall results of the Kennedy Round that the negotiations which were completed on June 3, 1967, fulfilled "the purpose and high hopes" of the Trade Expansion Act of 1962.[38]

On the agricultural negotiations John A. Schnittker, then undersecretary of agriculture, concluded that while the net result of the Kennedy Round which ended up being primarily a tariff negotiation could be characterized as "modest liberalization" of agricultural trade; more importantly, it also made the negotiators aware of the problems still pending in bringing increased order to world agricultural trade. To achieve order in agricultural trade, Secretary Schnittker indicated that efforts should focus on individual products or, at most, product groups, so that barriers, especially nontariffs, could be dealt with in depth.[39]

PROPOSED TRADE ACT OF 1970 AND RECENT AGRICULTURAL POLICY DEVELOPMENTS. From the time of the expiration in July 1967 of the presidential negotiating authority under the Trade Expansion Act of 1962 until August 1970, no major trade legislation was acted upon by Congress. At that time the proposed Trade Act of 1970 (HR 18970) received approval by the House Committee on Ways and Means. With the adjournment of the Ninety-first Congress in January 1971, the proposed act died since it did not receive Senate approval after having undergone many changes, additions, and deletions.

As interest continues high, further action on U.S. trade legislation is expected in Congress. In the Ninety-first Congress approximately nine hundred trade-related measures were introduced, of which nearly six hundred were import quota bills.[40]

THE PROPOSED TRADE ACT. Since the proposed trade act was based to a large extent on the Nixon administration's trade proposals, and it represented among the many measures introduced the major proposal on which agreement came closest, it is useful to sketch some of its principal provisions.

In his November 1969 message to Congress on the proposed trade bill, the president declared his intention of appointing a commission to examine the entire range of U.S. trade and related policies and to analyze the problems the United States would likely face in the 1970s. In April 1970 Albert L. Williams of New York was appointed chairman of the president's Commission on International Trade and Investment Policy.

In offering his proposals, President Richard M. Nixon stated that they represented "interim" legislation for developing "flexible" trade policies because of what he regarded as the need to reexamine the U.S. approach for the long range in recognition of rapid changes in production and in trade and investment patterns, and the rapid progress in communications, transportation, and technology. He stressed, however, that progress toward freer trade should continue and that his proposals would—

Restore the authority needed by the President to make limited tariff reductions. This authority [was] not intended for major negotiations, but rather to permit minor adjustments, such as would be required to extend compensation to other countries hurt by U.S. escape clause actions—thereby avoiding retaliations against U.S. exports.
Recognize the very real plight of particular industries, companies, and workers faced with import competition, but providing for a readier escape clause and adjustment assistance relief where justified.
Eliminate the American Selling Price System of customs valuation, a major obstacle impeding progress toward the reduction of nontariff barriers.
Strengthen the hand of the President in his efforts to ensure fair treatment for U.S. exports.[41]

After extensive public hearings and executive deliberations the House Committee on Ways and Means favorably reported in August

1970 the proposed Trade Act of 1970 (HR 18970) by Chairman Wilbur Mills of Arkansas.

The bill, considered to be the most significant trade measure since the passage of the Trade Expansion Act of 1962, included provisions for substantial revisions of and additions to the Trade Expansion Act of 1962 and other statutes. Revisions were made in the provisions pertaining to import relief for industries and adjustment assistance for firms and workers, easing the requirements which must be met to qualify. The imposition of import quotas on textiles and footwear with provision for negotiated agreements to supersede these quotas, and the creation of special tax provisions for "domestic international sales corporations" (DISC) constituted major proposed additions to laws affecting U.S. foreign trade.

Other important provisions included qualified authorization for the president to carry out trade agreements for elimination of the American selling price system of customs valuation which was applicable to a limited number of product groups; limited tariff-cutting authority; broader provisions for dealing with and retaliating against foreign import restrictions and other discriminatory practices; prohibition against the use of tariffs to regulate imports in national security cases; transfer to the secretary of agriculture from the secretary of the treasury the responsibility for determining what articles fall within the article descriptions subject to import restrictions under Section 22 of the Agricultural Adjustment Act; providing several changes in laws effecting unfair competition against the United States; and authorization of new authority to the president concerning drug traffic.[42]

Besides reporting favorably on the proposed Trade Act of 1970, the House Committee on Ways and Means also submitted proposals in a special report to the House of Representatives.

COMMITTEE PROPOSALS. The committee indicated that a number of other trade issues had come to its attention, in the course of its consideration of the bill, on which it had no legislative proposals but on which it did express its view.

Of particular note was its view on nontariff trade barriers and U.S. agricultural exports. The committee believed insufficient progress was being made in reducing or eliminating these barriers to international trade. In discussions with U.S. trading partners, it urged the administration to pursue vigorously the goal of lifting these burdens from U.S. exports. The committee recognized that unlike tariffs, prior congressional delegation of authority to the president to reduce nontariff trade barriers was difficult to embody in legislation because these restrictions were often the result of purely domestic concerns that were only indirectly related to foreign trade. They would require legislative actions to accomplish their removal, and the committee felt this should await the time when negotiations had shown more clearly what would be possible and what specific details were needed in legislation.

The committee believed that the administration should consult with members of Congress as to possible changes in domestic law which might be called for as a result of international negotiations in lowering of barriers. Subject to such consultation and the subsequent enactment of implementing legislation, the committee reported that the president should continue to discuss with other countries the means by which nontariff barriers to trade could be reduced or eliminated.

The committee stated that it was seriously disturbed by the trade problems created by the agricultural policies of some U.S. trading partners, particularly by variable levies and/or import quotas and export subsidies.

Views were expressed also by the committee on the need for action and improvements relating to a number of other items including a voluntary steel arrangement, international labor standards, articles assembled abroad with U.S. components, meat imports, U.S.-Canadian automotive agreement, and comparability of trade data.[43]

AGRICULTURAL POLICY DEVELOPMENTS. Of significance among the more recent agricultural policy developments are the price support changes and producer payments of the 1960s, the Agricultural Act of 1970, and the new International Wheat Agreement.

Price Supports. In the decade of the 1960s price support changes affected particularly feed grains, wheat, and cotton. The changes accompanied by acreage diversion programs and stepped-up aid shipments resulted in a sharp reduction of U.S. grain stocks. The downward adjustment in CCC loan rates for wheat and cotton eliminated the need for large U.S. export payments to facilitate exports. In fiscal year 1969, for example, export payments (those made in cash and those representing the difference between domestic market prices and CCC export sales prices in exports from CCC inventory) totaled $63 million as compared to over $600 million anually for the fiscal years 1960–61 to 1962–63.

Producer Payments. As a means of price support such payments were used in the 1960s for grains and cotton. At the same time farmers were required to participate in an acreage diversion program designed to reduce U.S. surplus stocks. This approach represented an extension of the program first used in the fifties for wool in order to achieve the objective of price support without raising the import duty on apparel wool above the rate bound by GATT or without restricting wool imports by quotas.

The Agricultural Act of 1970. This act, a significant new policy development, is aimed at inaugurating a more market-oriented farm policy, both domestic and foreign.

Domestic price support loan rates under authority of the act will be set close to world market price levels. That is expected to result in a continued lower need for export payment assistance.

Under the "set aside" provisions of the act, a producer will set aside his share of the national land diversion requirement and then be free to plant whatever he likes on his remaining land (except rice, peanuts, sugar, tobacco, or extra long staple cotton). This change is intended to result in more regional specialization and greater farm specialization, and bring about increased efficiency.

Developments given for undertaking the shift to the market-oriented policy include the increase in output of synthetic and substitute products, increases in production in other countries, the rise in competition for world farm product markets, and the growth in productive capacity of U.S. agriculture.

The New International Wheat Agreement. A further development that has significant trade policy implications is the International Wheat Agreement concluded on February 20, 1971, in Geneva. The three-year agreement replaces the International Grains Arrangement that expired June 30. The agreement became effective on July 1, 1971, after ratification by the U.S. Senate.

The wheat agreement contains two major parts: a wheat trade convention provides for cooperation and international consultation on supplies and prices, and a food aid convention in which the United States agrees to provide 1,890 thousand metric tons of wheat to needy countries during the three years of the agreement—the same level of U.S. contributions as under the 1967 agreement.

CONCLUSIONS. A review of the background and historical trends of U.S. trade policy during the past half century provides a useful perspective for analyzing present and future U.S. trade problems and opportunities.

Serious damage was done to U.S. and world trade and investment by the enactment of trade-inhibiting high tariffs in the twenties and early thirties.

The policy of trade expansion, inaugurated with the reciprocal trade agreements program of the thirties, continued in the post-World War II period in the multilateral framework of GATT, and climaxed with the Kennedy Round in 1967, in general brought substantial benefits to the American economy. These benefits resulted from the great growth that took place in U.S. trade. A reversion to protectionism in the case of an industry or group of industries would mean the loss of these benefits from a decrease of export opportunities by reason of retaliatory policies and also higher costs to domestic buyers who could not benefit from operation of the principle of comparative advantage. Further, a reversion to protectionism would prevent essential economic adjustments necessary to maintain competitive productive efficiency and would also tend to break up the unity of an increasingly interdependent world the United States has devoted so much effort to establish.

While Congress should determine U.S. trade policy against the broader background of U.S. foreign policy objectives, the implementation of such policy, as history has shown, is best handled by a delegation of specified authority to the president. Congress is not as well equipped in undertaking trade negotiations as is the executive branch of the government.

Domestic economic policies of market restriction have conflicted with foreign trade policies of market expansion for several decades, particularly in the agricultural sector, and a need still exists for remedial action in this area.

Despite a decline in average duties (see Appendix tables 1 and 2), tariffs in a number of specific instances still represent formidable barriers to trade. In those cases where tariffs have been reduced over time, fewer negotiating opportunities have remained for further reductions. As a consequence, nontariff barriers (NTB) which remain or which have been used for replacing the tariff have gained in importance. These barriers represent some of the most difficult and complex obstacles confronting present and future U.S. trade policy, because their trade and investment distorting effects are often not clearly apparent.

The nontariff barriers of the United States and its trading partners (see Appendix 2 to this chapter for an inventory of U.S. barriers) take varied and diverse forms. The U.S. barriers include quantitative restrictions; valuation practices; customs and administrative entry procedures; government procurement policy; and health, safety, and other nontariff practices.

Bilateral representations through diplomatic channels have been the traditional means for dealing with NTB affecting U.S. exports. Now an effort is being made on a multilateral level through the GATT Committee on Trade in Industrial Products (CTIP) for possible solutions to the major problems identified with NTB in the hope it will result in establishing a basis for multilateral negotiations for removal or modification of many restrictions. Besides the effort undertaken in GATT, the OECD is attempting to develop rules relating to government procurement policies that would put limits on discrimination in favor of national producers.

Progress in multilateral negotiations to eliminate NTB is expected to be slow and difficult as restrictions resulting from them generally are not covered by countries' negotiating authority as are tariffs, but are incorporated in statutes often unrelated to foreign trade and requiring action by national legislation. As in tariff negotiations the principle of reciprocity applies, and meaningful progress can therefore only be achieved depending on the ability of each country to offer reciprocal concessions.

The conditions of trade, relative tariffs, the structure of world economies, and industries have changed markedly in the past half century. The increased emphasis on nontariffs, the changing effect of existing factors, and the emergence of new developments affecting world trade must be continually and effectively reviewed and analyzed to achieve the optimal U.S. trade policy. The list to be considered is long and includes such significant items as subsidies, trade adjustment assistance, quotas, multinational corporations, labor conditions, border taxes, variable levies, generalized and special preferences, market disruption, the U.S.-Canadian automotive agreement, trade area enlargement negotiations, and relaxation of U.S.-mainland China trade relations.

APPENDIX 2.1

SELECTED STATISTICS ON TARIFFS OF THE UNITED STATES

TABLE 2.1. U.S. Imports, Dutiable and Duty Free, and Duties Collected, 1934–70 (Dollar Amounts in Millions)

Year	Imports*			Percentage Distribution			Calculated Duties	
	Total	Dutiable	Duty free	Dutiable	Free	Total	As percentage of total imports	As percentage of dutiable imports
1934	1,636	645	991	39	61	301	18.4	46.7
1939	2,276	879	1,397	39	61	328	14.4	37.3
1946	4,825	1,890	2,935	39	61	478	9.9	25.3
1947	5,667	2,212	3,455	39	61	428	7.6	19.3
1948	7,093	2,918	4,175	41	59	405	5.7	13.9
1949	6,591	2,708	3,883	41	59	365	5.5	13.5
1950	8,743	3,976	4,767	45	55	522	6.0	13.1
1951	10,817	4,824	5,993	45	55	591	5.5	12.3
1952	10,748	4,491	6,257	42	58	570	5.3	12.7
1953	10,779	4,859	5,920	45	55	584	5.4	12.0
1954	10,240	4,572	5,668	45	55	529	5.2	11.6
1955	11,337	5,300	6,037	47	53	633	5.6	11.9
1956	12,516	6,281	6,235	50	50	710	5.7	11.3
1957	12,950	6,914	6,036	53	47	746	5.8	10.8
1958	12,740	7,398	5,342	58	42	821	6.4	11.1
1959	14,994	9,170	5,824	61	39	1,052	7.0	11.5
1960	15,014	8,872	6,142	59	41	1,078	7.2	12.2
1961	14,658	8,735	5,923	60	40	1,057	7.2	12.1
1962	16,242	10,026	6,216	62	38	1,220	7.5	12.2
1963	17,001	10,743	6,258	63	37	1,240	7.3	11.5
1964	18,600	11,579	7,021	62	38	1,339	7.2	11.6
1965	21,283	13,849	7,434	65	35	1,643	7.7	11.9
1966	25,367	16,023	9,344	63	37	1,921	7.6	12.0
1967	26,732	16,529	10,203	62	38	2,016	7.5	12.2
1968	32,992	20,725	12,267	63	37	2,341	7.1	11.3
1969	35,870	22,809	13,061	64	36	2,551	7.1	11.2
1970	39,768	25,890	13,878	65	35	2,584	6.5	10.0

SOURCES: *Historical Statistics of the United States; Statistical Abstract of the United States,* U.S. Department of Commerce. Figures for 1967–70 from U.S. Department of Commerce.
* Imports for consumption.

TABLE 2.2. U.S. Tariff Reductions, 1934–67

Legislation	Percentage Reductions Authorized	Maximum Reduction Authorized on Basis of Actual Use of Tariff-Cutting Authority			Actual Change in Average Ad Valorem Equivalent (%)	
		Authorized reduction in tariff level (%)		Average "percentage point" reduction authorized		
		From	To		From	To
1934 act	50 percent (of 1934 rates)	47.0	23.5	23.5	47.0	28.0
1945 act	50 percent (of 1945 rates)	28.0	14.0	14.0	28.0	12.0
1955 act	15 percent (of 1955 rates, over 3 years)	12.0	10.2	1.8	12.0	11.0
1958 act (Dillon Round)	20 percent (of 1958 rates, over 4 years)	11.0	8.8	2.2	11.0	12.0
1962 act (Kennedy Round)	50 percent (of 1962 rates, over 5 years)	12.0	6.0	6.0	12.0	7.8*

SOURCE: *Congressional Record*, June 21, 1968, p. E5718.
*Assuming no change in price levels.

APPENDIX 2.2

INVENTORY OF NONTARIFF BARRIERS OF THE UNITED STATES. This inventory, taken from *International Commerce,* September 21, 1970, represents U.S. practices other countries have called to the attention of the General Agreement on Tariffs and Trade (GATT) as the most commonly mentioned impediments to their trade. The United States in like fashion also submitted an inventory of foreign nontariff barriers (NTB) affecting U.S. exports. The inventories of seventy countries including the United States were submitted to GATT as part of a comprehensive GATT-wide inventory.

QUANTITATIVE RESTRICTIONS. Presidential authority to impose quotas or fees on imports of agricultural commodities; restrictions are in effect on wheat and wheat flour, cotton, peanuts, and several dairy products.

Presidential authority to limit any imports for national security reasons, currently applied only to petroleum shipments.

Sugar quota reserving 65 percent of the national market to domestic producers.

Provision of the Meat Import Act for automatic import controls once a certain level (not yet reached) is attained.

Restrictions on firearms imports which are allegedly more stringent than regulations on interstate shipments or mail order sales.

A tariff rate quota on brooms, whereby all imports in excess of a stipulated number are assessed at higher rates of duty.

Ban on purchase of foreign-built containers by U.S. flag vessels if the vessel's operations are governed by an operating differential subsidy contract.

Provision that vessels engaged in U.S. coastal trade must be U.S.-built and U.S.-manned.

A provision of the Long-Term Cotton Textile Agreement, whereby the United States controls imports of cotton textiles under separate bilateral agreements with twenty-four countries, accounting for more than 80 percent of U.S. cotton textile imports.

Banning of imports of ermine, fox, kolinsky, marten, mink, muskrat, and weasel fur skins produced in the USSR or mainland China.

The Atomic Energy Act of 1954 prohibiting uranium enrichment servicing for nuclear materials of foreign origin intended for use in a facility within or under the jurisdiction of the United States.

VALUATION PRACTICES. The U.S. system of customs valuation provides nine different methods of establishing the value of articles, of which the two most frequently used employ f.o.b. (free on board) values. Other countries contend that complexity of U.S. valuation provisions is itself a barrier to trade, and some have proposed adoption of the Brussels definition of value—the landed c.i.f. (cost, insurance, and freight) value.

Under the American selling price system imported benzenoid chemicals, some rubber footwear, clams, and certain wool knit gloves have duties assessed on the value of competing U.S. products rather than the value of the imported article.

Certain products are valued on the old system of appraisement rather than the method established in the Customs Simplification Act of 1956.

OTHER CUSTOMS AND ADMINISTRATIVE ENTRY PROCEDURES. The Special Customs Invoice used to report entries valued at more than $500 requests some data which foreign suppliers consider unnecessary and burdensome.

Tariff Schedules of the United States (TSUS) vary from the Brussels Tariff Nomenclature, used by more than one hundred countries including all our major trading partners except Canada. Among other things, foreigners say that TSUS classifies items so that many parts are no longer listed with the product to which they belong.

Special dumping duties may be imposed under the Antidumping Act of 1921, which by law in case of conflict takes precedence over the International Dumping Code, to which the United States adheres.

United States countervailing duty practice provides for no injury requirement, which is called for by GATT.

Certificates of origin are required for importation of commodities into the United States when goods of Communist Chinese, North Korean, or North Vietnamese origin may be involved.

United States practice does not fully conform to the provisions of the international convention to facilitate imports of samples. The convention limits deposits on samples to the amount of import duties plus 10 percent, whereas the United States requires a deposit of double the estimated duties. (U.S. rules are being revised to bring them into line with the convention.)

GOVERNMENT PROCUREMENT POLICY. The Buy American Act of 1933 requires the federal government to buy only domestic materials unless (1) they are not available, (2) their purchase would not be in the public interest, or (3) the cost would be unreasonable. "Unreasonable" is defined as being more than 6 percent higher than the foreign bid. Another 6 percent is added if the material will be produced in a depressed area or by a "small business." The Defense Department currently applies a 50 percent differential due to balance-of-payments problems.

The Department of Defense cannot buy any article of food, clothing, cotton, wool, silk, or spun silk yarn for cartridge cloth, or synthetic and coated synthetic materials not produced in the United States.

SAFETY STANDARDS. Regulations affecting motor vehicles, boilers and pressure vessels, steel processes, plumbing, heating, lumber, firefighting and electrical equipment, and U.S. Coast Guard inspection of safety equipment have all been subject to complaint.

The Flammable Fabrics Act authorized the Federal Trade Commission to test merchandise believed to be in violation of established requirements. (This law applies equally to domestic and imported products.)

HEALTH STANDARDS. Certain provisions of the Quarantine and Food and Drug Law, the Wholesome Meat Act, and the Agricultural Marketing Agreement Act have been viewed as trade barriers by foreign suppliers.

OTHER STANDARDS. The Fair Packaging and Labeling Act of 1966 prescribes the manner in which certain consumer commodities are to be packaged and labeled. (This law also applies equally to domestic and imported products.)

The name of the country of origin must be marked in a conspicuous place on all imports coming into this country. Exceptions are permitted, but in such cases the container must be marked.

OTHER NONTARIFF PRACTICES. Escape clause actions allow the president to increase duties or otherwise restrict imports of items found to be injuring or threatening to injure a domestic industry.

Imports of bottled distilled spirits are assessed as though they were 100 proof, so that in effect a bottle of 86-proof Scotch is assessed for an additional 14 proof.

Legislation prevents the entry into the United States of more than 1,500 copies of any English language book authored by a U.S. citizen. It is not applicable to books authored by nationals of countries adhering to the Universal Copyright Convention.

All subsidized ship construction must be done in U.S. shipyards, and equipment purchased must be of U.S. origin.

Corporations that conduct all their business in the Western Hemisphere and derive 95 percent of their gross income from outside the United States are eligible for certain tax rebates.

Post exchanges at armed forces bases overseas may enter duty-free into host countries any goods, regardless of country of origin, and sell them tax-free to authorized customers.

The president may exclude goods imported through unfair acts when the effect of the acts is to destroy or substantially injure any industry, prevent establishment of an industry, or restrain or monopolize trade in the United States. This authority has been invoked once, against imports of Furazolidone, an antibacterial agent.

The Internal Revenue Service classifies sparkling cider as a sparkling wine. The law sets 0.277 grams or CO_2 per 100 milliliters as the upper limit for still wines, and sparkling cider generally has more than

0.4 grams of CO_2 per 100 milliliters. (Once again, this law applies with equal force to foreign and domestic products.)

The above list, among other things, does not include foreign assets control regulations which apply to U.S. trade with Communist China, North Korea, North Vietnam, and Cuba; voluntary export controls imposed by foreign governments to avoid disruption of the U.S. market; state and local government measures; and private practices.

NOTES

1. Oscar Zaglits, "Agricultural Trade and Trade Policy," *Foreign Trade and Agricultural Policy* (Washington, D.C.: National Advisory Commission on Food and Fiber, 1967), pp. 137–38.
2. Paul H. Douglas, "A History of the Tariff," *American Trade Policy* (Columbia, Mo.: Artcraft, 1962), p. 313.
3. George N. Peek and Hugh S. Johnson, *Equality for Agriculture*, 2nd ed. (Moline, Ill.: H. W. Harrington, 1922).
4. Robert L. Tontz, "Evolution of the Term Parity in Agricultural Usage," *Southwestern Social Science Quarterly*, 35(March 1955):348–50; "Origin of the Base Period Concept of Parity—A Significant Value Judgment in Agricultural Policy," *Agricultural History*, vol. 32, no. 1, 1958, pp. 3–13.
5. Alex F. McCalla, "Protectionism in International Agricultural Trade, 1850–1968," *Agricultural History*, 43(July 1968):329–43.
6. Douglas, p. 314.
7. Robert E. Baldwin, "Toward the Seventh Round of GATT Trade Negotiations," *Issues and Objectives of U.S. Foreign Trade Policy*, Joint Committee Print, 90th Cong., 1st sess. (Washington, D.C.: USGPO, 1967), p. 22.
8. Zaglits, pp. 141–42.
9. For a discussion of proposed corrective measures including lowered price supports which have been made recently, see D. Gale Johnson, "A Sound Trade Policy and Its Implications for Agriculture" in *Foreign Agricultural Trade: Selected Readings*, Robert L. Tontz, ed. (Ames: Iowa State Univ. Press, 1966), pp. 46–51.
10. Zaglits, p. 149.
11. Ibid., p. 148.
12. William Diebold, Jr., "Trade Policies Since World War II," in Tontz, ed., pp. 31–32.
13. Ibid., p. 32.
14. Ibid.
15. Baldwin, p. 22.
16. Ibid.
17. "U.S. Foreign Trade Policy From 1789–1958," in Tontz, ed., p. 28.
18. Baldwin, p. 22.
19. "U.S. Foreign Trade Policy," in Tontz, ed., p. 28
20. Ibid.
21. Ibid.
22. Baldwin, p. 23.
23. Zaglits, pp. 145–46.
24. Diebold, in Tontz, ed., pp. 34–35.
25. Ibid.
26. Zaglits, p. 152.
27. Public Law 480, adopted in 1954, may be regarded as the successor to Section 550 of the Mutual Security Act of 1951.
28. Cf. Willard W. Cochrane, "Public Law 480 and Related Programs," Erik Mortensen, "Foreign Surplus Disposal—The Competitor's Perspective," and Earle S. Hoffman, "The Economics of Surplus Disposals," in Tontz, ed., pp. 185–91, 235–45, 261–77; Clarence D. Palmby, *U.S. and World Agricultural Trade*, statement before the Subcommittee on International Trade Committee on Finance, U.S. Senate, May 20, 1971, p. 26.

29. Eugene M. Braderman, "Commercial Policies Safeguard U.S. Industry and Agriculture—While Promoting Trade Growth," in Tontz, ed., p. 295.

30. Zaglits, pp. 150–51.

31. Ibid., p. 151.

32. Ibid.

33. Cf. "Summary of the Trade Expansion Act of 1962," *Current History*, 43 (July 1962):50–51, 55, and Edwin M. Martin, "American Agriculture in Foreign Trade," *Department of State Bulletin*, 46(March 19, 1962):471–79.

34. "Trade Expansion Act of 1962," *Selected Provisions of the Tariff and Trade Laws of the United States and Related Materials*, Committee Print, 91st Cong., 2nd sess. (Washington, D.C.: Committee on Ways and Means, U.S. Congress, House, 1970), pp. 31–39.

35. Peter R. Kenen, *International Economics* (Englewood, N.J.: Prentice-Hall, 1964), p. 46.

36. Committee on Ways and Means, U.S. Congress, House, *Selected Provisions of the Tariff and Trade Laws of the United States*, Committee Print, 90th Cong., 2nd sess. (Washington, D.C.: USGPO, 1968), pp. 1–39, 67–71.

37. Office of the Special Representative for Trade Negotiations, *Report on U.S. Negotiations, GATT 1964–67 Trade Conference, Geneva*, vol. 1, pts. 1–2 (Washington, D.C.: USGPO, 1967).

38. "Message from the President of the United States," *General Agreement on Tariffs and Trade*, Document No. 184, as reported in *Selected Provisions of the Tariff and Trade Laws of the United States*, 90th Cong., 1st sess. (Washington, D.C.: USGPO, 1969), p. 42.

39. Hearings before the Subcommittee on Foreign Economic Policy of the Joint Economic Committee, *The Future of U.S. Foreign Trade Policy*, vol. 1, 90th Cong., 1st sess. (Washington, D.C.: USGPO, 1967), pp. 32–36.

40. *Commerce Today*, 1(January 11, 1971):48.

41. "Letter from the President to Chairman Mills, May 11, 1970," Committee Print, *Written Statements and Other Material Submitted by Administration Witnesses . . .* , 91st Cong., 2nd sess. (Washington, D.C.: USGPO, 1970), pp. 1–2.

42. *International Commerce*, 76(September 7, 1970):6–10.

43. Ibid.

[3]

What Difference Does Trade Make in World Community Welfare?

D. Gale Johnson

ALTHOUGH trade is important, those of us who have special interests as scholars or direct participants in exporting and importing should not be guilty of overestimating its importance. Achieving free trade in all products, agricultural as well as nonagricultural, will not bring the millenium; poor countries will not immediately or even in the longer run become rich as a result, nor will high income countries realize major gains in national income that can be used to meet the costs of curing their social ills such as poverty, urban congestion, crime, or pollution. Achieving free trade is only one of a number of policy measures governments can undertake in order to improve the efficiency with which their economies function and thus increase national welfare. I do not imply that the only component of national welfare is "more output—more income." But most social and economic problems besetting all countries, rich and poor, can be met more easily from a larger rather than a smaller national output.

While reducing barriers to international trade is only one of several measures all countries can consider, this in no way depreciates the importance of moving toward free trade nor the favorable consequences of so doing. But it is in fact desirable that achieving free trade would have fairly modest effects upon the world's real output of goods and services— its real income—since the rather limited effects of moving to free trade imply the largely misguided trade restriction policies of most governments have done only limited damage. Damage has been done, but its extent has been minimized by the very substantial flexibility existing in all economies. Economies appear to have the capacity to largely offset many mistakes due either to ignorance or avarice.

D. GALE JOHNSON is Professor of Economics, University of Chicago.

49

While it is true that most serious problems of the world would still be with us if there were free trade or something close to it, it is evident that if benefit-cost analysis were applied to the acts of politicians and their advisers, few would compete for the prize that went to the highest benefit-cost ratio. I refer not only to benefits that can be measured in gains in real output. But, if we had proper instruments for measurement, the gains in the value of real output might be only a small part of the total gains from free trade. Nor do I refer to the benefit that may come from increased discipline of the market that results in increased productive efficiency.

I have in mind primarily two other kinds of important benefits. One is that protection involves substantial income transfers that are often quite inconsistent with any notions of equity many societies claim to adhere to. The other is that protection has all too often provided an excuse for avoiding or ignoring important social and economic issues. This is especially true of agriculture. Governments have found barriers to trade, either direct or indirect, involving the use of subsidies, to be the politically most acceptable instruments even though the difficulties that are ameliorated do not have their origins in the low farm prices increased by trade restrictions. Low farm incomes, either in a relative or absolute sense, are the result of many difficulties facing farm people, and of these difficulties low farm prices are among the least important.

COSTS OF PROTECTION—TO THE PROTECTED. In this section concern will be solely with the costs of protection to the nation imposing restrictions on trade; the next section will consider the costs borne by external victims, namely those foreigners who lose the opportunity to sell and to buy. Primary emphasis is upon protection resulting in an interference with trade. Interference, however, includes measures other than tariffs, quotas, or export subsidies. A reduction in imports is no less real or significant if it occurs as a result of output expansion engendered by dificiency payments rather than from a tariff or quota. Similarly exports can be encouraged by input subsidies or deficiency payments related to output as well as by direct use of export subsidies. Thus protection is here defined to include techniques that may be used to increase domestic production above the level that would prevail if farmers received world market prices and nothing more.

The costs of protection may fall into three main categories: (1) loss in consumer welfare due to the consumption alternatives that consumers forego because the prices they face do not represent real cost alternatives; (2) excess production cost of domestic production compared to the cost of acquiring the same marginal output through trade; and (3) transfer of income from consumers and taxpayers to farmers and perhaps to resource owners who supply inputs to farmers. In the literature in international trade as well as in the study of the economics of welfare, only the first two of these costs are considered to be "real" costs. And this is a correct approach if the only or primary concern is that of the value of goods and services a nation loses through imposition of trade-interfering devices; these are the losses directly associated with a nation not taking advantage of the opportunity to obtain all its goods and services at the lowest possible cost.

In such analyses, and there are too many to cite, transfers of income from consumers and taxpayers are not considered to be a "real" cost of protection. It is true that apart from the effects of resource use of collecting taxes related either to income or expenditure the income transfers do not result in a loss in real output. In other words, apart from the exception noted, income transfers do not impose a reduction in real output over and above the excess production costs and loss of consumer welfare.

It is both reasonable and necessary to view income transfers as a cost of protection, though the perspective from which one starts is different from that underlying usual and appropriate analyses of welfare costs of protection. The perspective that permits, perhaps one should say requires, consideration of income transfers as a cost of protection is that taxpayers and consumers are required to make the income transfers and the income transfers are made for some purpose. Thus the relationship between costs of the transfer and benefits derived from the purpose or end of the transfer is a legitimate focus of inquiry.

In arguing that the transfer should be considered as a cost, there is not a presumption that there is no gain associated with the cost; the gain can presumably be greater than, equal to, or less than the cost involved. In this sense, there would be a net cost if the value of the gains from the transfer, however measured, were less than the cost. Presumably the decision to require the income transfer was based upon the conclusion that the gain exceeded the cost. What is involved is whether the assumption of gain exceeding cost is valid in particular circumstances.

Figure 3.1 illustrates the various components of cost under these conditions: (1) the domestic price is set above the import cost; (2) the country continues to import the farm product; and (3) the support price, P_2, is achieved by a tariff or variable levy. If there were no price support program, the domestic price would equal the world price or import cost, P_1; total consumption would be OX_2 of which OX_1 would be produced domestically and the remainder imported. With the higher price for producers, domestic production increases to OX_3, domestic consumption declines to OX_4, and imports are substantially reduced. In the example it is assumed that the world price is not affected by the reduction of imports.

The various cost elements referred to above can now be estimated

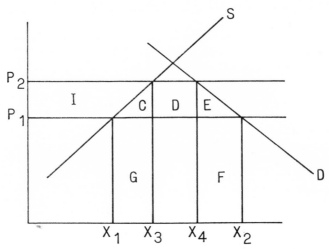

FIG. 3.1.   Components of cost.

from the labeled areas in Figure 3.1. If the price elasticity of demand for the farm product is less than one, consumers will pay more money for less of the product. The increase in consumer money costs would be $(I + C + D)-F$ of which D represents the funds collected by the treasury from the import tariff or variable levy. Thus the combined money cost to consumers and taxpayers would be $(I + C)-F$.

If one looks at the costs more analytically, he sees that I represents the increase in net income to producers—the presumed increase in rent or income farm resource owners would receive in excess of what they would receive if the product price were P_1. The triangle C is the additional resource cost due to the increase in output and represents the wastage of resources due to domestic production rather than importation. The triangle E is the loss in consumers' surplus—the loss incurred by consumers because the opportunity to purchase more of this product is foreclosed by the higher price. Thus the *real* costs are $C + E$ while two transfers are involved. One is the transfer from consumers to farmers, I, and from consumers to taxpayers, D, since, assuming a constant total governmental expenditure, other taxes may be reduced by D. Consumers may also consider C as a part of the transfer, though it would not be so viewed by the farmer. If the general tax structure is progressive and if the farm commodity is one with low income and price elasticities, the income transfer from consumers to taxpayers is likely to involve a net transfer of income from low income to high income citizens.

Figure 3.1 can be used to illustrate the distribution of costs if the difference between P_1 and P_2 is achieved by a deficiency payment rather than by control of imports. The average return to farmers would be the same—P_2. The increase in total return to farmers would also be the same as would the components—an income transfer of I and an increase in real costs of C; these two areas would represent the cost of the deficiency payment to taxpayers. The consumers would not suffer either a money cost or a loss of consumer welfare since their consumption would be the quantity OX_2 at the lowest available price, P_1. The resource cost, C, is the real cost of the program, as conventionally measured, to the economy if it is assumed the reduction of imports due to the increase in domestic production, X_1X_3, has no adverse effects upon the export sector of the economy.

A few words should be said about the two rectangles G and F in Figure 3.1. The first, G, is a component of the increase in the gross income of farmers. It represents a part—the major part—of the cost of increasing output by X_1X_3 and is a measure of what those costs would be if additional output could have been produced at a marginal cost of P_1, the import price of the product. The fact that G is one of the elements in the increase of the gross income of farmers may be one of the reasons the effectiveness of increased prices in improving the income position of farmers is generally overestimated by policy makers. The increase in returns due to higher farm prices, over what such resources would earn if employed elsewhere (that is, due to expansion of output by X_1X_3), is very small—approximately the value of the triangle C.

The other rectangle, F, represents the value of the reduction in consumption of food when the food is valued at import prices. What is the appropriate economic interpretation of this rectangle? From the standpoint of the economy as a whole it can be said the area represents neither a gain nor a loss since the expenditure represented by the area can be made for other goods and services without a loss of consumers' surplus. The individuals receiving the area I would spend their additional income for other goods and services and the loss in consumers' surplus for the economy is already reflected in E. But if one takes the viewpoint of the consumer *qua* consumer, or the viewpoint of all consumers except those who are recipients of I, F represents a loss. Such consumers are paying more and getting less food and less of all consumer goods and services.

The last sentence is correct only if the price elasticity of demand for food is less than unity, but even if the price elasticity is greater than unity, F represents a loss to consumers *qua* consumers though part of F could be offset by reduction in total expenditure for food. (Assume that at world prices, consumption was 60 billion units at a price of one, the price elasticity of demand is —2, and price is increased by 10 percent by the imposition of a tariff. Consumption falls to approximately 48 billion units and the value of the area F is 12 billion. However, consumer expenditure on food falls from 60 billion to 52.8 billion. The net value of the change in consumer expenditure and F is 4.8 billion. The loss in consumers' surplus [the triangle E] is 0.6 billion monetary units so the total cost to consumers is 5.4 billion.)

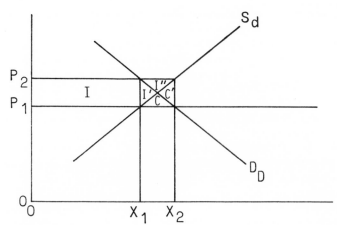

FIG. 3.2. Price support level and trade.

Taken together, F and G represent the reduction in the value of imports of the commodity if it is assumed that the elasticity of supply of imports to the country is perfectly elastic.

Figure 3.2 is similar to Figure 3.1 except that it depicts a situation in which the country would import if the farm price were the world price, P_1, and would export with a subsidy if the domestic price were P_2. It is assumed that the higher price would be achieved by import controls and export subsidies; thus even if there were variable levies there would be no net revenue to the treasury—any imports that came in and on which a levy was collected would be offset by an equal export subsidy on an equal volume.

To simplify the figure, it is assumed that domestic consumption at the higher price would exactly equal domestic production at the lower world price; this could happen, although it would be a quite accidental outcome. The income transfer to farmers is $I + I' + I''$. The real resource cost due to expanding high cost of domestic production is $C + C'$. The increase in consumer expenditures is $I - F$, but since the volume consumed has been reduced, the loss in consumers' surplus is $I' + C$. The cost of the export subsidy is equal to the difference between the domestic price, P_2, and world price, P_1, multiplied by the amount exported, X_1X_2. As far as this economy is concerned the part of increased resource costs and the part of consumers' surplus that overlap, C, should be counted twice. The loss to consumers would exist regardless of where S_d intersects the world price line.

In Figure 3.1 rectangle F also represents savings in foreign exchange achieved through reducing imports. If the nation has an appropriate exchange rate, it also represents loss of foreign exchange earnings suffered by the export sector of the economy. However, when a nation has an overvalued currency the rectangle F is often assigned a substantial positive value, in fact a value approximately equal to the number of currency units involved.

The examples depicted in the two figures indicate that the costs represented by the resources wasted and the loss of consumers' surplus are substantially smaller than the income transfer imposed upon consumers. This is not just an artifact of the particular examples, but appears to be generally true. The reason for the much greater magnitude of the income transfer is that the income transfer is the product of the tariff and the quantity consumed after the tariff is imposed, while the excess resource cost, C, is a part of the transfer as seen by the consumer, and the loss in consumers' surplus is (approximately) one-half the tariff rate multiplied by the decline in quantity consumed due to the increase in price.

The above approach to the comparison of the income transfer imposed upon consumers and the real income foregone, $C + D$, may be criticized because of the apparent double counting of C. C is a real cost since it measures the excess production cost but in the framework accepted here this is one of the outcomes paid for by the excess money cost imposed upon the consumer. In one sense it is irrelevant to the consumer whether the increased money handed over to the producer goes for additional real costs or for additional rents. If the consumer is convinced that farmers deserve higher incomes, the consumer would be saddened to learn that part of his gratuity is wasted on additional costs that benefit no one. If the consumer wants his income transfer to result in a benefit to a fellow citizen, he would prefer a policy measure that held output at OX_1 and transferred the amount, $I + C$, to the farmers. This would make farmers better off and consumers no worse off.

Some empirical estimates have been made of loss in real income due to trade restrictions. Arnold C. Harberger estimated that during the 1950s the various trade restrictions in Chile restricted trade equivalent to that of a tariff of 50 percent. Assuming trade would double if trade restrictions were removed, he estimates the welfare gain would be "no more than $2\frac{1}{2}$ percent of the national income."[1] Harry G. Johnson made an estimate of the gains to the United Kingdom if there were free trade with Europe, based on projections of the value of trade in 1970. His conclusion was that the gain to Britain was a maximum of 1 percent of the national income of the United Kingdom.[2] A study of the short-run effects of lowering import duties on industrial products in Germany in the 1950s concludes that when duties were lowered by half, or by about ten percentage points, the gain amounted to 0.18 percent of national income.[3] The period of adjustment was short (about two years) and the demand curve for all industrial products was assumed to have zero price elasticity though, since the increase in imports was based on actual change in imports after the tariff reductions, the assumption with respect to demand was quite unimportant in affecting the estimated gain. A study directly related to agricultural trade has recently been published by T. E. Josling of the London School of Economics, "Agriculture and Britain's Trade Dilemma."[4] He makes four estimates of various costs of British agricultural and trade policy: (1) the present system with deficiency payments; (2) substitution of variable levies for the deficiency payments; (3) variable levy system with the United Kingdom inside the European Economic Community (EEC) but with U.K. prices; and (4) variable levy system with the United Kingdom inside the EEC but having EEC prices for farm products. His estimates of various costs and transfers are given in Table 3.1. The period for the estimates is the late 1960s. As background, consumption of farm food products is £3,050 million, of which £1,500 million is imported. The current deficiency payment scheme has increased average returns to producers by 10 percent, and joining the EEC would increase market prices by 25 percent and produce average returns over the current level including the deficiency payments by about 15 percent. Under the present system deficiency payments are £150 million and domestic gross farm receipts are

TABLE 3.1.   Economic Costs and Returns of Various British Agricultural Policies Relative to Free Market Conditions

	Deficiency Payment System with U.K. Outside EEC	Variable Levy System with U.K. Outside EEC	Variable Levy System with U.K. Inside EEC but U.K. Prices	Variable Levy System with U.K. Inside EEC and EEC (High) Prices
	(million)			
Extra producer gross returns	212	212	212	560
Cost of extra resources	65	65	65	174
Net additional returns to British producer	147	147	147	386
Extra consumer food expenditure	...	246	246	605
Loss in consumer valuation	...	51	51	137
Loss in consumer welfare	...	297	297	742
Internal transfer from consumers	...	295	150	405
Net loss in consumer welfare	...	2	147	337
Gross internal transfer to producer	150	150	150	405
Net producer returns	147	147	147	386
Cost of transfer	3	3	3	19
Net cost of policy to Britain	3	5	150	356
Net real cost of policy	3	5	5	34

SOURCE: T. E. Josling, *Agriculture and Britain's Trade Policy Dilemma*, Thames Essay No. 2, Trade Policy Research Centre (London, 1970), p. 24.

£1,700. The higher producer returns under the deficiency payment system are estimated at £212 million, of which £65 million goes for extra resources, leaving a net additional return of £147 million (col. 1, Table 3.1).

Further assumptions based on available estimates of demand and supply elasticities were made. With respect to supply, it is estimated that with a supply elasticity of 0.4 for domestic farm production the present system increases farm output by 4 percent and EEC prices would increase output by an additional 6 percent or 10 percent above domestic supply at world prices. The U.K. price elasticity of demand is estimated to be —0.16, so that current U.K. producer prices achieved by a variable levy system that would increase consumer prices by 10 percent would reduce consumption by 1.6 percent, and raising prices to the EEC level would reduce consumption by an additional 2.4 percent.

We may now turn to Josling's estimates given in Table 3.1. The last row of the table gives the estimates of the resource cost for the first and second policies. The loss in real income from the deficiency payment system is estimated at £3 million, which is 0.1 percent of the total British consumption of food or 0.2 percent of domestic gross farm receipts or only about 2 percent of the net additional returns to British farmers (row 3, col. 1). Thus the resource cost of the transfer involved in the deficiency payment system is very small. A change to the variable levy system would shift the costs from the treasury to consumers; in fact, the treasury would come out ahead, which may explain why tariffs and variable levies are more popular than deficiency payments. The additional real cost of the variable levy system compared to the deficiency payment system is very small—only £2 million or a total of £5 million. The loss in real income of the variable levy system would be less than 4 percent of the net additional returns received by the producer.

The last row of Table 3.1 reflects the resource cost of these two policies in the same sense it does for the first two policies. Without transfer of the variable levy receipts to the EEC, the loss in real income to the United Kingdom under the variable levy system with U.K. prices and membership in the EEC would remain at £5 million. What is involved is a *transfer* of £145 million from the United Kingdom to the other members of the EEC. As Josling indicates this is a cost of EEC membership for the United Kingdom, but it is a cost in the same sense that a transfer from the British treasury or consumers to British farmers is a cost. One can readily understand why a British citizen would view the two costs rather differently.

The last row of Table 3.1, derived from Josling's estimates, shows the sum of the excess resource cost and the loss of consumers' surplus. These costs are those normally referred to as the real costs of protection. The next to the last row in the table indicates the net cost of the various programs to Britain and this row includes both real costs and, when

58 CHAPTER THREE

applicable, transfers that would be made to the EEC. If the United Kingdom were a member of an EEC that adopted the U.K. prices, the transfer would be £145 million; if a member of EEC with current EEC farm prices, the transfer to the other members of EEC would be £322 million.

Resource or real costs (excluding transfer to the EEC) due to EEC membership with EEC prices are much higher absolutely than for either the deficiency payment scheme or a variable levy scheme with U.K. prices. In fact, the real cost becomes rather large at £34 million. The increase in prices from 10 percent in excess of world prices to 25 percent in excess is responsible for the increase in real cost from £5 million to £34 million. With EEC prices the British producer would realize an increase in income of £386 million and the resource cost would be about 9 percent of the income transfer. In one sense it might appear that an efficient means had been found for increasing farm income, since the apparent increase in income is eleven times the real cost. However, the consumer of food might take a different viewpoint since his cost is £741 million. Even if you subtract the transfer to the EEC, the cost to the consumer is £420 million which is greater than the increase in return to farm resources. And so it must be greater by the amount of the real resource costs. As is sometimes said, there is no such thing as a free lunch.

Given the general structure of Josling's example, the resulting relationship between the magnitude of the transfer and the real costs would be moderately affected by significant variations in the elasticities of supply and demand. If the elasticity of domestically produced food were unity instead of 0.4, the excess resource cost with U.K. prices increases from £3 million to £7.5 million and under EEC prices from £19 million to £47.5 million.

The largest of the estimates of excess resource costs, however, is still less than 12 percent of the gross transfer to producers and only about 7 percent of the total cost to consumers. The upper limit of the price elasticity of demand for food products in the United Kingdom or other high income countries can hardly be more than double the elasticity used (−0.16), or about −0.3. If the larger price elasticity of demand were used, this would double the value of the loss in consumers' surplus and it would still be relatively small for either U.K. or EEC prices. However, the estimates of the real cost of protection presented are underestimates of the actual costs, though the magnitude of the underestimate is not known. Three sources of underestimation may be noted: (1) all the examples assume there are no intermediate products or a protected product is not used as an input; (2) the elasticities of supply and demand that have been used are generally for the short run; if the long-run elasticities, especially of supply, are substantially higher than in the short run the real losses are increased significantly; and (3) the estimates generally assume a single rate of protection and if varying degrees of protection exist, the real costs become higher. The first point is another way of saying that protection is likely to move an economy away from its production possibility curve to an interior position.

COSTS OF PROTECTION—TO THE EXCLUDED. The previous section viewed the cost of protection imposed upon the country that restricts trade in one sector of its economy, such as agriculture. In the analysis it was assumed that trade restrictions did not change the terms of trade in favor of that country. If that assumption is maintained, the analysis applies equally to the costs that would be imposed upon countries that have lost part of their opportunity to export as a result of protection imposed by another. Assume that all exporters impose an export tax upon products subject to trade restrictions in importing countries, with the size of the export tax set to maintain world prices at the level that would prevail with free trade. In this way the terms of trade would not be affected by the trade restrictions.

If the usual assumptions are made about elasticities of supply and demand, an exporting country would suffer a loss of exports and internal prices of export products would fall relative to prices of both domestic and imported goods. Output of goods formerly imported will increase in response to their higher relative prices, while output of the export product will fall in response to its lower price. There will be both excess resource costs and consumers' surplus losses compared to the free trade situation. The relative prices that would prevail in the domestic market would not reflect the real opportunity costs of obtaining imported goods through exportation.

The primary difference between the two cases is the source of the income transfers. In the exporting countries the transfer will be from producers of the exported product to consumers of that product who will not only receive some gain in consumers' surplus due to increased consumption but will also be recipients of a substantial saving in expenditure on their previous level of consumption. Consumers will lose some or all the gain in consumers' surplus on the exported product as a result of reduced availability of imported products, but this statement probably would not be true of consumers other than those who were also producers of the exported product. If the export tax is used in the manner described above, producers will also be making a transfer to other taxpayers.

But the conclusion reached earlier will hold, namely that the income transfer would be much larger than the real costs of restricted opportunity to export so long as some exports continue. Thus when industrial countries restrict trade in agricultural products they are not only imposing income transfers from consumers to producers in their own countries but are also imposing income transfers from producers to consumers (and to some degree to producers of imported products) in other countries. And if the exported good is an agricultural product, it is highly probable a significant part of the income transfer would be from low income farm families to higher income urban families if the country involved is a developing one.

While accepting the conclusion that the real losses due to restrictions on the opportunity to export are modest compared to the income transfers and the national income of the exporting country, certain other costs should be recognized if a developing country is involved. It is highly improbable that any single developing country or developing countries as a group can prevent the decline in their terms of trade. It is theoretically possible to do so, but experience indicates the virtual practical impossibility of doing so. If it were easy to prevent such declines in the terms of trade, we would see many more commodity agreements entered into by developing countries. For sugar producers outside any preferential arrangements, the terms of trade have been changed in an adverse direction, and yet the sugar producers have been unable to modify the situation. So it is reasonable to expect that protection of agricultural producers in the industrial countries will result in transfers from the developing to the industrial countries for those farm products produced in both types of economies. For a limited number of farm products the transfers could be and are substantial.

Another real cost imposed upon developing countries by trade restrictions would arise if the costs of borrowing are substantially higher for developing than for industrial countries. The lost opportunity to earn foreign exchange may impose substantially higher costs on developing countries than it does on industrial countries for each dollar of foreign exchange lost. When a developing country is dependent on importation of capital goods and services, a loss of export opportunities requires a reduction in the purchase of such goods and services or an increase in foreign borrowing. If the rate of interest is substantially higher than that paid by the industrial countries, the earlier analysis may have seriously underestimated the real costs of trade restrictions.

A further substantial cost is the loss of export opportunities, which would enhance the popularity of an industrialization policy based on import substitution.[5] Such programs impose further real losses in national income. While it could be argued that developing countries embark upon industrialization based on import substitution of their own volition and adoption of the policy should not be blamed upon trade restrictions imposed by industrial countries, the point can hardly be made in good grace by industrial countries that protect their agricultures to the extent they do. It may also be noted that such inefficient industrialization involves further additional income transfers from farm to urban areas. Most import substitution activities are located in urban areas and most of the loss in export opportunities still affects rural areas in developing countries; taken together the income transfers from rural to urban areas may reach large magnitudes.

The lower prices of agricultural products would slow down the adoption of new inputs and modernization of agriculture in the developing countries. This cost may well be substantial in real terms over the long run. If the import substitution policy is extended to industries producing new farm inputs, the impact of trade restrictions will be significantly enlarged.

It would be erroneous to assume the only real costs of trade restrictions upon the countries that lose export opportunities are the excess production costs and loss of consumers' surplus as these are usually measured. The costs delineated above may well be substantially greater than the total of the excess production costs and loss of consumers' surplus.

WHO BENEFITS FROM THE TRANSFERS? In Figure 3.1 the transfer from consumers to farmers equals the new total output multiplied by the difference between the domestic price and the world price. While triangle *C* represents excess resource costs, the remainder is large absolutely and relatively to the previous level of gross farm income if the price increase is of the order of magnitude of 20 or 25 percent. Can it be said that net farm income would be increased by area *I* in Figure 3.1? If net farm income is defined to include income going to the owners of all agricultural resources and if the time period under consideration is the one appropriate to the particular supply function for agriculture, the answer is in the affirmative. Thus the analysis seems to imply that if the tariff or levy revenue were used to reduce other taxes, the consumer plus taxpayer would find a large fraction of the transfer would go to increase the incomes to farm resource owners, including labor. But more probing indicates that such an impression would be largely erroneous.

The first consideration would be the distribution of the short-run gains to the various categories of resource owners. As is well known, the largest increases in return would be to the resources with the lowest elasticities of supply, which in the case of agriculture is land. Under reasonable assumptions a 20 percent price increase could result in at least a 25 percent increase in the current return to land; the increase in return per unit of labor would be substantially less even if the elasticity of supply is 0.5, perhaps about 17 percent. The return to reproducible capital (farm machinery, for example) would increase in the short run, but only until the supply of such capital increased to a new equilibrium level.

In the case of labor, the short-run increase in returns would soon be eroded away. In part this would be because the long-run elasticity of supply of labor to agriculture is larger than the short-run elasticity, and more workers would be engaged at agriculture and at a lower wage rate then immediately following the output price increase. While the response to the higher return to farm labor would somewhat reduce farm wages, the major consequences would be a greater increase in output than depicted in Figure 3.1 and an even further increase in the return to land as more labor, as well as other resources, are used with the land. But this is only part of the story and a minor part at that. What should be recognized is that the effect of the higher output prices on the return to labor is a once-and-for-all effect.

This is not to say that the maximum effect on wages is necessarily achieved at once, though this is in fact the case. Wages would increase most in the short run; if there is a reasonable degree of mobility of resources (except land) all other adjustments tend to reduce the return to farm labor though such effects would be relatively small. But increasing the output price results in a single shift in the demand for labor if the supply functions for other inputs remain unchanged. Any further shift in the demand for farm labor must be due to another change, such as a shift in the supply function for another input or a change in methods of production. With a fixed output price, a reduction in the price of a purchased input would almost certainly increase the demand for farm labor.

But such changes as would have the effect of shifting the demand curve for labor to the right are small compared to another influence, namely shifts in the supply function for labor that occur as alternative earnings in the rest of the economy increase. In an economy with rising real per capita incomes, the supply function for labor to agriculture is continuously shifting to the left. This shift in conjunction with an approximately stable demand curve results in a rise in real wages in agriculture that would fairly soon overtake the increase in returns to labor due to an output price increase of the magnitude referred to earlier.

What the transfer from consumers to farmers achieves is a permanent increase in the return to land and a temporary and declining increase in the return to labor compared to what that return would have been in the absence of the price increase. Gradually more and more of the income transfer is required to pay for the excess resources retained in agriculture, and the only net income transfer that will remain is to land and perhaps to some small fraction of the farm labor force whose alternative earnings in nonfarm employment are low because of age or some particular impairment, such as lack of education..

Agriculture in the United States during the 1960s provided a test of the above conclusions that came close to being an experiment one would design if he could. Farm product prices increased by 19 percent during the decade; the index of prices paid for production items increased by 18 percent. Real farm prices as measured by the ratio of the index of prices received to the index of prices paid for production items did not change though if one adds the government payments to farmers the index of adjusted prices received increased about 6 percent relative to the prices paid for production items. In either case the change in real farm prices was small.

According to USDA estimates of changes in the ratio of total output to total input, productivity as conventionally measured changed hardly at all during the decade, namely by 3 percent. Since quality changes in some of the inputs are inadequately reflected in the input indices, it is safe to assume that no change in resource productivity occurred over the decade.

If changes in farm wage rates are used as a proxy for changes in the return to farm labor we may estimate that in absolute dollar terms returns per farm worker increased by 71 percent between 1960 and 1970. (While not directly relevant to the present discussion, it may be noted that between 1960 and 1970 the cost of living in farm areas increased by 24.5 percent, making a 37 percent increase in farm wages during the decade, or an annual increase of 3.2 percent.)

This compares to an increase in farm product prices of only 19 percent. Thus only a small part of the increase in returns to farm labor can be attributed to higher output prices or increases in resource productivity. Most of the increase in real returns to farm labor has been due to changes in the ratio of all other inputs to labor or, put differently, to the increase in the marginal physical product of labor. The increase in the average physical product of labor is due to the increase in farm output of 15 percent during the decade and a reduction of the farm labor force of 30 to 35 percent. If it is assumed that the production function has an elasticity of substitution between labor and all other inputs of unity and the production function coefficients did not change over the decade, the increase in the marginal physical product of farm labor between 1960 and 1970 was 65 percent. (The increase in the average physical product was derived by dividing 115, the output level in 1970 relative to 1960, by 70, the labor input index in 1970 relative to 1960.)

The increase in the estimated marginal physical product of farm labor of 65 percent, if adjusted for the change in farm product prices, is a larger increase than is implied by the 71 percent increase in money returns to labor. The difference can be a result of one or more of the following: the 71 percent increase in returns to farm labor is an underestimate of the return to all farm labor; the labor coefficient in the production function showed a small decline; or the elasticity of substitution between labor and all other inputs was greater than unity. Rough estimates based on a residual method of estimating the returns to farm labor indicate the general increase in the average return per farm worker was approximately 70 percent, or almost identical to the increase in farm wage rates; thus the first reason can probably be ruled out. Only a rather small decline in the labor coefficient in the production function is required to bring the changes in estimated value of the marginal product of labor and the increase in farm wage rates into approximate equality. A reduction of 10 percent in the labor coefficient—for example, from 0.20 to 0.18—is large enough to eliminate almost all the difference. Given the large increase in purchased inputs during the decade and past trends in the labor coefficient, a reduction of 10 percent in the coefficient over the decade does not seem unreasonable.

It is clear that during the 1960s adjustments through the labor market were primarily responsible for the substantial increase in money and real returns to farm labor. Neither significant changes in output prices nor total productivity change could have had a significant role. The implication of this conclusion is that the large income transfer from consumers and taxpayers to farmers has done very little to improve the earnings of farm workers. If we assume that farm prices, including all direct payments as an addition to prices, have been increased by about 15 percent by government programs, the transfers could have resulted in a once-and-for-all increase in the return to farm labor of 15 percent at most, and probably more nearly 10 percent.

It is quite unlikely that government programs increased farm prices by as much as 15 percent during the decade. Much of the increase in prices was due to higher prices for animal products and oil-bearing crops. The prices received from crop products covered by governmental programs actually declined.

If an increase of farm product prices of 15 percent resulted in an increase in returns to farm labor of 15 percent, this means that the elasticity of labor returns to output price is unity. This elasticity appears to be lower than this and may be more nearly 0.75 in the short run and perhaps somewhat lower in the long run.[6] Thus a continuing annual series of transfers that have now persisted for well over two decades are required to achieve a one-time increase in returns to farm labor of 10 to 15 percent, an increase that has been achieved not once but repeatedly by labor transfers in two to three years.

There is no doubt that returns to land are higher because of the transfers as well as total capital investment in reproducible assets. In fact, rough calculations of the increase in the national income produced by agriculture in 1970 compared to 1960 show that at least two-thirds of the increase of $6.6 billion can be attributed to increased return to land and capital.

An analysis of the consequences of large income transfers from consumers and taxpayers to farmers in other industrial countries would duplicate the analysis for the United States. Farm incomes have been increasing in real terms during the past decade, but the primary source of the increase has been labor migration and not enormous income transfers. In fact, the governments of the industrial countries, with only two important exceptions, were unable to significantly increase real farm prices during the 1960s. The two exceptions are Japan and France, and only in the former case has a significant increase (40 percent) been realized; partly at the expense of its partners in the EEC France achieved an increase of about 12 percent.

If the governmental efforts made in many industrial countries were not successful in increasing real farm prices in the 1960s with the noted exceptions, it seems unlikely that the 1970s will show a different picture. Thus very large transfers have been and will be required just to maintain the present level of real farm prices and by now the labor markets have rather fully adjusted and returns to farm labor are approximately what they would have been in the absence of the farm programs. The remaining net income transfers go to the owners of land and to pay for the larger volume of investment in buildings, machinery, and equipment.

Estimates of the magnitude of the transfers made by consumers and taxpayers to farmers have been made for the EEC and the United States. For the EEC in 1968 estimates of total costs imposed on consumers and taxpayers range from $11 to $14 billion.[7] I have estimated that in 1968 costs imposed on U.S. consumers amounted to $3.4 billion and an additional $6.2 billion came from taxpayers. Thus in the EEC and the United States the total transfers amount to more than $20 billion; less than fifteen million farm workers are involved and thus the transfer per worker is $1,330. The cost of the transfers is very close to half the value added by agriculture of $48 billion in 1968. These costs are mentioned to indicate that transfers have reached what I can only describe as a very large figure.

While one can argue that if the protection of agriculture in the industrial countries has little, if any, long-run effect upon the return to farm labor, it may not be possible to be so firm in the conclusion that if the excluded producers are primarily in the developing countries, the return to farm labor would soon return to the level prevailing before a reduction in exports. The reason for the difference in view is not that the mechanisms of adjustment are different in the two types of economies but that the elasticity of supply of labor to agriculture may be more inelastic and shifts at a slower rate over time in the developing countries.

These differences are due to the much greater relative importance of farm employment in the developing countries. A larger part of the resource adjustment to lower prices must occur through shifts within agriculture in the form of shifting from export products to those consumed domestically and returns to labor may be depressed for a very substantial period of time. While this may seemingly benefit consumers in such countries, the long-run effect may be to significantly slow the modernization of agriculture, with a consequent rise in real costs to the economy. If loss of export markets slows the pace of modernization of agriculture, the case for import substitution will be strengthened, and if efforts are made in this direction both the magnitude of income transfers from farmers to consumers and the real costs will grow over time.

BENEFITS OF FREE TRADE. What difference does trade make in world community welfare? Several approaches have been taken in an attempt to answer this question. It is fairly clear that at least in the short run the losses in national income or welfare resulting from restrictions of trade are a small fraction of national output. Income transfers from consumers to farmers and taxpayers or from consumers and taxpayers to farmers are many times as large as the probable real costs of protection in industrial countries. Similarly it is probable the transfers that occur in developing countries because of the loss of export opportunities are significantly greater than the real costs.

It was also argued that total costs of the loss of export opportunities to the developing countries may be substantially larger than the value of the excess production costs of expanding the production of imported goods plus the loss of consumers' surplus. Difficulties and costs in borrowing to acquire foreign exchange for investment purposes, the loss of income due to deterioration of the terms of trade, the impetus given to a policy of industrialization based on import substitution, and the long-run effects of lower farm products on modernization of agriculture probably would result in losses in real national income over time that would be substantially larger than conventionally measured welfare losses resulting from trade restrictions. And of these four potential sources of loss, loss of real income due to deterioration of the terms of trade might well be the least important, since long-run supply adjustments appear to gradually redress the deterioration in the terms of trade for farm products.

It was also argued that long-run increases in farm incomes achieved by protection were relatively small compared to the magnitude of the income transfers. Real income gains to farm labor are quite rapidly overtaken by normal outmigration of labor from agriculture. In any case, the percentage increase in returns to farm labor that can be achieved by higher farm prices is quite small compared to actual increases in real returns occurring as a result of economic growth. Real income transfers that do occur in agriculture are primarily increased returns to farmland and so far as I know no one has been able to attribute a large social benefit to such a transfer. If the discussion of the distribution of gains from protection presented earlier is approximately correct, that discussion implies that, as protection is maintained over a fairly long period, the real costs increase relative to the magnitude of the income transfers.

Income transfers associated with protection of agriculture in industrial countries appear to go on more or less indefinitely, largely without analysis of what groups are adversely affected or of what net social gains, if any, are achieved. It would appear that after such protection has been maintained for a period of time the main argument for continuation is that substantial losses would be imposed upon resource owners in the protected sector. In the case of agricultural protection, large losses would occur in the capital value of land and other relatively long-life assets and readjustment in the labor supply would be painful and serious. It is difficult for governments that have misled a significant and vocal fraction of their citizens to admit the programs they have been following have been of relatively modest benefit, most of the net benefits go to relatively high income groups, and continuation of the present high transfer costs, or even higher costs, is necessary to merely maintain the status quo with respect to real product prices.

Perhaps the major cost of protection is that it all too often precludes consideration and implementation of more effective means of achieving desired goals. Where farm incomes are low, the primary reasons are limited resources rather than the level of prices or availability of nonfarm jobs. In almost all societies education of farm people has been woefully neglected. If there is any lesson developing countries should learn from the experience of industrial countries it is that enormous social and economic costs can and do result from discrimination against farm and other rural people in the provision of educational opportunities.

Interference with international trade results in large income transfers, both in countries engaging in protection and in other countries that lose export opportunities. At least as far as agriculture is concerned, transfers do not achieve significant social or economic benefits. But unfortunately the transfer process is such a subtle one when it is achieved through higher farm and consumer prices that there is seldom any effort made to relate the sacrifices imposed upon consumers to the modest benefits eventually accruing to the farm population.

And nowhere in the political process of the world does any mechanism appear for considering the loss of welfare that import restrictions impose upon agricultural producers in developing countries, either directly or through long-run effects upon economic growth in such nations. But since so little concern exists about the relative benefits and costs of income transfers within the industrial countries, the lack of concern about the effects upon those who are a long distance away should not be surprising.

NOTES

1. Arnold C. Harberger, "Using the Resources at Hand More Effectively," *American Economic Review,* 49(May 1959):135.

2. Harry G. Johnson, "The Gains from Free Trade with Europe: An Estimate," *Manchester School,* vol. 26, September 1958.

3. J. Wemelsfelder, "The Short Run Effects of the Lowering of Import Duties in Germany," *Economic Journal*, 70(March 1960):100.

4. T. E. Josling, "Agriculture and Britain's Trade Policy Dilemma," Thames Essay No. 2 (London: Trade Policy Research Centre, 1970), p. 24.

5. Harry G. Johnson, *Economic Policy Toward Less Developed Countries: A Survey of Major Issues* (Washington, D.C.: Brookings Institute, 1967), p. 111.

6. John E. Floyd, "The Effects of Farm Price Supports on the Return to Land and Labor in Agriculture," *Journal of Political Economy*, 72(April 1965):148–58.

7. The Atlantic Institute, "A Future for European Agriculture: A Report by a Panel of Experts," *Atlantic Papers* 4(1970):8–9, 62; G. R. Kruer and B. Bernston, "Cost of the Common Agricultural Policy to the European Economic Community," *Foreign Agricultural Trade in the United States*, October 1969, pp. 7, 12.

[4]

Patterns of World Agricultural Trade

Arthur B. Mackie

P ATTERNS of world agricultural trade have undergone major changes in the postwar years—changes that have gone relatively unnoticed until recently. A heavy emphasis on imports of agricultural raw materials for industrial use that characterized the 1920s and 1930s has shifted to (in the 1950s and 1960s) an emphasis on products for direct consumption or imports used in the production of food, such as feeds and feed grains for livestock. These changes have been in response to the structural changes in world import demand associated with postwar economic growth. As a result of these changes in the commodity composition of import demand, the patterns of world trade in agricultural products have been altered between countries. These changing flows of world agricultural products have greatly altered export prospects for particular countries and commodities. I will identify these emerging patterns of agricultural trade and briefly suggest what they indicate for future world trade flows in agricultural products and especially for U.S. agricultural exports.

AGRICULTURAL TRADE IN PERSPECTIVE. The value of world trade in agricultural products in 1965–69 was $49 billion, or about one-fifth of the value of total trade (Table 4.1). At this level, world agricultural trade was 1.6 times the level in 1955 but about 3.0 times the level in 1925–29. "Agricultural trade" includes Standard International Trade Classification (SITC) Sections 0, 1, 2, and 4 but excludes Divisions 24, 25, 27, and 28 of Section 2 (6).[1]

ARTHUR B. MACKIE is Chief, International Monetary and Trade Research Branch, Economic Research Service, United States Department of Agriculture. Special acknowledgements are due Louise Perkins for her help in preparing the statistical data for this paper.

TABLE 4.1. World Trade in Agricultural Products,* 1955 and 1960–64 and 1965–69 Average

	Importing Region											
	Developed†			Less developed‡			Central plan§			World		
Exporting Region	1955	1960–64	1965–69	1955	1960–64	1965–69	1955	1960–64	1965–69	1955	1960–64	1965–69
	(Billion U.S. $, f.o.b.)											
Developed†												
Total exports	42.15	71.47	118.05	16.74	22.84	31.60	1.32	3.58	6.13	60.21	97.89	155.78
Agricultural	10.60	15.32	20.65	2.35	3.85	4.83	0.49	1.15	1.35	13.44	20.32	26.83
% agricultural	25	21	18	14	17	15	37	32	22	22	21	17
Less developed‡												
Total exports	17.10	21.61	30.56	5.79	6.52	8.62	0.58	1.58	2.34	23.47	29.71	41.52
Agricultural	10.48	10.59	11.70	2.51	2.47	2.92	0.51	1.38	1.88	13.50	14.44	16.50
% agricultural	61	49	38	43	38	34	88	87	80	58	49	40
Central plan§												
Total exports	1.71	3.31	5.87	0.62	2.06	3.41	6.90	11.76	15.47	9.23	17.13	24.75
Agricultural	0.84	1.40	2.32	0.23	0.51	0.85	1.95	2.33	2.52	3.02	4.24	5.69
% agricultural	49	42	40	37	25	25	28	20	16	33	25	23
World												
Total exports	60.96	96.39	154.48	23.15	31.42	43.63	8.80	16.92	23.94	92.91	144.73	222.05
Agricultural	21.92	27.31	34.67	5.09	6.83	8.60	2.95	4.86	5.75	29.96	39.00	49.02
% agricultural	36	28	22	22	22	20	34	29	24	32	27	22

SOURCES: "United Nations Conference on Trade and Development," *Handbook of International Trade and Development Statistics;* *Monthly Bulletin of Statistics.*

* Includes SITC Sections 0, 1, 2, and 4 but excluding Divisions 24, 25, 27, and 28 of Section 2.

† Includes United States, Canada, Western Europe (including Yugoslavia and Turkey), Republic of South Africa, Japan, Australia, and New Zealand.

‡ Includes all countries of Central and South America, Africa (except South Africa), Asia (except Turkey, Japan, mainland China, North Vietnam, North Korea, and Mongolia, and all the islands in the Pacific and Caribbean not elsewhere listed.

§ Includes U.S.S.R., Eastern Europe (except Yugoslavia), mainland China, North Vietnam and Korea, and Mongolia.

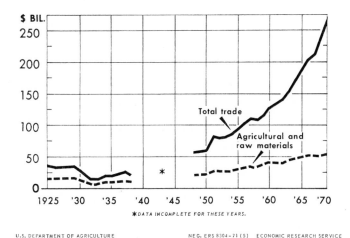

FIG. 4.1. Total world trade compared with trade in agricultural and raw materials.

World trade in agricultural products in the postwar years has represented a declining proportion of total world trade in all commodities (Figure 4.1). For example, in the 1920s and 1930s trade in agricultural products and agricultural raw materials accounted for about 50 percent of total world trade. (Crude fertilizers, ores, wood, and wood products were included in the data prior to 1938 because of incomplete details on commodities in this period.)[2] Agriculture's share decreased to about 32 percent by 1955 and to 25 percent by 1965.

Last year the value of world trade in agricultural products and raw materials was only one-fifth the value of total world trade. This relationship between agricultural and nonagricultural trade is well known and is related to the slowly expanding demand for agricultural products in developed countries. And since world trade in agricultural products, like total trade, is primarily between developed countries, the declining share of agricultural products in world trade is highly related to the inelasticity of demand for agricultural products in the developed countries.

In view of low income elasticity of demand for agricultural relative to industrial products in developed countries, one would expect world import demand for agricultural and raw materials would grow more slowly than for manufactured goods as these countries achieve higher levels of economic growth. Likewise, it would be logical to expect that within the slowly growing world import demand for agricultural products there would be differences in income elasticities for particular products. These differences in elasticities would result therefore in a substitution of some products with relative high income elasticities for those commodities with relatively low elasticities in the total demand for agricultural imports. An examination of historical trade data tends to support this hypothesis.

Substitution of industrial products in world trade for agricultural products is clearly illustrated by the data in Table 4.1. From 1955 to 1965–69 total trade increased 7.5 percent per year or from $92.9 to $222 billion while agricultural trade grew only 4.2 percent per year, or about $49 billion. These data also illustrate how important the developed countries are in world trade and the nature of the changes that are generated in the patterns of trade in agricultural and nonagricultural products between major regions of the world.

PATTERN OF TRADE BETWEEN ECONOMIC REGIONS. The three major economic regions of the world include the following countries:

Developed: United States, Canada, Developed Market Economies of Europe (including Turkey and Yugoslavia), Australia, New Zealand, South Africa, and Japan.

Central Plan: Union of Soviet Socialist Republics, Albania, Bulgaria, Czechoslovakia, East Germany, Hungary, Poland, Romania, mainland China, Mongolia, North Korea, and North Vietnam.

Less Developed: Countries other than Developed or Central Planned Economies.[3]

The central feature of current international trade is that the economically advanced countries are each other's best customers.[4,5] For example, in 1965–69 trade between the developed countries represented 53 percent of world trade and 42 percent of world agricultural trade (Table 4.2). In 1955, these percentages were 45 and 35 percent respectively. In 1965–69, the developed countries accounted for 55 percent of world agricultural exports (45 percent in 1955), but 71 percent of world agricultural imports.

On the other hand, the less developed countries (LDCs) accounted for 34 percent of world agricultural exports in 1965–69, but only 17 percent of world agricultural imports. While the LDCs' share of world agricultural imports has remained rather constant since 1955 (about 17 percent) their share of world agricultural exports has declined eleven percentage points (from 45 percent in 1955 to 34 percent in 1965–69). Since the central plan countries' share of world agricultural imports and exports has remained rather constant since 1955, the loss in the LDCs' share of world agricultural exports has been due primarily to the gain in world market share by the developed countries. In other words, a definite trend has been underway in the postwar years, substituting agricultural exports from the developed countries for exports from the LDCs in world markets.

From the standpoint of market outlets for agricultural exports of

TABLE 4.2. Distribution of World Total and Agricultural Exports, 1955 and 1960–64 and 1965–69 Average

	Importing Region (%)											
	Developed			Less developed			Central plan			World		
Exporting Region	1955	1960–64	1965–69	1955	1960–64	1965–69	1955	1960–64	1965–69	1955	1960–64	1965–69
Developed												
Total exports	45	49	53	18	16	14	2	3	3	65	68	70
Agricultural	35	39	42	8	10	10	3	3	3	45	52	55
Less developed												
Total exports	18	15	14	6	4	4	1	1	1	25	20	19
Agricultural	35	27	24	8	6	6	2	4	4	45	37	34
Central plan												
Total exports	2	2	3	1	2	1	7	8	7	10	12	11
Agricultural	3	4	5	1	1	1	6	6	5	10	11	11
World												
Total exports	65	66	70	25	22	19	10	12	11	100	100	100
Agricultural	73	70	71	17	17	17	10	13	12	100	100	100

SOURCES: "United Nations Conference on Trade and Development," Handbook of International Trade and Development Statistics; Monthly Bulletin of Statistics.

TABLE 4.3. Distribution of World Total and Agricultural Imports, 1955 and 1960–64 and 1965–69 Average

(%)

Exporting Region	Importing Region											
	Developed			Less developed			Central plan			World		
	1955	1960–64	1965–69	1955	1960–64	1965–69	1955	1960–64	1965–69	1955	1960–64	1965–69
Developed												
Total imports	69	74	76	72	73	72	15	21	25	65	67	70
Agricultural	48	56	59	46	56	56	17	24	23	45	52	55
Less developed												
Total imports	28	23	20	25	21	20	7	9	10	25	21	19
Agricultural	48	39	34	49	36	34	17	28	33	45	37	34
Central plan												
Total imports	3	3	4	3	6	8	78	70	65	10	12	11
Agricultural	4	5	7	5	8	10	66	48	44	10	11	11
World												
Total imports	100	100	100	100	100	100	100	100	100	100	100	100
Agricultural	100	100	100	100	100	100	100	100	100	100	100	100

SOURCES: "United Nations Conference on Trade and Development," *Handbook of International Trade and Development Statistics; Monthly Bulletin of Statistics.*

the LDCs, the developed countries have been historically the major market. In 1955 almost half (48 percent) of the agricultural imports of the developed countries were from the LDCs; 48 percent were from other developed countries (Table 4.3). This historical pattern has been changing rapidly over the past decade so that the LDCs in 1965–69 supplied only 34 percent of the agricultural imports of the developed markets. This loss in market share by the LDCs was taken up primarily by the developed countries themselves, since intradeveloped-area trade increased from 48 percent in 1955 to 59 percent in 1965–69. During this time, there was a small increase by central plan countries in the market share of the developed countries' agricultural imports, from 4 to 7 percent.

Similar trends have been underway in the agricultural import market of the LDCs. For example, in 1955 the LDCs supplied 49 percent of their own agricultural imports while 46 percent came from developed countries. At this time only 5 percent originated in central plan countries. By 1965–69, however, intra-LDC trade as a proportion of LDC imports had decreased to 34 percent while the developed countries' share of the LDCs' agricultural import market had increased from 46 to 56 percent from 1955 to 1965–69. Even central plan countries increased their market share from 5 to 10 percent of the LDCs' agricultural import market during this period.

While the LDCs have been losing out in their own and developed countries' markets, their agricultural exports to central plan countries have represented an increasing share of the import market in these countries since 1955. This change has been due primarily to the slow growth of intrabloc trade and greater reliance upon LDCs and the developed countries for a major source of their agricultural imports.

In summary, there has been a significant change in the pattern and trade flows of agricultural products between the three major economic regions since 1955. These shifts in world trade patterns between the three major economic regions since 1955 have—

1. Increased the developed countries' market share in all three economic regions;
2. Decreased the LDCs' market share in the developed countries;
3. Made the LDCs more dependent upon agricultural products from developed countries;
4. Increased the dependency of the central plan countries upon world supplies of agricultural products, primarily from LDCs;
5. Effected a substitution in world markets of developed countries' agricultural products for those from LDCs.

These changes in world trade patterns between the three major economic regions have been associated with a change in commodity composition of world imports.

TABLE 4.4. Regional Commodity Composition of Agricultural Trade, 1955 and 1960-64 and 1965-69 Average

Exporting Region	Importing Region									World exports		
	Developed			Less developed			Central plan					
	1955	1960-64	1965-69	1955	1960-64	1965-69	1955	1960-64	1965-69	1955	1960-64	1965-69
						($ bil)						
Developed												
Food	7.5	11.3	16.0	2.1	3.3	4.2	0.3	0.8	1.0	9.9	15.4	21.2
Raw materials	3.0	4.1	4.7	0.3	0.6	0.6	0.2	0.3	0.3	3.5	5.0	5.6
Total agricultural	10.5	15.4	20.7	2.4	3.9	4.8	0.5	1.1	1.3	13.4	20.4	26.8
% food	71	73	77	88	85	88	60	73	77	74	75	79
Less developed												
Food	6.9	7.5	8.8	1.6	1.7	2.1	0.2	0.8	1.2	8.7	10.0	12.1
Raw materials	3.6	3.0	3.0	1.0	0.7	0.7	0.3	0.7	0.7	4.9	4.4	4.4
Total agricultural	10.5	10.5	11.8	2.6	2.4	2.8	0.5	1.5	1.9	13.6	14.4	16.5
% food	66	71	75	62	71	75	40	53	63	74	69	73
Central plan												
Food	0.5	0.8	1.3	0.1	0.4	0.9	1.2	1.4	1.6	1.8	2.6	3.8
Raw materials	0.4	0.6	1.0	0	0.1	0.1	0.8	0.9	1.0	1.2	1.6	2.1
Total agricultural	0.9	1.4	2.3	0.1	0.5	1.0	2.0	2.3	2.6	3.0	4.2	5.9
% food	56	57	57	100	80	90	60	61	62	60	62	64
World imports												
Food	14.9	19.6	26.1	3.8	5.4	7.2	1.7	3.0	3.8	20.4	28.0	37.1
Raw materials	7.0	7.7	8.7	1.3	1.4	1.4	1.3	1.9	2.0	9.6	11.0	12.1
Total agricultural	21.9	27.3	34.8	5.1	6.8	8.6	3.0	4.9	5.8	30.0	39.0	49.2
% food	68	72	75	75	79	84	57	61	66	68	72	75

SOURCES: "General Agreement on Tariffs and Trade," *International Trade, 1969;* "United Nations Conference on Trade and Development," *Handbook of International Trade and Development Statistics.*

TABLE 4.5 Distribution of World Agricultural Exports, 1955 and 1960–64 and 1965–69 Average

(%)

Exporting region	Developed			Less developed			Central plan			World		
	1955	1960–64	1965–69	1955	1960–64	1965–69	1955	1960–64	1965–69	1955	1960–64	1965–69
Developed												
Food	37	40	43	10	12	11	2	3	3	49	55	57
Raw materials	31	37	39	3	5	5	2	3	2	36	45	46
Total agricultural	35	39	42	8	10	10	2	3	3	45	52	55
Less developed												
Food	34	27	24	8	6	6	1	3	3	43	36	33
Raw materials	38	27	25	10	6	6	3	6	6	51	40	36
Total agricultural	35	27	24	8	6	6	2	4	4	45	37	33
Central plan												
Food	2	3	3	1	1	2	5	5	4	8	9	10
Raw materials	4	5	8	0	1	1	8	8	8	13	15	18
Total agricultural	3	4	5	1	1	2	6	6	5	10	11	12
World												
Food	73	70	70	19	19	19	8	11	10	100	100	100
Raw materials	73	70	72	14	13	11	13	17	17	100	100	100
Total agricultural	73	70	70	17	17	18	10	13	12	100	100	100

SOURCES: "General Agreement on Tariffs and Trade," *International Trade, 1969;* "United Nations Conference on Trade and Development," *Handbook of International Trade and Development Statistics.*

COMMODITY COMPOSITION OF AGRICULTURAL TRADE. The changing nature of world import demand for agricultural products has altered the relative importance of trade flows in food and agricultural raw materials during the past fifteen years.[6,7]

For example, the value of world exports in food products increased about $17 billion from 1955 to 1965–69, while the value of trade in agricultural raw materials increased only $2.5 billion. As a result of this disparity in growth, the importance of food exports in world agricultural trade increased from 68 percent in 1955 to 75 percent in 1965–69.

As with total and agricultural trade, the developed countries loom large in world food trade—accounting for 57 percent of world exports and 70 percent of world imports in 1965–69. The dominance of the developed countries is more pronounced for imports than for exports of raw materials—accounting for 72 percent of world imports, but only 46 percent of world exports in 1965–69.

The impact of the developed countries on the patterns of world trade in food and agricultural raw materials can be shown by an examination of market share data as shown in Table 4.6.

TABLE 4.6. Market Share of Agricultural Imports, 1955 and 1960–64 and 1965–69

Importing Regions	Food Products			Raw Materials			Annual Rate of Growth 1955 to 1965–69		
	1955	1960–64	1965–69	1955	1960–64	1965–69	Food	Raw Material	Total
				(%)					
Developed from									
Developed	50	58	61	43	53	54	6.5	3.8	5.8
Less developed	46	38	34	51	39	34	2.0	−1.5	1.0
Central plan	4	4	5	6	8	12	8.3	7.9	8.1
World	100	100	100	100	100	100	4.8	1.8	3.9
Less developed from									
Developed	55	61	58	23	43	43	6.0	6.0	5.9
Less developed	42	31	29	77	50	50	2.3	−2.9	0.6
Central plan	3	8	13	0	7	7	20.1	0.0	21.2
World	100	100	100	100	100	100	5.5	0.6	4.5
Central plan from									
Developed	18	26	26	15	16	15	10.6	3.4	8.3
Less developed	12	27	32	23	37	35	16.1	7.3	11.8
Central plan	70	47	42	62	47	50	2.4	1.9	2.2
World	100	100	100	100	100	100	6.9	3.6	5.5
World from									
Developed	49	55	57	36	45	46	6.5	4.0	5.9
Less developed	43	36	33	51	40	36	2.8	−0.9	1.6
Central plan	8	9	10	13	15	18	6.4	4.8	5.8
World	100	100	100	100	100	100	5.1	1.9	4.2

SOURCES: "General Agreement on Tariffs and Trade," *International Trade, 1969;* "United Nations Conference on Trade and Development," *Handbook of International Trade and Development Statistics.*

For example, from 1955 to 1965–69 the developed countries supplied an increasing proportion of their own food imports—increasing their market share from 50 to 61 percent—while the less developed countries' market share of the food imports of the developed countries declined from 46 to 34 percent. That is to say, intrafood trade increased 6.5 percent per year from 1955 to 1965–69, while food imports from the LDCs increased only 2 percent per year.

Similar trends have developed in the market shares of developed countries' raw material imports during this period. Intratrade in raw materials increased from 43 to 54 percent of the market—growing 3.8 percent per year—while the LDCs' market share of the developed market declined from 51 to 34 percent—decreasing 1.5 percent per year from 1955 to 1965–69.

While the developed countries have been turning increasingly to other developed countries for more of their food and raw material imports, the LDCs have done just the opposite. They have turned increasingly to the developed countries for more of their food and raw material imports. For example, LDCs' imports of food and raw materials from the developed countries each increased 6 percent per year since 1955 while intratrade in food products grew only 2.3 percent. Intratrade in raw materials actually declined (−2.9 percent per year). This slow growth in intratrade combined with a rapid growth in imports from the developed countries is related in part to the food aid programs of the developed countries, especially the United States.

The pattern of trade for the central plan countries had been similar to that for the LDCs since 1955. That is, intratrade had grown very slowly while trade with other regions increased rapidly, especially with the LDCs. The central plan countries, particularly those of Eastern Europe, have sharply increased their imports from the LDCs in the 1960s so that the LDCs' market share of the central plan countries' food imports has increased from 12 to 32 percent since 1955. The LDCs' share of their raw material imports increased from 23 to 35 percent since 1955—growing at a rate of 7.3 percent per year. The central plan countries have also increased their imports from the developed countries. The emerging patterns of food and raw material imports of the central plan countries during the 1960s indicate that they have been looking increasingly to the West for a larger portion of their agricultural products.

So far we have been examining the effects of changing patterns of world import demand on only two major commodity groups in agricultural trade—food and agricultural raw materials. While it has been possible to show that major changes in the patterns of world agricultural trade have occurred in the postwar years by using highly aggregative data, these commodity breakdowns are not adequate to show the more fundamental trends in trade that have occurred within the food cate-

TABLE 4.7. World Imports of Selected Food Products, 1963 and 1968

Commodity	1963	1968	Absolute Change 1963–68
	($ bil)		
All grains	6.34	7.53	1.19
Food	4.39	5.12	0.73
Feed	1.95	2.41	0.46
Corn	(1.22)	(1.66)	(0.44)
Meat products	4.07	5.51	1.44
Feeding stuff	1.19	1.80	0.61
Feed grains and feeding stuff	3.14	4.21	1.07
Including soybeans	3.69	5.13	1.44
Beverage crops	3.36	4.11	0.75
Sugar	2.67	1.98	0.69
Fruits and vegetables	2.32	2.99	0.67
Oilseeds	1.43	1.86	0.43
Soybeans	0.55	0.92	0.37
Oil cake and meal	0.62	0.83	0.21

SOURCE: *Trade Yearbook 1969.*

gory during the 1960s—namely, trade in feeds and feed grains. Some of the more significant changes in world imports of agricultural products during the 1960s have been associated with rapid expansion of livestock production in Japan and Western Europe. As a result of this expansion, significant changes have taken place in world trade in feed grains and feed products.

While trade in feed and feed grain products in 1968 represented only about 8 percent of world trade in agricultural products and 12 percent of world trade in food products, their absolute values have increased about $1 billion since 1963 (Table 4.7). And, if soybeans are included as feed, the increase since 1963 has been $1.44 billion.[8]

The absolute increase in world imports of feed products (including soybeans) was equal to the $1.44 billion increase in world imports of meats and meat products. The major commodities accounting for this increase in feed imports were corn, oil cake and meal, and soybeans. Corn and soybeans together accounted for 57 percent while soybeans and soybean oil cake and meal accounted for 40 percent of the total increase in world feed imports between 1963 and 1968. These products have been highly influential in affecting world agricultural trade patterns during the 1960s and have significantly influenced the commodity composition of world imports of agricultural products and particularly those of the developed countries.

A complete breakdown of world agricultural trade statistics by all regions is not possible because of incomplete reporting by some countries. Therefore, analysis of the changes in feeds and feed grains cannot be made on a world basis. However, trade data for most developed countries are available. A tabulation of agricultural imports for feed

TABLE 4.8. Commodity Composition of Agricultural Imports, Selected Major Markets 1960 and 1969

Major Market and Region of Origin	Food*		Annual Rate of Change	Feed†		Annual Rate of Change	Raw Materials‡		Annual Rate of Change	Total Agricultural		Annual Rate of Change
	1960	1969		1960	1969		1960	1969		1960	1969 or 1970	
						($ bil c.i.f.)						
EEC from												
World	4.32	8.76	8.1	1.29	2.97	9.7	3.53	3.43	−0.3	9.14	15.16	5.8
Developed	2.13	5.50	11.1	0.84	2.10	10.7	2.08	1.90	−1.0	5.05	9.49	7.3
Less developed	1.89	2.73	4.2	0.36	0.62	6.4	1.29	1.34	0.4	3.53	4.70	3.2
Central plan	0.31	0.52	5.9	0.10	0.24	10.9	0.16	0.20	2.7	0.56	0.96	6.2
EFTA from												
World	4.06	5.56	3.5	0.93	0.99	0.6	2.30	1.70	−3.3	7.29	8.24	1.4
Developed	2.50	3.62	4.3	0.64	0.75	1.8	1.24	1.00	−2.4	4.37	5.87	2.3
Less developed	1.23	1.63	3.2	0.20	0.20	−0.2	0.97	0.61	−4.9	2.40	2.45	0.2
Central plan	0.35	0.30	−1.7	0.08	0.03	−10.4	0.10	0.09	−0.7	0.53	0.42	−2.5
Japan from												
World	0.54	1.41	11.3	0.20	0.94	18.7	1.03	1.33	2.9	1.78	3.68	8.5
Developed	0.25	0.77	13.5	0.13	0.71	21.0	0.60	0.65	0.9	0.97	2.13	9.6
Less developed	0.28	0.58	8.4	0.06	0.17	11.7	0.42	0.58	3.5	0.76	1.32	6.3
Central plan	0.01	0.07	18.5	0.01	0.05	19.8	0.02	0.11	24.0	0.04	0.23	21.2
United States from												
World	3.37	3.91	1.7	0.13	0.20	5.4	1.20	1.05	−1.5	4.70	5.17	1.1
Developed	0.92	1.26	3.6	0.08	0.10	2.2	0.46	0.41	−1.4	1.46	1.77	2.2
Less developed	2.42	2.59	0.8	0.05	0.10	9.6	0.72	0.63	−1.6	3.19	3.33	0.5
Central plan	0.03	0.05	6.1	neg	neg	...	0.02	0.02	0.0	0.05	0.07	4.4

SOURCE: *Commodity Trade Statistics*, 1961, 1970, Statistical Papers, series D, vol. 11 (4).

* Food is all of Section 0 except Divisions 001, 043, 044, 045, 08; Section 1 except Division 12; Section 22 except Division 221.4; and Section 4 except Division 422.

† Feed includes Divisions 001, 043, 044, 045, 08, and 221.4.

‡ Raw materials include Divisions 12, 21, 23, 26, 29, 422, and 511.1.

products for some of the major developed markets is shown in Table 4.8 for 1960 and 1969. These four major developed markets—the European Economic Community (EEC), Japan, European Free Trade Association (EFTA), and the United States—have highly influenced the patterns of world trade in the postwar years.[9] For this reason, they have been selected for more detailed analyses.

The definitions of agricultural trade in Table 4.8 remain the same as previously used.[10] Only the commodities have been changed and reorganized to create imports by three end-use categories: food consumption, farm consumption, and industrial use.[11] For example, tobacco has been taken out of food and put into industrial use, while feed grains, feeds, fodders, oil cake and meal, as well as soybeans, have been taken out of food and put into a separate feed grouping. This new grouping should make it easier to identify the changes in import demand and end uses that have occurred for food and raw materials in these markets.

Since changes in end use are one measure of assessing the changing nature of the import demand for these products, these groupings should make possible a better identification of actual trends under way in the patterns of world imports. The nature of growth in imports for these commodity groupings by the various regions can also be identified.

An inspection of the data in Table 4.8 shows that Japan and the EEC have been among the largest contributors to the growth in world import demand for food products in the 1960s. The growth in feed imports in Japan has been outstanding. In fact, of the four major markets being considered here, Japan is the only region expanding its imports in all three commodity groupings. The second major growth market for foods and feeds has been the EEC. The United States and EFTA have both lagged far behind in their import growth for these products. These two major markets are also distinguished by their negative growth rates for raw material imports.

The major source of supplies for the growth in feed imports by Japan and the EEC has been the developed countries. The LDCs have participated in their import growth of feed products, but to a much lower degree than have the developed countries such as the United States. Japan has endeavored to balance its growth in feed imports between these two major sources of feed supplies. Since the United States has been a major source of world supplies of most food and feed products in the postwar years, it might be useful to take a closer look at the commodity composition of U.S. agricultural exports.

U.S. AGRICULTURAL EXPORTS AND WORLD TRADE PATTERNS. The patterns of U.S. agricultural trade and changes in the commodity composition of U.S. agricultural exports since the 1920s have been significant. These changes have been highly related to the

TABLE 4.9. Commodity Composition of U.S. Agricultural Exports, 1925–70

Commodity	1925–32	1933–40	1940–44	1945–49	1950–54	1955–59	1960–64	1965–69	1970
				($ mil)					
Food products	577	216	1,003	2,150	1,504	1,906	2,607	2,732	2,929
Dairy and eggs	17	8	295	339	111	229	172	143	142
Meat and products	159	47	406	264	138	164	211	213	268
Food grain and preparations	232	55	109	1,091	846	901	1,493	1,548	1,502
Fruits, vegetables, and preparations	124	87	130	278	224	358	420	476	524
Other foods	45	19	63	178	185	254	311	352	493
Feed and farm input products	72	41	34	244	411	728	1,312	2,248	2,888
Feeds and fodders	24	9	3	18	24	63	138	342	497
Feed grains and preparations	40	26	16	172	275	412	693	1,059	1,059
Soybeans	0	2	2	25	91	211	425	763	1,216
Seeds and breed stock	8	4	13	29	21	42	56	84	116
Industrial raw materials	863	453	270	892	1,337	1,304	1,447	1,353	1,359
Cotton and linters	695	322	139	525	871	675	737	431	378
Tobacco	131	111	98	265	294	350	392	485	488
Animal products	8	5	1	25	85	162	195	278	320
Vegetable products	21	10	17	55	72	99	101	118	121
Essential oils	8	5	15	22	15	18	22	41	52
Total exports	1,512	710	1,307	3,286	3,252	3,938	5,366	6,333	7,176
				(% composition)					
Food products	38	30	77	65	46	48	49	43	41
Feed and farm input products	5	6	3	7	13	18	24	36	40
Industrial raw materials	57	64	21	27	41	33	27	21	19

SOURCES: *United States Exports and Imports Classified by OBR, End-use Commodity Categories, 1923–68; U.S. Foreign Agricultural Trade.*

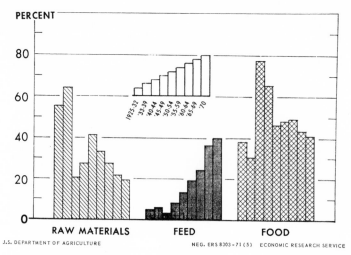

FIG. 4.2.   Composition of U.S. agricultural exports.

changing structure of world import demand in the postwar years. The changes in the commodity composition of U.S. exports has, in effect, acted as mirror image of the various changes in world demand for agricultural imports during the past forty years.

In the 1920s and 1930s U.S. agricultural exports were primarily raw material oriented.[12,13] That is, during these two decades about 60 percent of U.S. agricultural exports were agricultural raw materials for industrial use in other countries (Table 4.9 and Fig. 4.2). During the war years, however, this composition was drastically altered in favor of food exports to feed the war-devastated countries of Western Europe. For example, in 1940–44, food exports increased to 77 percent from 30 percent in 1933–40, while the proportion of raw material declined from 64 to 21 percent of total U.S. agricultural exports.

In the immediate postwar years, the proportion of food exports remained high, but this proportion decreased throughout the 1950–64 period to less than 50 percent. The effect of the PL 480 programs was no doubt instrumental in these years in holding up the proportion of food exports. However, more recently (1965–69) this proportion steadily declined—reaching 41 percent in 1970, or about the level existing in the 1920s.

While food exports as a percentage of total U.S. agricultural exports have decreased in the postwar years, this decline was not offset by a proportionate increase in exports of agricultural raw materials for industrial use. Rather, the share of raw materials of total agricultural exports steadily declined throughout the whole postwar period, reaching an all-time low of 19 percent in 1970.

The real story underlying the decline in the relative shares of U.S. food and raw material exports has been the dramatic increase in exports of feeds and feed grains, increasing from 5 percent of total exports in 1925–32 to 40 percent in 1970. Half this increase occurred since 1955–59. These rapid changes in the commodity composition of U.S. agricultural exports have been related to the rapid expansion in demand for feeds and feed grains in Japan and Western Europe in the 1960s to fuel their rapid growth in livestock production.

In summary, the rapid growth in U.S. exports of feeds and feed grains has vastly altered the picture of the United States as a raw material exporting economy, that characterized the prewar years, to one emphasizing exports of food and feed products in the postwar years. Future changes in world demand should continue this trend and may, in the years ahead, increase the export share of feed products relative to food products. In terms of the original definition of agricultural trade at the beginning of this chapter, the current composition of U.S. agricultural exports is 81 percent food and feed and 19 percent raw materials—a picture not materially different from the commodity composition of world agricultural trade in 1965–69 shown in Table 4.4.

IMPLICATIONS FOR FUTURE ECONOMIC GROWTH AND TRADE. The complementary relationship between economic growth and trade has been well established.[14] That is, economic growth increases the actual and potential level of trade between countries as consumers achieve more purchasing power and begin to demand a variety of products not widely grown or produced in their countries. Under the impact of sustained economic growth in Japan and Western Europe during this past decade, consumption has become more diversified and specialization of production has increased. The net effect of these developments has been to increase trade between countries. The changing nature of the demand for and supply of food associated with postwar economic growth in Japan and Western Europe has also affected the level and commodity composition of actual and potential trade between most countries, and particularly with the United States.

The rapid growth in their demand for food and feed products, as well as the ability of Japan and Western Europe to meet their demand either by their own agricultural production or trade, has varied greatly from country to country, depending upon their supply of agricultural land resources and other resource endowments. For example, Japan with its limited supply of agricultural land available for production of feed grains and feeds has relied heavily upon imports to meet its demand. This reliance on imports has increased their imports almost in direct proportion to increases in total demand for feeds.

In Western Europe, on the other hand, available land resources for feeds and feed grain production are relatively more abundant, thereby making possible a greater reliance on domestic supplies for a large proportion of their total feed consumption. The availability of larger land supplies relative to Japan has directly affected the level and commodity composition of agricultural imports in these two major markets. These factors have strongly influenced the changing patterns of world agricultural trade in the postwar period and will, no doubt, continue in the years ahead.

NOTES

1. Arthur B. Mackie, "1965 Foreign Economic Growth and Market Potential for U.S. Agricultural Products," *Foreign Agricultural Economic Report,* no. 24, April 1965.
2. *Trade Yearbook, 1969* (Rome: Food and Agriculture Organization, 1970).
3. "General Agreement on Tariffs and Trade," *International Trade, 1969* (Geneva: United Nations, 1970), pp. 20–21.
4. "United Nations Conference on Trade and Development," *Handbook of International Trade and Development Statistics* (Geneva: United Nations, 1967), pp. 45–55.
5. *Monthly Bulletin of Statistics* (New York: United Nations, March 1971), pp. xx–xxiii.
6. "General Agreement on Tariffs and Trade," pp. 20–21.
7. "United Nations Conference," pp. 45–55.
8. Mackie.
9. *Commodity Trade Statistics,* Statistical Papers, Series D, vol. 11, pt. 4 (New York: United Nations, 1970).
10. *Standard International Trade Classification,* Revised, Statistical Papers, Series M, no. 34 (New York: United Nations, 1961), pp. 5–21.
11. *United States Exports and Imports Classified by OBR, End-use Commodity Categories, 1923–68,* OEB-SUP 70–71 (Washington, D.C.: U.S. Department of Commerce, Office of Business Economics, November 1970), pp. 6–8.
12. Ibid.
13. *U.S. Foreign Agricultural Trade,* a supplement to the monthly *Foreign Agricultural Trade of the United States* (Washington, D.C.: USDA, June 1971), pp. 1–10.
14. Mackie.

[5]

Trends and Structure
of U.S. Agricultural Trade

Raymond A. Ioanes

U NITED STATES agriculture in fiscal year 1971 enjoyed the
best export year in history. Shipments of U.S. farm products set three
separate records by substantial margins. First, the total value of exports
reached $7.7 billion—far above the previous high mark of $6.8 billion.
Second, exports sold commercially approximated $6.7 billion—the high-
est dollar total ever registered. Third, the physical volume of goods
shipped was well in excess of previous levels. Agricultural imports also
rose, though not as sharply as exports. United States agricultural imports in fiscal year 1971 were about $5.7 billion—a new high record for
the second year in a row.

The U.S. balance of payments continues to benefit from a favorable
commercial agricultural trade balance plus certain returns from foreign
aid programs. The net contribution of agriculture to the balance of
payments in 1970 was $760 million while the gross contribution was
$6.4 billion.

How did our agricultural trade get where it is today?

A dominant factor has been the general economic improvement
taking place around the world. This has increased the demand for agricultural products almost everywhere, though not to the same degree in
all countries or for all commodities. Also, the generally upward trend
of U.S. agricultural exports has been influenced by trade barriers, competition of other producing areas, improved agricultural technology in
many developing countries, U.S. export market promotion effort, and
other factors. These shifting trends and patterns are revealed graph-
ically by the following charts, which show what has been happening
with respect to agricultural exports and export destinations, imports

RAYMOND A. IOANES is Administrator, Foreign Agricultural Service, United States Department of Agriculture.

87

TABLE 5.1. U.S. Agricultural Exports, Total, Commercial and Concessional, Broken Down to Show Both Commercial and Concessional Shipments

Fiscal Year	Concessional	Commercial	Total
		($ bil)	
1960	1.3	3.2	4.5
1961	1.5	3.4	4.9
1962	1.6	3.6	5.1*
1963	1.5	3.6	5.1
1964	1.4	4.6	6.1*
1965	1.6	4.5	6.1
1966	1.4	5.3	6.7
1967	1.3	5.5	6.8
1968	1.3	5.0	6.3
1969	1.0	4.7	5.7
1970	1.0	5.7	6.6*

* Discrepancy of $100 million due to rounding.

and import origins, commodity composition, and the agricultural trade balance.

In Table 5.1 we see the generally upward trend of total exports and shipments sold for dollars. All the gain in total exports resulted from the expansion in commercial shipments, represented by the middle line. The increase in commercial shipments more than offsets the decline in concessional exports.

The sharp dip shown for 1969 was the result of several unfavorable factors. There was a longshoremen's strike. The Japanese temporarily withdrew from the U.S. wheat market for several weeks when sprout damage developed in some of our grain. On top of all that, good growing weather over most of the world stimulated big crops, which meant increased competition. But in 1970 the United States recovered some lost ground, and now is pushing up to new high records.

While dollar sales have risen, concessional exports—relief shipments of farm products to the less developed countries—have tapered off from their high point in 1965. There are three main factors in this situation:

1. Some of the developing countries are producing more of their own food. That is particularly true in south and east Asia, where improved technology, increased use of high yielding wheat and rice, and expanded agricultural inputs have brought what has been referred to as the "Green Revolution."
2. Other countries, notably Canada, Japan, Australia, and the European Economic Community (EEC), have diverted some of their surpluses to needy peoples.
3. The United States has hardened its agricultural assistance terms

by shifting most sales from foreign currencies to dollars, and insisting as a condition for food assistance that recipient countries do more to produce more of their own food. Table 5.2 shows the commodity breakdown. The most impressive feature of this table is the gain shown for every major commodity category except cotton.

Soybeans and products show a consistent and rather sharp upward trend. This is an excellent example of the way American agriculture benefits when it has good access to foreign markets for a product that is in strong demand. Soybeans have duty-free access to the world's largest market—the EEC—and to several other countries including Canada, Denmark, Norway, and Israel. We also sell substantial quantities of soybeans to other countries, including Japan and Taiwan, where duties are relatively low.

Feed grains, the raw material for countries expanding their poultry and livestock production, also are doing well. But feed grain exports would do even better if the EEC would follow more liberal agricultural policies. The EEC's variable import levies on feed grains not only limit our access to that market, but they also, at times, stimulate surpluses which the EEC puts onto world markets, in competition with our own farmers, through use of export subsidies. Our trade is hit by a double blow when that happens.

Tobacco exports have expanded sharply over the decade. A key factor in this situation is the United Nations embargo on Rhodesian tobacco, which has created a world supply gap that the United States is helping to fill.

The interesting category called "other" has just about doubled in the decade of the 1960s. "Other" includes such commodities as rice, nuts, alfalfa meal, seeds, and a variety of minor items such as fatty acids, casein, and essential oils.

Cotton exports are feeling two types of competition: increased output of synthetic fibers and expanded cotton production in foreign countries. Short U.S. cotton crops in recent years also have kept this country from realizing its full export market potential.

Table 5.3 answers the question: Have we gained more in the export of raw farm products requiring considerable further processing abroad than we have in the shipment of finished and semifinished items more nearly ready for consumption?

This table shows that exports of the items roughly classified as "raw" have expanded somewhat more than exports of "finished" products. For raw, the increase from 1960 to 1970 was about 50 percent, whereas the gain for the finished goods was about 40 percent.

It is rather surprising that exports of finished items have done as well as they have, taking into account what the rise in wage costs have been in this country. Between 1960 and 1970, compensation per man

TABLE 5.2. Total U.S. Agricultural Exports (Commercial and Concessional) Value of Selected Commodities and Groups, Fiscal Years 1960–70

Fiscal Year	Soybeans and Products	Wheat and Products	Feed Grains and Products	Rice (Included in "Other")	Animals and Products	Fruits and Vegetables and Products	Cotton	Tobacco	Other	Total
						($ mil)				
1960	450.7	869.4	574.5	139.6	570.7	412.4	825.7	341.9	473.7	4,519.0
1961	480.4	1,151.1	563.9	135.1	599.5	392.1	936.8	385.2	437.0	4,946.0
1962	547.5	1,285.9	730.7	133.2	613.6	429.7	662.8	407.5	464.3	5,142.0
1963	673.3	1,157.9	766.6	163.5	591.9	457.3	491.4	378.2	561.4	5,078.0
1964	720.6	1,517.8	851.5	215.1	758.3	454.4	670.4	420.7	674.3	6,068.0
1965	936.9	1,240.3	973.8	203.6	799.8	459.6	583.9	395.3	707.4	6,097.0
1966	1,074.8	1,402.2	1,378.8	221.5	768.7	512.9	385.8	394.7	758.1	6,676.0
1967	1,148.4	1,311.8	1,189.1	306.8	708.7	508.6	542.3	549.7	812.4	6,771.0
1968	1,111.0	1,277.4	1,036.4	339.0	618.2	468.5	474.8	493.7	831.0	6,311.0
1969	1,127.7	893.2	805.6	319.9	731.1	474.8	328.6	506.9	873.1	5,741.0
1970	1,522.1	941.6	1,023.5	321.7	773.0	550.3	346.6	539.6	949.3	6,646.0
1971 (est)*	1,870.0	1,200.0	1,070.0	297.0	849.0	549.0	455.0	530.0	1,077.0	7,600.0

* 1971 figures provided by Ed Karpoff, FAS, following a canvass of FAS commodity divisions early in May 1971.

TABLE 5.3. Total U.S. Agricultural Exports Broken Down to Show Exports of "Raw" and "Finished" Products in Fiscal Years 1960 and 1970

Raw Products	1960	1970	Finished Products	1960	1970
	($ mil)			*($ mil)*	
Wheat	707	831	Fruits and preparations	250	341
Feed grains	542	995	Vegetables and		
Soybeans	300	1,069	preparations	162	209
Cotton	826	347	Wheat flour	163	102
Tobacco	342	540	Rice	140	322
Inedible tallow, waxes,			Edible fats and oils	240	229
etc.	312	380	Dairy products	114	109
Oilcake and meal	57	323	Meats	62	141
Other	150	350	Other	152	358
Total	3,236	4,835	Total	1,283	1,811

hour in the United States rose by 72 percent. (*Economic Report of the President,* February 1971, Table C–34, p. 236.)

The shift among the raw products is also revealing. Wheat and cotton were dominant in 1960. In 1970, however, feed grains and soybeans had moved to the fore, and the margin in their favor continues to expand as the foreign world steps up poultry and livestock production.

Table 5.4 indicates where our total agricultural exports go. Europe was our biggest market in 1960 and as a result of some expansion in exports over the decade it remained the biggest market in 1970.

But our Asian market has shown remarkable expansion. The gain in Asia, paced by Japan and other industrializing countries of the Far East, was greater than the combined gain of all other areas of the world.

This table illustrates the prime importance of economic development in the agricultural export picture. Europe and the Far East are our biggest markets because their rapid and consistent economic growth has supported the employment and purchasing power that create a

TABLE 5.4. U.S. Agricultural Exports, Total—Commercial and Concessional—1960 and 1970 Fiscal Years

	1960	1970
	($ bil)	
EEC	1.12	1.38
Other Europe	1.01	1.13
Total	2.13	2.51
Japan	0.44	1.09
Other Asia	0.78	1.36
Total Asia	1.22	2.45
Latin America	0.55	0.64
Canada (adjusted for transshipments)	0.40	0.53
Africa	0.18	0.23

TABLE 5.5.   U.S. Agricultural Exports Sold for Dollars—Principal Dollar Areas and
Countries

Fiscal Year	EEC	Other Europe	Japan	Canada (for Consumption in Canada)	Other*	Total
1960	1.02	0.68	0.42	0.40	0.72	3.24
1961	1.04	0.76	0.53	0.40	0.71	3.44
1962	1.15	0.79	0.45	0.44	0.74	3.57
1963	1.06	0.83	0.49	0.40	0.83	3.61
1964	1.33	1.10	0.73	0.46	1.01	4.63
1965	1.36	0.90	0.75	0.48	1.01	4.50
1966	1.59	1.09	0.91	0.48	1.22	5.29
1967	1.49	1.08	0.93	0.48	1.48	5.46
1968	1.40	0.98	0.90	0.46	1.28	5.02
1969	1.30	0.85	0.84	0.50	1.21	4.70
1970	1.38	1.08	1.09	0.53	1.59	5.67

* Includes undistributed transshipments through Canada.

high demand for our farm products. Canada, which has a high degree
of economic development, illustrates the same tendency. Note that our
exports to Canada for consumption in Canada have been almost as
large as to the entire Latin American area, where economic growth has
been slow, and larger than shipments to all of Africa, where economic
development also has lagged.

In view of the recent relaxation of the trade embargo with mainland China, it should be noted that our agricultural exports to all
communist countries as a whole declined from about $260 million in
1960 to $150 million in 1970. The big factor in this decline is our con-
tinuing embargo on trade with Cuba. In 1960 we sold Cuba $125 mil-
lion worth of farm products, mainly for dollars. That was more than
we sold to France in 1960. Our trade with the communist countries in
recent years has been primarily with Poland and Yugoslavia, although
sales are beginning to pick up with Romania, Czechoslovakia, Hungary,
and East Germany.

Table 5.5 shows the major markets where we sell our farm products
commercially—for dollars, that is. A few major markets, primarily industrialized countries, account for the bulk of agricultural exports sold for
dollars. Europe—the EEC and "other Europe"—is by far our biggest
dollar market, but Japan, as you can see, is rapidly increasing as a dollar
market for U.S. agricultural exports.

Canada is an important market for such U.S. products as citrus
fruit, other fruits, juices, vegetables, soybeans, oil cake and meal, rice,
corn, peanuts, and cotton. The growth rate in our exports to Canada,
although appreciable, is not as large as the rates to some other markets.
This traces to the fact that Canada and the United States are much alike.

Both are strong agricultural countries. Both produce most of the staple foods, such as wheat, meat, and dairy and poultry items. Sometimes we exchange the same things across the border—for instance, potatoes for potatoes and pork for pork.

The rapidly expanding "other" category takes in a number of countries, some of which, notably several Far East countries and the Caribbean Islands, are emerging as significant markets.

Table 5.6 is a magnification of our market in Europe. One feature that stands out is the export gain we chalked up in the rest of Europe as contrasted with our gain in the EEC. Between 1960 and 1970 our trade with other Europe rose almost 60 percent; with the EEC it rose only 35 percent.

Our exports to the EEC obviously have been hurt by that area's Common Agricultural Policy, which became effective in 1966. Note that our shipments to the EEC gained rather consistently between 1960 and 1966 but following initiation of the Common Agricultural Policy, continued to decline.

In fiscal year 1971 our agricultural exports to the EEC set a new record above the 1966 peak. But we can't take too much comfort from that. The big demand in Europe that year represented an unusual situation. Europe's harvests were hurt by bad weather in 1970 and the area has had to look to outside sources for some supplies. Also, an overambitious commodity disposal program in 1969 and 1970 reduced the EEC's stocks position to a lower level than has turned out to be desirable. But the EEC is still following a protectionist policy that works against consistent expansion of that market.

Finally, Table 5.6 is really a spectrum of U.S. agriculture's current concern about EEC developments. A strong possibility exists that

TABLE 5.6.   U.S. Agricultural Exports—Dollar Sales to Europe as a
Whole and the European Economic Community

Fiscal Years	EEC	Other Europe	Total Europe
		($ bil)	
1960	1.02	0.68	1.70
1961	1.04	0.76	1.79*
1962	1.15	0.79	1.94
1963	1.06	0.83	1.89
1964	1.33	1.10	2.42*
1965	1.36	0.90	2.27*
1966	1.59	1.09	2.68
1967	1.49	1.08	2.57
1968	1.40	0.98	2.38
1969	1.30	0.85	2.15
1970	1.38	1.08	2.46

* Discrepancy due to rounding.

TABLE 5.7. U.S. Agricultural Exports—Dollar Sales to Japan and the European Economic Community

Fiscal Year	Japan	EEC
	($ bil)	
1960	0.42	1.02
1961	0.53	1.04
1962	0.45	1.15
1963	0.49	1.06
1964	0.73	1.33
1965	0.75	1.36
1966	0.91	1.59
1967	0.93	1.49
1968	0.90	1.40
1969	0.84	1.30
1970	1.09	1.38

some of the market now represented by "the rest of Europe" will enter the EEC fold and embrace its protectionist policy. The United Kingdom, Ireland, Denmark, and Norway have applied for membership. That is a sobering thought, considering that Europe in 1970 accounted for 43 percent of our total dollar sales of farm products to all destinations.

Table 5.7 shows another perspective on the EEC. United States agricultural trade to the EEC has been flattened out by the area's Common Agricultural Policy, but Japan is becoming an increasingly important buyer of the U.S. farm products. Our trade with the EEC increased only 35 percent between 1960 and 1970, whereas with Japan the gain was 160 percent.

Table 5.8 shows another reason we talk so much about Japan and

TABLE 5.8. U.S. Agricultural Exports Sold for Dollars to Japan and the Rest of Asia, Fiscal Years 1960–70

Fiscal Year	Japan	Other Asia	Total Asia
	($ bil)		
1960	0.42	0.19	0.62
1961	0.53	0.23	0.76
1962	0.45	0.24	0.69
1963	0.49	0.26	0.75
1964	0.73	0.31	1.04
1965	0.75	0.30	1.05
1966	0.91	0.32	1.23
1967	0.93	0.45	1.38
1968	0.90	0.46	1.36
1969	0.84	0.49	1.33
1970	1.09	0.63	1.72

its emergence as a market: Total Asia is a vast land area, sweeping eastward from the Mediterranean Sea all the way cross the Middle East, South Asia, and Southeast Asia to the Pacific Ocean. Japan, though occupying only a string of little islands, accounts for a substantial part of the Asian total. And Japan, in all probability, will be the world's first $2 billion market for U.S. farm products.

Table 5.5 points out gains being registered in areas outside our major dollar markets. Included in that total are increasing shipments to several industrializing Far East countries other than Japan. Table 5.9 shows the total dollar sales to Taiwan, Hong Kong, South Korea, Thailand, Singapore, Malaysia, Okinawa, and the Philippines. Some of the gains are quite impressive. For example, U.S. dollar sales of farm products to Taiwan increased from $12 million in 1960 to $114 million in 1970—a ninefold gain. Dollar sales to South Korea have risen from $16 million to $54 million.

The Foreign Agricultural Service is alert to these developments. Agricultural attache offices have been opened in this set of new markets and promotion effort is being stepped up elsewhere in the Far East. For example, we have staged food trade fairs in Hong Kong and Singapore.

The Caribbean area also is an emerging market included in the "other" total in Table 5.5. As you can see (Table 5.10), dollar sales of U.S. farm products to this area have more than doubled in the last decade. Some of this is due to the rapid rise of tourism, but much of it is based on the solid foundation of comparative advantage. Earnings

TABLE 5.9.   U.S. Agricultural Exports Sold for Dollars to Far East Countries Other than Japan, Fiscal Years 1960–70

Fiscal Year	Major Far East Markets Other than Japan
	($ bil)
1960	0.13
1961	0.14
1962	0.15
1963	0.14
1964	0.20
1965	0.20
1966	0.23
1967	0.26
1968	0.42
1969	0.38
1970	0.36

NOTE: Includes Taiwan, Hong Kong, South Korea, Thailand, Singapore, Malaysia, Okinawa, Philippines.

TABLE 5.10. U.S. Agricultural Exports
Sold for Dollars to Countries
in the Caribbean Area, Fiscal
Years 1960–70

Fiscal Year	Dollar Sales to Caribbean Area
	($ mil)
1960	47
1961	52
1962	55
1963	57
1964	65
1965	68
1966	77
1967	90
1968	98
1969	107
1970	113

NOTE: Principal markets are Bahamas, Bermuda, British Honduras, Guyana, Jamaica, Netherlands Antilles, Surinam, Trinidad, and Tobago.

from such sources as Jamaican bauxite and Dominican Republic sugar are financing sales of U.S. rice, meats, and canned foods.

Proof positive that trade moves on a two-way street is given in Table 5.11. While our total agricultural exports, commercial and concessional, have been trending upward, so have agricultural imports. This is natural and normal. Our population is expanding. Our gross national product is on the rise. Increased agricultural imports are helping us meet our greater needs and wants.

TABLE 5.11. Agricultural Trade Balance—Total U.S. Agricultural Exports vs. Agricultural Imports

Fiscal Year	Total U.S. Agricultural Exports, Commercial and Concessional	Total Agricultural Imports
	($ bil)	
1960	4.52	4.01
1961	4.95	3.64
1962	5.14	3.76
1963	5.08	3.91
1964	6.07	4.10
1965	6.10	3.99
1966	6.68	4.45
1967	6.77	4.45
1968	6.31	4.66
1969	5.74	4.93
1970	6.65	5.48

TABLE 5.12. U.S. Agricultural Imports by Areas or Countries of Origin, Fiscal Years 1960 and 1970

Fiscal Year	1960	1970
	($ bil)	
Canada	0.18	0.28
Latin America	1.89	2.21
Europe	0.51	0.95
Africa	0.34	0.58
Asia	0.85	0.87
Australia and New Zealand	0.24	0.58

Table 5.12 shows that one thing is certain: The United States buys a great many agricultural products from Latin America—more than from any other area of the world. High on the list are coffee, cocoa beans, bananas, and other items not produced in this country, but we also import competitive products, such as sugar, beef, tomatoes, and strawberries.

From Europe we import cheese and other dairy products, canned hams, wines, chocolate products, and breeding animals. But the total from Europe is much smaller than from Latin America.

From Australia and New Zealand, the big category is livestock products—mainly meat, but also wool and some dairy items.

Table 5.13 shows that our agricultural exports do not balance out with agricultural imports. For example, we export a great volume of agricultural commodities to Japan, but import only a small volume of farm products from Japan. And we export a relatively small volume to Latin America but import a great deal. These imbalances explain why, in a trade negotiation, industrial products must also be considered in striking trade bargains.

Table 5.14 shows total imports broken down into two general categories—noncompetitive (complementary) and competitive (supplementary). Virtually all the growth in the past decade has been in the competitive category. The gain, in terms of value, was from $1.98 billion to $3.37 billion—a rise of about 70 percent. The sharpest increase was in imports of meats, which almost tripled, but gains also were recorded for sugar, fruits, vegetables, and breeding animals.

TABLE 5.13. U.S. Agricultural Trade, Commercial, Fiscal Year 1970, Destination of Exports and Origin of Imports

	Exports	Imports
	($ bil)	
Europe	2.46	0.95
Japan	1.09	0.04
Latin America	0.54	2.21
Other	1.58	2.28
Total	5.67	5.48

TABLE 5.14. Total Agricultural Imports, Competitive and Noncompetitive

Fiscal Year	Competitive (Supplementary)	Noncompetitive (Complementary)	Total
		($ bil)	
1960	1.98	2.03	4.01
1961	1.81	1.83	3.64
1962	2.05	1.71	3.76
1963	2.21	1.70	3.91
1964	2.22	1.87	4.10*
1965	2.13	1.86	3.99
1966	2.47	1.98	4.45
1967	2.67	1.79	4.45*
1968	2.84	1.81	4.66*
1969	3.07	1.86	4.93
1970	3.37	2.11	5.48

* Discrepancy due to rounding.

Noncompetitive imports consist of items we do not produce in this country—crude rubber, hard fibers, bananas, coffee, cocoa beans, tea, spices. On a value basis, imports of these products rose only from $2.03 billion in 1960 to $2.11 billion in 1970.

Table 5.15 compares interestingly with Table 5.3, which broke down shifts in 1960 and 1970 exports of raw and finished products, and showed that dollar values of raw product exports had outgained shipments of finished items, but not by much.

Here, on imports, we see a different trend. Volumes of raw product imports changed little between 1960 and 1970, but imports of finished goods increased sharply. It is clear that lower wage rates in foreign countries are making it profitable for foreign suppliers to ship us larger supplies of beef, strawberries, pineapples, oranges, tomatoes, and mushrooms.

On meats, Table 5.16 shows that the United States has been on a

TABLE 5.15. U.S. Agricultural Imports Broken Down into "Raw" and "Finished" Products, Fiscal Years 1960 and 1970 in Billion Dollars

Raw Products	1960	1970	Finished Products	1960	1970
Green coffee	1.04	1.10	Meats	0.34	0.97
Sugar	0.51	0.69	Fruits (including bananas)	0.14	0.32
Rubber	0.38	0.28	Breeding animals	0.08	0.14
Wool	0.21	0.12	Vegetables	0.10	0.28
Cocoa beans	0.15	0.21	Other	0.31	0.58
Other	0.74	0.82	Total	0.97	2.28*
Total	3.04	3.20			
Total imports, 1960	4.02		Total imports, 1970	5.48	

* Small discrepancies due to rounding.

Trends and Structure of U.S. Agricultural Trade 99

TABLE 5.16. Comparison of Exports and Imports of Meats, Fruits, and Vegetables in Fiscal Years 1960 and 1970 in Million Dollars

	Exports		Imports	
	1960	1970	1960	1970
Meats	62	140	340	967
Fruits and preparations (excludes bananas)	250	341	64	141
Vegetables and preparations	150	209	99	275

net import basis for some time, but meat imports in relation to exports increased sharply over the past decade.

Exports of fruits increased between 1960 and 1970 by about $90 million, or 35 percent. Citrus juices going to Western Europe and lemons going to Japan increased sharply. Exports of dried fruits also increased. But imports of fruits and preparations increased by $77 million—a gain of 120 percent. Imports of strawberries, pineapples, and mandarin oranges among other products also increased.

Both exports and imports of vegetables and preparations increased, but the shift to vegetable imports was much more drastic than for fruits. Actually the United States shifted in the decade from a net export basis to a net import basis by a wide margin. In this shift Mexico looms large. Tomato imports from Mexico increased from $24 million in 1960 to a record $96 million in 1970. We also imported substantial quantities of cucumbers and peppers from our neighbor to the south. On the processed side, the big increases have been in canned mushrooms—mainly from Taiwan—and in tomato products, primarily from the Mediterranean area.

The big story in the livestock area is the substantial expansion of meat imports. This expansion (Table 5.17) has evolved over a period of several years.

Meat imports by the United States became unusually heavy in 1963. This meat, primarily frozen beef from Australia and New Zealand, was looking for a market. Markets elsewhere—notably Japan, the EEC, and the United Kingdom—were either closed or were less attractive than the American market because of their import or domestic systems.

TABLE 5.17. Exports and Imports of Livestock and Products in 1960 and 1970

	Exports		Imports	
	1960	1970	1960	1970
	($ mil)			
Live animals (excluding poultry)	26	26	82	139
Hides and skins	69	157	79	53
Meats	62	140	340	967
Lard	62	36	. . .	. . .
Tallow (all)	109	152	. . .	. . .
Total	328	511	501	1,159

TABLE 5.18. U.S. Agricultural Exports Sold for Dollars vs. Agricultural Imports

Fiscal Year	Agricultural Exports Sold for Dollars	Agricultural Imports
	($ bil)	
1960	3.24	4.02
1961	3.44	3.64
1962	3.57	3.77
1963	3.61	3.91
1964	4.63	4.10
1965	4.50	3.99
1966	5.29	4.45
1967	5.46	4.45
1968	5.02	4.66
1969	4.70	4.93
1970	5.67	5.48

As imports continued to rise rapidly, it became obvious that orderly importing procedures were needed. The Meat Import Law of 1964 provided a basis for this orderly importing, but since late 1968 a voluntary restraint program has been in effect. Under the restraint program the United States, in lieu of quotas, has worked out arrangements with foreign meat exporting countries to limit their shipments to us voluntarily. In 1970 voluntary restraints provided the basis for our estimate of imports of 1,160 million pounds. The same level was in effect for calendar year 1971. These import levels are higher than our imports in 1963, the year that brought on the quota legislation.

Table 5.18 shows how the commercial component of our agricultural exports, the part sold for dollars, compares with imports. Agriculture obviously did not pay its way in the early years of the decade. However, a favorable bulge developed in the mid-1960s. Exports dropped in 1969, but recovered in 1970. In 1971, dollar exports exceeded imports by a wide margin.

Figure 5.1 shows, on a calendar year basis, what U.S. agriculture has contributed to the U.S. balance of payments. The gross contribution, represented by the ton line, is made up of two dollar-inflow categories: First, there is the inflow coming from dollar sales of farm products in commercial channels. Second, there are certain funds accruing under PL 480 that the United States uses for embassy expenses, military outlays, market promotion, and the like, as well as Export-Import Bank principal and interest repayments. From this gross contribution is subtracted the total represented by agricultural imports. The remainder is the net contribution, represented by the bottom line. Since 1963 this net contribution has aggregated $5.5 billion.

THE FUTURE. What do these charts point to with respect to the future of our agricultural trade? By and large they are encouraging.

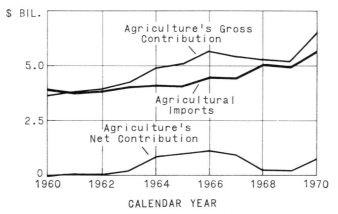

FIG. 5.1.   U.S. agriculture's contribution to the balance of payments.

If we can judge the future by the past, the future looks encouraging.

Since 1960 the United States has set five new export records. New marks for exports were established in 1961, 1962, 1964, 1966, and 1967. Shipments in fiscal 1971, as already emphasized, far and away set a new record.

A look at our trade patterns shows that our largest commercial sales are being made to countries where economic growth is taking place on an expanding scale. This should mean that our commercial agricultural exports will continue to increase because economic growth is on the upgrade almost everywhere.

President Richard M. Nixon recently called attention to the desirability of $10 billion agricultural export years—an achievable objective. Between 1960 and 1970 total agricultural exports rose by 47 percent—an average of 4.7 percent a year. At that average rate, we would hit the $10 billion level by 1977.

We live in an impatient world. People were willing to put up with poverty twenty or thirty years ago, but the people who inhabit this globe today want to improve their standards of living more. They know that science and technology can lead the way to higher living standards.

The United States is in a strategic position to capitalize on this universal yearning for better living. As the charts on the makeup of our exports showed clearly, much of our export volume is oriented toward the raw products—feed grains, oilseed cake and meal soybeans as such, and wheat. These are the products America can produce with great efficiency, and will continue to produce.

Some problems remain, however. Some world areas—Africa and South America—probably will not be big markets for many years to come. In these areas, per capita incomes are small and we must wait for economic growth to support demand. In some developed countries, such as Canada, the United Kingdom, and Mexico, diverse forces are at work—competition of other producing areas, preferential arrangements, a drive for self-sufficiency, a desire to improve a balance of payments position. Trade barriers, of course, play a role. The protectionist policies of the EEC are hurting our trade, and are hurting the best interests of Europeans.

By and large, however, I believe that the forces pressing for better living are in the ascendancy everywhere. These forces cannot long be held in check. Inexorably they will push our agricultural export totals upward to the $10 billion level envisioned by the president. It is a matter of time until they get there.

[6]

Trade Restrictions and U.S. Consumers

Dale E. Hathaway

IN THE TRADE POLICY area, lip service is paid to consumers, but political pressures are always on behalf of producers. Farmers themselves and most citizens nearly always look at trade policy as producers, not as consumers. Even though this book is primarily concerned with U.S. farm exports, it is appropriate to include a chapter on the impact of trade restrictions on U.S. consumers.

Despite the sporadic efforts of the Ralph Naders, consumers' interests in many policy questions are ignored, for there is no effective political organization to express them. This is especially true of those in our economy who are consumers but not producer oriented: many housewives, the young, the retired, welfare recipients, and others. They are consumer oriented, but they lack effective organization and political power as consumers.

In general, the things mentioned are "old hat" to economists, so much so that we sometimes tend to forget them in our policy analysis. In any case, this chapter attempts to interpret these factors in terms of the current U.S. economy, which does not exactly fit some of the textbook models. The items discussed will be (1) resource use efficiency, (2) product availability, (3) protection against economic blackmail and political irresponsibility, (4) competition apart from resource use efficiency, and (5) international relations.

RESOURCE USE EFFICIENCY. The concept of resource use efficiency is, of course, the cornerstone of international trade. Comparative advantage is what trade is all about and why consumers gain from trade. We are all familiar with the studies of what our trade restrictions and

DALE E. HATHAWAY is Professor and Chairman, Department of Agricultural Economics, Michigan State University.

protection programs have cost the American consumer in cheese, butter, sugar, and tobacco products.

While these costs are often real, in some cases they are not. Our theories assume resource mobilities between agriculture and other industries that do not exist. In the absence of such mobility, resources may not move to other industries but stay in the production of farm or other products that would produce low returns in the event of the absence of trade restrictions. Thus, some of our trade restrictions merely become mechanisms for income transfers through the market price, a mechanism which has some economic and political advantages as well as disadvantages. One disadvantage is that such income transfers tend to encourage further poor allocation of resources which are a real cost to the economy and which in turn increase the political pressures for continued trade restrictions.

In general, however, the argument cannot be made that the resource cost of poor allocation due to our present level trade restrictions is large. Indeed, it must be relatively small in comparison to the resource losses of 6 percent unemployment and the widespread underemployment in many rural areas, or of the resource loss from racial discrimination. To fight trade policy wars on this battlefield is a losing cause. Our economy has many greater and more obvious resources losses, and many of these are not net losses.

In order to put this point in perspective we should remember that the total merchandise imports into the United States in 1970 were $40 billion. Of these, food, beverages, and tobacco amount to $6.2 billion; crude material and fuels, $6.6 billion; and manufactured goods, $25.9 billion. Total merchandise imports were about 4 percent of the gross national product (GNP). Merchandise imports are about 7 percent of total personal consumption expenditures and food and beverage imports are 5 percent of consumer expenditures on those items. Since many imports are items which we cannot produce, the rest would not appreciably lower resource use efficiency if produced at home.

Even if the cost were twice as much for domestic production as for importation, we are talking about less than 2 or 3 percent of the GNP after excluding those products we do not produce at all. From this loss we would have to subtract the value of additional GNP obtained by expanding domestic employment, so the net loss would be half or less of that amount. Import restrictions on all competitive products would probably cost no more than 2 percent of the GNP, at most, in terms of resource use efficiency. This, of course, still amounts to $20 billion, a figure that could have a major impact on poverty, environment, health, and other major problems in our society. Because it is so small and hard to measure, producer groups meet very little consumer resistance when they push for restrictionist policies.

Having said all this, we should remember that our exports are dependent upon imports, and nearly 4 percent of our labor force is employed in production of merchandise exports. Moreover, workers in export industries average 8 percent higher wages than do workers in industries that would provide import subsidies.

AVAILABILITY OF GOODS. In this area, trade restrictions have powerful effects upon U.S. consumers. It is not possible for Americans to enjoy the unheated British inn or the pleasantries of French taxi drivers without tourist trade. Nor could the American consumer enjoy coffee, tea, bananas, scotch, and numerous other food products not produced in this country in the absence of trade. Large parts of the world do live without some or all of these items, but I believe they are a significant and important part of our standard of living and as such are important to American consumers.

Perhaps even more important to American consumers are products which could be produced here but are not because of the structure of our economy. The U.S. economy is a mass production economy and only the Lord and imports can save the consumer who wants something which does not fit within the consumer market as seen by our corporate planners. Perhaps the best case in point is the U.S. auto industry. Not until foreign imports exceeded a million units a year did it occur to our manufacturers that it does not require 300 horsepower and two tons of metal to propel an individual professor three miles to the office or his wife three miles to the faculty tea. No technological, economic, or climatic reason has prevented U.S. manufacturers from producing small, lower priced cars.

Imports have become the consumer's main defense against corporate stupidity and the obsession with the middle of the market. And this protection works at both ends of the income scale. In our economy it is virtually impossible for those who can afford it to find the individually handcrafted items they want for their homes and personal use. Conversely, as the average consumer becomes wealthier, mass production processes upgrade the quality and price of many items to meet the changing market. The consumer who cannot afford the higher quality and higher priced item depends upon imports which have filled the low end of the market gap.

It is ironic, but I believe true, that the greatest purchases of imported consumer goods are at the two ends of the income scale. The man who eats Kobe beef and the one who eats at McDonald's have something in common, just as do the one with the $25 English cotton shirt and the one with the $1.95 discount house shirt from Hong Kong. Both are consumers for whom the mass market is not large enough to activate the U.S. production process, and in the absence of imports they would be forced into less satisfactory consumption patterns. These kinds of imports seem especially important to me, for while they are closed as competitive, in many cases they really are not. We increase consumer satisfaction and expand our markets abroad without really displacing U.S. producers.

PROTECTION AGAINST ECONOMIC POWER. Increasingly we recognize that major sectors of the U.S. economy are dominated by giant institutions: the large corporation and the industrywide trade union. More and more we see these two giants, traditionally deadly rivals, acting in consort to wield their joint economic power against the American consumer. The game plan is generally this: The industrywide union demands, and by strike if necessary, receives wage increases well in excess of the growth in industry productivity. The corporation in turn has power to determine its market price level, and the wage demands are passed on in higher consumer prices. The final piece of this drama is a joint effort by industry and the unions to demand protection from imports which might undermine their ability to extract higher prices and wages from the domestic economy.

We are generally more familiar with the traditional theories of the relationship between domestic inflation control and international trade. A country faced with excess demand finds imports useful in soaking up some of that excess demand—avoiding inflation caused by too much money demand and a highly inelastic supply of goods and services.

This kind of inflation, however, is not the major problem facing U.S. consumers. Instead we find simultaneously high unemployment, excess industrial capacity, and what has come to be known as cost-push inflation. This inflation exists largely as the result of economic concentration in unions and industry, and which I choose to call the exercise of economic power, or to put it less politely, economic blackmail.

Even our present Republican administration has come to support this conclusion. In their *Third Inflation Alert,* the Council of Economic Advisors said: "The terms of the agreement reached in the can industry are clearly in excess of any realistic assessment of the long-term productivity growth prospects."[1]

This statement followed a discussion of the forthcoming nationwide steel negotiations and related to the fact that the steel wage settlements might follow the can industry. That statement also said: "One important element in the price-cost situation has been a voluntary restraint arrangement which restricts European and Japanese steel shipments to the United States."[2]

The Joint Economic Committee in their short unanimous statement made the case more explicit:

Import competition offers a practical means for promoting efficiency and combating wage-price increases in industries that are highly concentrated in the United States. Every industry in this country that is dominated by a few firms also has a strong, industry-wide union. Thus, without import competition, the industry and its corresponding union would be free to bargain collusively and to agree to combination of wage and price increases at the expense of firms and employees in less-concentrated industries. In this respect, the contrast between the automobile and steel industries, both of which are highly concentrated, is instructive.

Imports of automobiles and parts have not been restricted. The firms have instead responded to competition from abroad by introducing small cars to compete directly with imports, and the auto workers have evidenced concern for increasing productivity and holding down costs per unit of output. Over the long run, both American consumers and the employees of auto producers are likely to gain from this constructive response to competition from abroad.

In contrast, both management and labor in the steel industry have in recent years advocated the restriction of imports. Their pleas induced the Executive, in December 1968, to persuade other producing countries to voluntarily limit their steel exports to the United States. From 1960 through December 1968, wholesale prices of iron and steel products increased 5.5 percent; from December 1968 to November 1970—following the introduction of voluntary import quotas— wholesale iron and steel prices increased 13.8 percent. (The wholesale price index for all industrial commodities rose 8.8 percent and 7.7 percent in these same two periods.) Thus, iron and steel price increases in the two years following the introduction of import restrictions were more than twice the increases in the previous nine years. The industry is currently urging that existing import limitations be tightened.[3]

One of the greatest values of a liberal import policy is that for goods it can serve as a substitute for or perhaps even more effectively as a kind of government wage-price-income policy. Unfortunately we cannot import constructed buildings or personal services. We must use restraints other than trade to deal with these areas of economic power.

The implications up to now have been that import restrictions are not likely to seriously harm the consumer if they occur in industries where the economic structure is reasonably competitive, inasmuch as such industries are incapable of using import restrictions to protect their power positions in the economy. However, important exceptions to this do occur within agriculture.

A number of agricultural products subject to price support programs and some in which import restrictions become important elements allow the program to be pushed to unrealistic levels. A case in point is the dairy industry. It has an elaborately rigged market structure of milk marketing orders and federal price supports. In order to maintain this price support system, it has become necessary to impose quotas on manufactured dairy products, and more recently, reinstitute the export subsidy program.

The concept of an income transfer program for the dairy industry is not basically wrong. Most data indicate that resource returns in dairying are near the bottom in agriculture, so if there is any justification for income transfers to agricultural producers, the dairy producers have a case.

The error is in the method used to achieve the transfer: protecting it by import restrictions and raising consumer product prices, which puts most of the cost on the lower income family with children, the consumers of dairy products. It is almost certain to erroneously induce additional expansion of dairy product output, with further poor management of resources and continuing pressure for higher price supports and import restrictions. It can be clearly shown that in the U.S. economy a move to limited direct payments on manufactured milk could make some groups better off without reducing producers' income.

Other producers who use protective import restrictions lack economic power or a government market intervention program but wish to reduce or entirely avoid competition from foreign producers who may have lower costs. These, for example, would include U.S. fruit and vegetables producers, and possibly the shoe and textile manufacturers. It is true that tariffs or quotas would increase consumer costs on these products, but since these groups lack either the market structure or political power to extract monopoly profits from the U.S. economy, the consumer loss would be relatively small. The domestic supply elasticity in most such industries would be quite high, at least in expansion, and consumer losses from protecting such groups would be those incurred in taking advantage of better resource allocation under freer trade.

Finally, international trade and finance can and does put some real limits upon irresponsible domestic monetary and fiscal policy. Some would argue that we should not let our domestic economy be influenced by trade and international finance, but in its absence there would be an irresistible poltitical pressure to inflate the economy excessively in lieu of handling the problems of the unemployed and disadvantaged in other ways.

COMPETITIVE PRESSURE. Those who have had the dubious pleasure of traveling on an airline which has a monoply on a given route or in a particular country are well aware that elements other than price are involved in competition. Competition not only induces economic efficiency, it also tends to encourage innovation, attention to consumer complaints and needs, and response to change. It is possible that the necessity for international competition by our major airlines explains in part their closer attention to passenger welfare than has been the case in the U.S. railroad industry.

Competition and innovation may also be major factors contributing to long-run gains in static resource use efficiency. Many have made the point that protection for European agriculture for several decades is a major factor in its relative inefficiency today. The same point has been made about the U.S. steel industry. This means that, over time, consumers are less well served than they might be, even if their consumption is largely from domestic production.

This issue of innovation and trade cuts two ways. Not only do consumers benefit as such by the pressure of foreign goods in the domestic market but they also benefit from better performance at home by companies that compete abroad. I am certain that German and Japanese consumers get better products at home because their producers must compete in world markets. Conversely, the poor Russian consumer gets goods that are shoddy by their own judgment, because their consumer goods manufacturers never have to compete with other producers in any market.

INTERNATIONAL RELATIONS. Our trade *theory* is cast in economic terms but our trade *policy* is cast in political terms. An important political fact of life is that trade can be an important positive or negative aspect of international relations. The United States is spending billions of dollars in foreign aid and many times as much in trying to win and maintain friends around the world through military alliances. Neither policy is doing very well abroad and neither is especially popular at home, although the unpopularity varies from group to group.

The American public has been slow to recognize that a major importation from politically unstable or even hostile countries may do more to keep them from irresponsible action than either aid or alliances. Anyone with oil, coffee, sugar, or bananas to sell is much more likely to be reasonable to deal with if they have a major market to protect in the United States.

More recognition should be given to the fact that we can buy some things in the international political arena, and that we can buy them cheaper than foreign aid, defense expenditures, or CIA agents. United States consumers would get something besides guilt complexes and student unrest at home from purchasing goods, and foreign producers would gain as well.

SUMMARY AND CONCLUSIONS. As economists we point out that nations should and do trade in order to get more from a given bundle of resources. But looking realistically at the figures and import flows, I doubt that this general reason is very powerful in the United States; this has never been a politically viable argument, since producers are much better organized than consumers.

First, we want to trade because we want to sell abroad—the main focus of this book. We have an excess capacity in our economy and need foreign markets. About 4 percent of our labor force is employed in producing exports and receiving higher wages than the average of those producing only for domestic consumption. But we must buy in order to sell.

Second, we need imports to fill our need for products we cannot produce. Minerals, crude fuels, tropical products, and similar products fall into this category. Moreover we need imports to fill the market gaps our mass-producing industries do not fill. It would be possible to live without some of these items—the Russians do, for instance—but our level of living would be appreciably lower.

Third, and perhaps most important, imports may prove to be the only effective protection consumers have against the economic power of unions, corporations, and government-organized monopolies. The politics of trade are more favorable than the politics of antitrust against corporations, unions, or farm lobbies, in part because in almost every case there is a countervailing exporter interest in the trade area.

Fourth, consumers need trade to maintain competitive pressures beyond the price field. Competition forces innovation, change, and attention to consumers' wants.

Finally, we should recognize that import trade can have a significant international effect beyond providing exchange to sell more abroad. We can buy some international political stability, and probably cheaper through trade than through present methods.

In summary, yes, consumers have an interest and stake in a liberal trade policy. And it is an interest beyond that given in classical trade theory, in terms of both importance and complexity.

NOTES

1. *Third Inflation Alert,* Council of Economic Advisors, p. 30.
2. Ibid., p. 28.
3. Ibid., p. 30.

[7]

Interrelationships between the Levels of U.S. Exports and Imports

G. L. Seevers AND W. R. Keeton

I N THIS CHAPTER we examine aggregate interrelationships between U.S. exports and imports and provide quantitative estimates of the magnitudes of certain of these interrelationships. This subject has recently captured the attention of many who are concerned about the possible impact of new U.S. import restrictions on our sales abroad.

In the present context it is important to distinguish between *economic interrelationships* (how a change in exports would affect imports and vice versa through economic responses) and *policy interrelationships* (how our trading partners would react if the United States adopted policies to, for example, directly affect imports—the question of retaliation). Identifying and quantifying the economic interrelationships is itself a major undertaking, but analysis of policy interrelationships would be even more hazardous because it would involve speculation about political responses. While political reactions are surely no less important than economic responses in the present state of affairs, we have chosen to concentrate on economic interrelationships.

INTERRELATIONSHIPS AND COMMON CAUSAL FACTORS. A second distinction that we wish to make is between interrelationships on the one hand and common factors that influence both exports and imports on the other. This distinction deserves some amplification. At one extreme is the case of uranium imports which are permitted to enter this country for processing in U.S. enrichment plants only if they are subsequently exported. A similar interdependence of trade flows arises when a U.S. firm builds a plant overseas for the explicit purpose

---

G. L. SEEVERS and W. R. KEETON are Staff Economists at the Council of Economic Advisors. Mr. Seevers is on leave from Oregon State University. The views expressed are those of the authors, and should not be attributed to the Council of Economic Advisors.

of processing materials shipped from the United States and returning the end-products to this country. The importance of this phenomenon has been increasing in recent years. Imports under special tariff provisions that exempt from duty assessment the value of U.S. materials further processed overseas accounted for 6 percent of total U.S. imports in 1966.[1] By 1969 they had grown to 8 percent of total U.S. imports, with a duty-free content of 24 percent. While it is uncertain to what extent the special tariff provisions have encouraged firms to process U.S. materials or assemble U.S. components overseas, it appears a direct and growing interrelationship exists between the two trade flows.

In contrast to these two examples of direct interrelationships, factors working at the other extreme concurrently affect both exports and imports. Several examples are worth mentioning to illustrate the principal aggregate factors at work.

1. If investment in research and development leads to a major breakthrough in a domestic industry that both exports and competes with imports, this industry will become more competitive with foreign goods.
2. If the United States experiences slower general price and wage increases than its trading partners, the competitive position of U.S. exports will be strengthened and at the same time imports will become more expensive vis-a-vis domestic products.
3. On the other hand, a higher rate of real economic growth in the United States than in its trading partners will tend to raise the demand for U.S. imports more rapidly than for exports and increase pressures to transfer resources employed in export industries to domestic uses.
4. There is substantial evidence that the level of unemployment of domestic resources affects the competitiveness of both U.S. exports and domestic import-substitutes via delivery lags, credit terms, and other nonprice factors as well as through relative prices.

The interplay of these aggregate economic forces clearly has an important influence on U.S. trade patterns. Rather than pursue this theme further, however, more direct interrelationships will be examined.

IMPORTS CONTENT OF EXPORTS. About one-third of U.S. imports are raw materials and intermediate goods. To the extent these enter the production of export goods, imports and exports are directly related.

Estimates derived from the Input-Output Model of the U.S. Economy indicate that the 1958 export bill of goods contained 2.2 percent imports. The import content had risen to 3.0 percent by 1965 and to 3.6 percent for the 1969 bill of exports (both in 1958 dollars). About

TABLE 7.1.   Import Content of U.S. Exports, 1958, 1965, and 1969

	Value of Exports 1969	Import Content 1958	1965	1969
	($ mil)	*(%)*		
Total exports	33,358	2.2	3.0	3.6
Mining	615	1.6	2.1	2.7
Chemicals	1,699	3.9	4.0	4.7
Construction, mining and oil field machinery	1,125	2.4	3.4	4.1
Special industry machinery and equipment	693	2.8	3.5	4.4
Office, computing and accounting machines	965	1.8	2.2	3.1
Radio, television and communication equipment	613	2.2	3.2	4.1
Motor vehicles and equipment	2,732	3.8	4.2	6.3
Aircraft and parts	2,158	2.1	2.3	3.1

SOURCE: *Input-Output Model of the U.S. Economy,* U.S. Department of Labor.

one-fifth of the increase between 1965 and 1969 can be attributed to a change in the mix of exports and the remainder to greater dependence on imports by individual industries.

Table 7.1 gives aggregate results as well as changes for selected industries (with over $0.5 billion exports in 1969) that became substantially more import-intensive. Motor vehicles and equipment is the outstanding example of a major exporting industry that has a relatively high import content and has become more import-intensive, with imports of intermediate goods representing 6.3 percent of output in 1969. No important industry experienced a decline in import intensity. Agricultural and food exports had a relatively low import content—2.3 percent in 1969.

Charles Bowman, Bureau of Labor Statistics, provided these estimates. They are based on the average import content of production in each industry, and do not distinguish between the content of exported output and of output sold domestically.

The input-output relationships, even though they assume fixed coefficients, provide a framework for discussing influences on imports that are critically important to certain exporting industries. United States import policies that affect prices and quantities of imports which serve as raw materials or intermediate goods in export production also influence the competitiveness of exports. If tariffs are reduced, the price of imported and import-competing inputs will fall, and exports dependent upon these inputs will become more competitive abroad. Or if the United States adopts quantitative restrictions on imports that are used to produce export goods, a smaller total quantity of inputs will be available, prices of those inputs will rise, and exports using them will become less competitive. Our steel import restraint agreement with Japan and Europe affords an excellent illustration of how restrictive import policies can serve to reduce exports.

According to one estimate, "For every dollar's worth of steel kept out of the United States by import restrictions, over a half dollar is spent on increased imports or reduced exports in other product lines because of the higher cost of steel inputs."[2] The United States has quantitative restrictions either through voluntary restraint agreements or mandatory quotas on several important commodities, including some that are inputs for exporting industries: petroleum, sugar, dairy products, meat, cotton textiles, and steel.

The availability of imports on a competitive basis has another and perhaps more important impact in its exertion of pressure on domestic producers of inputs used in exporting industries to reduce costs and refrain from price increases.

U.S. IMPORT RESPONSE TO A CHANGE IN EXPORTS. The input-output results suggest that a change in aggregate U.S. exports would induce an offsetting response of only 3 to 4 percent in imports of raw materials and other intermediate goods. However, this understates the total response by ignoring the multiplier effects of a change in exports on the level of aggregate economic activity, which in turn influences the demand for imports of both intermediate and finished goods. In the next section we employ quantitative estimates of these total responses for each of the developed countries to estimate the economic import on U.S. exports of new U.S. import restrictions. First, however, it will be illustrative to quantify the relationship for the United States alone in the absence of foreign repercussions.

A simulation of the Data Resources Model of the U.S. Economy indicated that a $1 billion decrease in exports in 1968 prices would lead to a $1.9 billion fall in the gross national product (GNP). We therefore assumed an export multiplier of 2, which is consistent with the results of other macro-econometric models.[3] From recent statistical estimates of the income elasticity of demand for U.S. imports of both finished goods and intermediate products, we derived the marginal propensity to import.[4] Combining these results, we determined that a $1 billion contraction in exports would induce a $130 million decline in imports (both in 1968 prices). Imports of finished and semimanufactured goods would represent a substantial share of this decline, with only one-eighth of the total occurring in crude materials and foods. This highlights an important point with respect to agricultural products: the economic responses are likely to be relatively minor for products that have low income elasticities.

U.S. IMPORT RESTRICTIONS. With the recent growth in protectionist sentiment in the United States it is particularly appropriate to examine the potential impact of new import restrictions on U.S. exports. In this section we estimate the impact of restrictive measures operating through the income mechanism in other countries, extending the basic relationship discussed above for the United States to a multi-country trading framework.

The method employed to estimate the impacts was as follows:

1. It was assumed that new U.S. trade restrictions initially reduce U.S. imports by $1 billion. This reduction was allocated to countries that supply the restricted products in proportion to their 1968 or 1969 exports to the United States, depending on availability of data. Strictly speaking, these results correspond to an increase in tariffs sufficient to reduce imports by $1 billion. The distinction does not affect the first round "bilateral" estimates, and it makes little quantitative difference for the total estimates.

2. The effects of the reduced exports on each supplying country's imports were obtained from estimates of the relationship between imports and autonomous spending (including exports, government consumption, and investment) for the twenty-five developed countries. (Estimates were provided by Grant Taplin of the International Monetary Fund [IMF].) For each country a "reflection ratio" was derived, corresponding to the product of the export multiplier and the marginal propensity to import, and indicating the change in imports which would be caused by a given change in exports. (Adjustments were made to convert all ratios to constant dollars of the same year, chosen to be 1968.) These ratios ranged from a low of 0.14 for the United States to a high of 0.74 for Ireland. Many countries had reflection ratios between 0.3 and 0.4. All developing and Soviet bloc countries were assumed to have reflection ratios of unity. This is consistent with past studies which have employed reflection ratios for similar purposes[5] and assumes that the imports of such countries are limited by the availability of foreign exchange.

3. The next step was to allocate the reduced imports of each supplying country among its trading partners, including the United States, according to actual market shares. This yielded an estimate of the first round "bilateral effects" on U.S. exports of an import restriction —the initial direct impact which occurs as supplying countries decrease their imports from the United States. The bilateral effects exclude further bilateral feedback between the United States and its trading partners; i.e., the impact of the additional fall in U.S. imports induced by the reduction in its exports. This feedback would be relatively small because of the low U.S. reflection ratio.

4. Finally we estimated the "total effects," which include the impact of the U.S. import restriction on trade flows among our trading partners. When a country experiences a fall in its exports to the United States, its imports decline not only from the United States but also from other nations. The resultant fall in those countries' exports

TABLE 7.2. Estimates of the Bilateral Impact on U.S. Exports Resulting from a $1
Billion Restriction of Selected U.S. Imports

	U.S. Exports		
	Total	Developed countries*	Agricultural†‡
	($ mil)		
General restriction§	172.9	84.1	9.7
Radio and television receivers‖	104.0	46.7	21.0
Nonrubber footwear‖	71.0	46.4	15.9

* OECD members and Australia.
† Includes the following SITC categories:
  0—Food and live animals
  1—Beverages and tobacco
  2—Crude materials, inedible, except fuels
  4—Animal and vegetable oils and fats
  ‡ Based only on 21 developed market economies for which estimates of import responses were available for categories as well as total.
  § The $1 billion restriction is allocated to countries in proportion to their total exports to the U.S. in 1969.
  ‖ The $1 billion restriction is allocated to countries in proportion to their share of U.S. imports in 1969.

causes a reduction in their imports and thus a further decline in U.S. exports. The total effects also take into account all additional feedbacks after the first round of reduced spending.

BILATERAL EFFECTS. Table 7.2 shows the bilateral effects for three different hypothetical import restrictions: on U.S. imports in general, and on two categories of imports for which restrictive measures have been proposed—radios and television sets, and nonrubber footwear. These differ in the pattern by which the reduced imports are allocated to supplying countries. A general $1 billion restriction (1968 prices) operating only through the income mechanism would lead to an estimated U.S. export reduction of $173 million—17.3 percent of the initial decline in U.S. imports. About 50 percent of the fall in U.S. exports would come from reduced purchases by developed countries and the remainder from developing and Soviet bloc countries.

In the case of the two individual categories, the estimated bilateral effects are smaller than for a general restriction, because our imports of commodities in these two categories were distributed mainly to countries that have smaller than average feedbacks to the United States (Japan, Italy, Taiwan, Hong Kong, Mexico, and Spain).

AGRICULTURAL EXPORTS. We have also obtained crude estimates of the reduction in U.S. agricultural sales to the developed countries based on statistical estimates of the share of the total reflection ratios that would apply to agricultural commodities (Standard International Trade Classification [SITC] categories 0, 1, 2, 4).

These estimates were derived from the import equations estimated for four separate commodity groupings by Grant Taplin of IMF. SITC category 2 includes certain nonagricultural products (fertilizers and minerals, metal ores, and scrap) which accounted for 29 percent of U.S. imports in this category in 1969.

Unfortunately, comparable estimates were not available for other countries. The results indicate that agricultural exports to the developed countries would decline only $10 million with a general import restriction, compared with a reduction of total U.S. exports to those countries of $84 million. The impacts are substantially larger for restrictions on the two individual categories—$21 million for radios and television receivers and $16 million for nonrubber footwear—even though the decline in total U.S. exports to developed countries was less than for a general restriction. The reason is quite clear. Japan, Italy, and Spain have the three largest reflection ratios for agricultural imports relative to total imports of all the developed countries. And they are the principal developed countries that would be initially affected by restrictions on radios, television receivers, and nonrubber footwear.

TOTAL EFFECTS. Estimates of the total effects were obtained by combining all noncommunist countries into fourteen trading groups which are listed in Table 7.3. Because they include all the rounds of spending and respending, the total effects could be spread out over an extended period of time. The bilateral effects, in contrast, involve only the lags between a reduction of a country's exports, the resultant contraction

TABLE 7.3.   Estimates of the Impact on Exports and Imports Resulting from a $1 Billion Reduction of U.S. Imports

Country Group	General Restriction		Selective Restriction*	
	Imports	Exports	Imports	Exports
	($ mil)			
United States	1,032	229	1,026	187
Canada	97	305	65	205
Latin America	171	171	80	80
EEC	148	387	159	416
United Kingdom	47	120	51	128
Other EFTA	40	94	43	102
Other Western Europe	26	41	29	46
South Africa	3	11	3	12
Other Africa	49	49	34	34
Japan	37	216	54	317
Middle East	44	44	47	47
Other Asia	134	134	204	204
Australia and New Zealand	12	39	8	25
Rest of World	39	39	24	24
Total	1,879	1,879	1,827	1,827

* SITC 6 and 8.

of its domestic economy, and the full effect of this internal contraction on imports. These are probably short enough that most of the impact would be experienced in the first year or two.

The estimated total impacts of two hypothetical import restrictions are given in Table 7.3. A $1 billion general restriction on imports would reduce U.S. exports by $229 million. Calculated on the same basis, in a fourteen-region trading framework rather than by individual countries as in Table 7.3, the bilateral effects were $161 million. Thus the full repercussions on income and imports in all trading groups enlarges the impact on U.S. exports by over 40 percent. The regions suffering the largest reductions in exports as a result of a general restriction would be the European Economic Community (EEC), Canada, Japan, and Latin America.

Table 7.3 also reports the impact of a $1 billion selective restriction on imports in SITC categories 6 and 8 ("manufactured goods classified chiefly by material" and "miscellaneous manufactured articles"), which include products more likely to be restricted. It is estimated that U.S. exports would fall by $187 million as a result of such a restriction. The impact is smaller than in the case of a general restriction because Latin America and Canada, which have the largest feedback on U.S. exports, would not be as adversely affected initially, while Japan and "Other Asia," with lower feedbacks, would experience larger initial reductions in their exports.

The estimates above take into account only the economic repercussions of a fall in U.S. imports. But other countries could be expected to respond in kind if the United States were to impose new import restrictions, and any retaliatory measures adopted by our trading partners would probably discriminate either overtly or covertly against U.S. exports. It seems reasonable that countries would retaliate against those U.S. products for which alternative foreign or domestic sources of supply were available. Certain agricultural products fall in this category. In most years stocks of grain, or at least of wheat, are sufficiently large so that importing countries could readily turn to alternative suppliers. While it would be highly speculative to try to identify U.S. exports most likely to suffer from retaliation, this is a subject that deserves further study.

THE MULTIPLIER ASSUMPTIONS. What the above procedures estimate are the Keynesian income multiplier effects with foreign repercussions. The validity of the estimates depends on the multiplier assumptions that: (1) prices do not respond or, if they do, they do not affect trade flows; (2) monetary policy is managed in such a way the export reductions do not affect economic activity through money markets; and (3) countries do not use fiscal policies to offset the impact of reduced exports.

For an increase in export demand the constant-price assumption will be valid only when there is sufficient domestic excess capacity (unemployed resources) to absorb the expansion without increasing prices. Certainly not all countries could be expected to fulfill this requirement at any given time. However, our estimates apply to a *decrease* in export demand that would contract domestic economies. Since prices are often relatively inflexible downward, estimating only the effects operating through the income mechanism with prices constant is probably more realistic than as if the impact of increased exports were under consideration.

Reductions of exports can nevertheless be expected to put downward pressures on prices (possibly by slowing the rate of inflation), and therefore to affect imports through the price mechanism also. Although the methodology to take account of the joint price-income effects has not been developed, the price mechanism should not be ignored. Indeed in an economy experiencing excess aggregate demand, there would be no loss of real output (income) and therefore no real income effects at work. Only the price mechanism would operate to reduce imports, and whether this would exceed or fall short of the pure income effect estimated here is uncertain.

A second assumption of multiplier analysis is a constant rate of interest. This implies that the country finds itself in the Keynesian *liquidity trap,* or that the monetary authorities use the instruments at their disposal to maintain constant interest rates—for example, the rate of interest is regarded as a target of economic policy determined on the basis of the desired rate of economic growth. However, the use of monetary instruments to prevent changes in interest rates is only one of several possible policy responses to a fall in exports.

For example, if monetary authorities neutralize the effect of the decline in exports on the domestic money supply, the reduction in autonomous expenditures represented by the fall in exports would ordinarily lead to a decline in interest rates as a result of the lower transactions demand for cash balances. The decline in interest rates would in turn partially offset the deflationary impact on economic activity of the fall in exports. Consequently, the fall in imports would be less than if interest rates were maintained at constant levels: the reflection ratios would then be less than assumed in our analysis.

Suppose on the other hand that the authorities allow the money supply to fall in proportion to the loss in reserves brought about by the change in the trade balance. Interest rates rise, and income falls, until external balance is restored—the decline in the *rate* of imports just equals the downward shift in the level of exports. In this event, the new equilibrium level of income and imports would be lower than indicated by the traditional income multiplier approach.

Since we have subtracted from capital movements, balance of payments equilibrium requires equal levels of exports and imports. If there were interest-sensitive capital flows, a somewhat smaller decline in income and imports would be necessary to halt the decline in reserves and restore external balance. However, as long as capital flows are less than perfectly interest elastic, the equilibrium levels in income and imports would still be lower than if the authorities maintained a constant rate of interest.

Finally, our estimates would be reduced by dropping the assumption that a decline in a country's exports would not affect fiscal policy. For instance, if a country's exports decrease by $1 million as a result of a U.S. import restriction, and if as a consequence government expenditures are increased by the same amount, autonomous spending remains unchanged and no feedback on the country's imports, from the United States or elsewhere, takes place. The country's trade balance has deteriorated, of course, and this might eventually make it necessary for the authorities to tolerate some decline in domestic income or take other action to restore balance of payments equilibrium.

OTHER QUALIFICATIONS. The results given in Tables 7.2 and 7.3 correspond to trade flows in constant (1968) prices. They would apply to present or future conditions only if changes in the appropriate price indexes (unit export indexes for exports and import price indexes for imports) have moved together. Although current indexes are not available, it is unlikely that they would cause the estimates to deviate noticeably from those reported.

In appraising the results, several qualifications should be kept in mind. First, when restrictions are applied to individual import categories, the intended restrictive effect may be eroded by diversion of purchases to substitute import categories. An intended restriction of $1 billion may net out to a substantially smaller actual restriction. Experience with dairy import quotas illustrates how difficult it is to selectively restrict imports. As long as there are unrestricted substitute imports, the economic pressures can be expected to shift and raise imports elsewhere.

A second qualification pertains to our assumption that the actual market shares approximate the distribution of each country's marginal import response to a decrease in autonomous expenditures. To determine the importance of this assumption, market shares in the developed countries were adjusted on the basis of available statistical estimates of bilateral income elasticities of demand for imports, and the total effects of a $1 billion restriction on U.S. imports recalculated. The impact on U.S. exports was found to be only about $10 million less than reported above.

Finally, our estimates are somewhat understated in that they do not take into account the effects of reduced trade flows on the demand for freight and insurance services. A decline in output of services could be expected to have additional multiplier effects on income and imports in the developed countries.

SUMMARY. If the United States were to impose new restrictions on imports, the estimated impact on U.S. exports would range from 19 to 23 percent, depending on whether the restriction applied to all imports or, more probably, only to selected categories. These estimates include repercussions operating through changes in incomes in all countries affected directly or indirectly by the restriction. The impact on U.S. agricultural exports would be relatively small because imports of these products appear to be quite insensitive to changes in income for most countries.

Our estimates do not allow for any retaliation by other countries, either in the form of general import restrictions or measures directed specifically against U.S. exports. The repercussions would obviously be much larger in the event of retaliation, and could reduce U.S. exports by the full amount of the initial restriction, or more. It is probable that any retaliation would in some part be directed against U.S. agricultural exports.

NOTES

1. "Economic Factors Affecting the Use of Items 807.00 and 806.30 of the Tariff Schedules of the United States," U.S. Tariff Commission Publication 339, September 1970, p. 33.
2. Based on research by Gerald M. Lage, cited in Robert E. Baldwin, *Nontariff Distortions of International Trade* (Washington, D.C.: Brookings Institute, 1971), p. 43.
3. Michael K. Evans, *Macroeconomic Activity* (New York: Harper and Row, 1969), pp. 569, 583.
4. Stephen P. Magee, A Theoretical and Empirical Examination of Supply and Demand Relationships in U.S. International Trade Unpublished manuscript, Council of Economic Advisors, November 1970.
5. Walter S. Salant and Beatrice N. Vaccara, *Import Liberalization and Employment* (Washington, D.C.: Brookings Institute, 1961); W. Whitney Hicks, "Estimating the Foreign Exchange Costs of United Aid," *Southern Economic Journal*, 30(October 1963):168–74.

[8]

U.S. Agricultural Trade
and Balance of Payments

Raymond P. Christensen AND *O. Halbert Goolsby*

$\mathbf{A}$GRICULTURE has a long history of making important contributions to our international balance of payments. From the time of
the first shipment of agricultural products—2,500 pounds of tobacco
from Jamestown, Virginia, to England in 1616—until 1916, three hundred years later, agricultural products accounted for the bulk of our exports. As late as 1900, agricultural products accounted for two-thirds
of total merchandise exports. Not until after 1910 did the ratio of agricultural exports to total merchandise exports decline to less than 50
percent. These exports paid for most of our imports, including many
industrial goods necessary for our industrial development.

During most years prior to 1900, however, our foreign exchange
earnings were not large enough to pay for all our imports of goods and
services. Foreign investments in the United States supplied much of
the foreign currency needed to finance imports not paid for by exports.
We were a net debtor nation until World War I, when export earnings
rose greatly with rising prices. Agricultural exports paid for most of
the interest and other charges on our foreign debts until about 1910.
Large agricultural exports during and immediately following World
War I helped make us a net creditor nation, a position we have maintained most years since then.

Our agricultural exports dropped drastically in the 1920s and 1930s
as European countries put increased emphasis on self-sufficiency in agriculture. Also, we increased our tariffs and other barriers on imports,
making it difficult for foreign countries to earn dollars to finance imports from us. Not until the onset of World War II did our agricul-

RAYMOND P. CHRISTENSEN and O. HALBERT GOOLSBY are members of the Foreign Development and Trade Division, Economic Research Service, United States Department of
Agriculture.

tural exports again rise significantly. They declined in the early 1950s but moved upward quite steadily during the 1960s.

THE FIRST 150 YEARS AFTER INDEPENDENCE. Merchandise imports exceeded merchandise exports during the one hundred years from 1776 to 1875. Data are not available to show very precisely what share of the nation's output was exported or what share of consumption was imported before the Civil War. However, in the decade following the Civil War, the value of merchandise imports was equivalent to about 7 percent of the gross national product (GNP) and merchandise exports were equal to about 5.5 percent of the GNP. The corresponding ratio for net imports of merchandise was much less, about 1.5 percent. If it is assumed that services accounted for half of the GNP, imports amounted to 15 percent of the total value of products and net imports

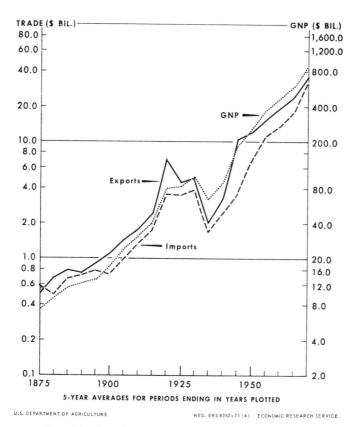

FIG. 8.1. Total merchandise trade and gross national product of the United States.

to 3 percent. Imports were large compared with domestic capital formation, perhaps equivalent to a third during 1866–75 and an even larger
share in earlier years.

Total merchandise exports and imports rose rapidly from 1875
until the early 1920s, as did the gross national product (Fig. 8.1). Exports were equivalent to 9 percent of the gross national product in
1916–20. Foreign markets took a large share of our products, perhaps
close to 20 percent in 1916–20.

We had a large favorable trade balance in agricultural products
during our early development. From 1870 to 1900, farm exports—mainly
tobacco, cotton, and wheat—averaged twice as large as agricultural imports (Fig. 8.2).

We had large net imports of industrial products during the 1700s
and 1800s, but not until after 1900 did we have a favorable trade balance on nonagricultural products (Fig. 8.3). Our favorable balance

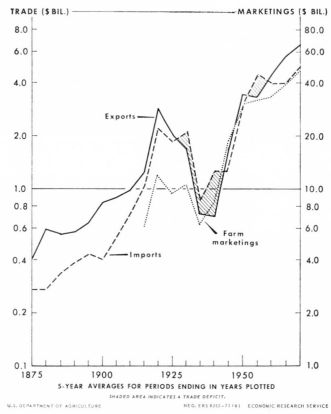

Fig. 8.2.   U.S. agricultural trade and farm marketings.

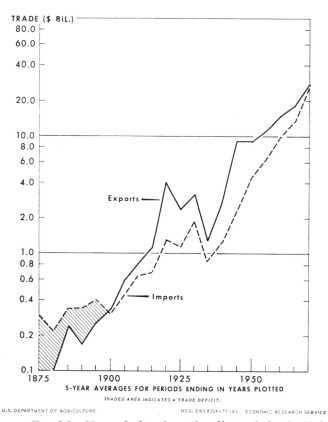

FIG. 8.3.   Nonagricultural merchandise trade by the United States.

on total trade until about 1900 was due to our favorable agricultural trade balance. We do not have good estimates of what share of our agricultural production was exported in early years, but during 1916–20, farm exports amounted to 21 percent of cash receipts from farm marketings.

Agricultural exports helped make possible imports of capital goods required during the 1700s and 1800s. For example, much of the iron used in the early construction of our railroads had to be imported. Agricultural products accounted for 80 percent or more of total exports in the 1870s (Fig. 8.4). The ratio was over 70 percent in the 1880s and 1890s and did not decline to less than 40 percent until after 1925.

Foreign countries made long-term capital investments in the United States during these early years. The cumulative net value of these investments reached $1.7 billion in 1875. This does not sound like much today, but it was equivalent to 20 percent of our gross national product

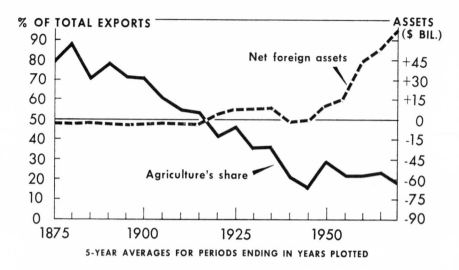

FIG. 8.4. Agriculture's share of U.S. merchandise exports and U.S. net foreign asset position.

and to 70 percent of gross farm output in 1875. Payments to service our external debts reached about $188 million in 1875, an amount equivalent to 1.3 percent of our gross national product.

Foreign exchange earnings from transportation and other services also helped finance imports of goods and services (Fig. 8.5). This category accounted for less than 20 percent of our foreign exchange earnings in most years. Fifty percent or more of our foreign exchange earnings were from agricultural exports before 1900.

The distribution of our foreign exchange spending did not change significantly until after 1925 (Fig. 8.6). From 1875 until 1925, agricultural imports accounted for about 40 percent, nonagricultural imports for about 35 percent, and transportation and other services for about 25 percent of our foreign exchange disbursements.

Our foreign exchange spending for transportation and other services has been larger than our foreign exchange earnings from this source throughout most of our history.

Although we had a favorable trade balance for nonagricultural products beginning in the early 1900s, it did not become larger than our trade balance for agricultural products until World War I. In 1916–20, we had a favorable merchandise trade balance of $3.3 billion a year—$2.7 billion for nonagricultural products and $600 million for agricultural products. Rising prices and a rapidly expanding export market for food and other products caused our exports and foreign exchange earnings to rise rapidly.

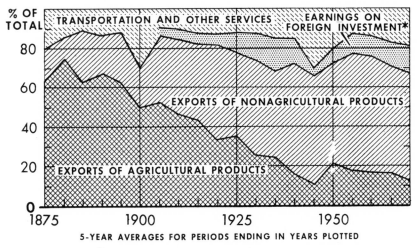

U.S. DEPARTMENT OF AGRICULTURE   NEG. ERS 8356-71 (6)   ECONOMIC RESEARCH SERVICE

FIG. 8.5. Foreign exchange earnings by the United States.

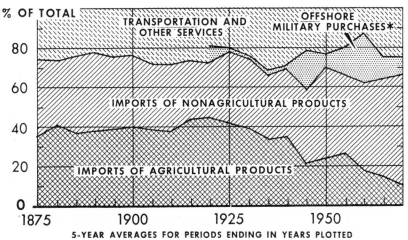

U.S. DEPARTMENT OF AGRICULTURE   NEG. ERS 8357-71 (6)   ECONOMIC RESEARCH SERVICE

FIG. 8.6. Foreign exchange disbursements by the United States.

We paid off foreign debts and made investments abroad at a rapid rate during the early 1900s. In 1914, U.S. investments abroad were $3.5 billion while foreign investments here were $7.0 billion. By 1919, the situation was exactly the opposite. U.S. investments abroad amounted to $7.0 billion while foreign investments here were only $3.5 billion. Our balance of trade for agricultural products was large during 1910–14 and continued to be important during the war years. But a favorable trade balance for nonagricultural products was mainly responsible for our shift from a net debtor to a net creditor position. About the same time we became a net creditor nation, agriculture's share of total exports declined to less than 50 percent (Fig. 8.4).

It is important to recognize that European countries financed much of their large merchandise trade deficits by liquidating their foreign investments, including many in the United States. Also, some foreign countries financed their trade deficits with the help of large loans from us during World War I and early postwar years. Many of us are old enough to remember the publicity given to the failure of foreign countries to repay these loans in the late 1920s and 1930s.

EXPORT-IMPORT BALANCES DURING 1925–70. Our foreign trade dropped drastically during the late 1920s and early 1930s (Fig. 8.1). Total merchandise exports fell from $5.3 billion in 1928 to $1.4 billion in 1932 (fiscal years). Our merchandise imports fell from $4.1 billion in 1928 to $1.3 billion in 1932 (calendar years).

We were not well prepared for playing our new role as a large creditor nation after World War I. If foreign countries were to repay the loans we made them, they would have needed a favorable merchandise trade balance with us. However, we put into effect higher tariffs on imports during the 1920s and 1930s in the effort to maintain a favorable merchandise trade balance.

We had an unfavorable trade balance on agricultural products from 1925 to 1940. Agricultural exports declined to only $350 million in fiscal 1940, the lowest amount since 1871. Our protectionistic trade policies did not expand farm exports or improve farm incomes.

We continued to have a favorable trade balance on nonagricultural products during the 1925–40 period. We also had a small positive trade balance on all merchandise. The dollars with which foreign countries purchased our merchandise came from increases in our investments and loans abroad and our dollar spending for transportation, tourism, and other so-called invisible items. In addition, U.S. purchases of gold in the 1930s supplied foreign countries with dollars.[1]

Agricultural exports increased greatly after 1940 with the onset of World War II. They continued high until 1949. Most of this growth was financed by U.S. government programs. In 1950 Lawrence Witt pointed out that, of our total agricultural exports of $20 billion during fiscal years 1941 through 1949, nearly $11 billion was financed by government programs—Lend-Lease, United Nations Relief and Rehabilitation, Army Civilian Supply Programs, European Cooperation Administration, and others.[2] The remaining $9 billion was financed by dollars foreign countries received from our imports, sales of assets they held in the United States, sales of gold to the United States, and invisible items. Without the financing provided by government programs, our exports of both agricultural and industrial products would have been much smaller.

Our net foreign assets moved from a positive amount in 1935 to a negative amount in 1940 and continued to be negative until after World War II (Fig. 8.4). With the uncertainty associated with war, there was a flight of capital out of Europe to the United States. This of course reduced the amounts of dollars foreign countries had available to pay for imports. But U.S. capital moved abroad rapidly after 1945, and net foreign assets increased greatly in the 1950s and 1960s.

Our agricultural exports declined in the early 1950s but increased after passage of PL 480, the Agricultural Trade Development and Assistance Act of 1954. We had an unfavorable trade balance for agricultural products in the early 1950s as agricultural imports increased (Fig. 8.2). Imports of complementary products (coffee, cocoa, rubber, etc.) doubled from $1.4 billion in 1949 to $2.8 billion in 1951. High prices for coffee and other tropical products contributed to the rise in total value of agricultural imports.

Exports of nonagricultural products rose greatly during the early 1940s and have continued to rise since then (Fig. 8.3). Our merchandise trade balance on nonagricultural products averaged over $6 billion annually in the 1941–45 period. It remained high until about 1965 and then decreased to $1.3 billion annually in the last five years.

We have had a favorable overall merchandise trade balance each year since 1940 (Fig. 8.1). It averaged over $5 billion annually from 1945 to 1960, increased to $6.2 billion annually during 1960–65, and then declined to $2.9 billion during 1965–70. These large favorable merchandise trade balances were financed in many different ways.

We supplied our allies with large amounts of food and other materials during and after World War II for reconstruction. Most of these materials were supplied as grants—not loans, as was the case during and after World War I. We did not repeat the mistake of making large loans that could not be repaid.

Large exports of farm products were financed under the Food for Peace Programs authorized by PL 480 beginning in 1954. Shipments under this program reached a record high of $1.6 billion in 1964.

Loans and grants under foreign economic aid programs helped finance our exports during the 1950s and 1960s. Military aid programs financed large exports during the Korean War and more recently during the Vietnam War.

United States investments abroad also have helped finance exports.

They reached a record high of $140 billion in 1969, nearly three times the amount foreigners had invested in the United States. In addition, dollars spent abroad for tourism and other purposes helped finance our favorable merchandise trade balance.

We built up our gold stocks to a record high of nearly $25 billion in 1949, but they declined to $11 billion in 1970. Shipments of gold to the United States before 1949 helped finance our exports, but since 1949 we have, in effect, used gold to pay for imports and our net investments abroad. Our balance on goods and services dropped drastically after 1949. This balance averaged about $7 billion a year during the 1940s compared with only $2 to $3 billion during the 1950s.

Several factors caused this decline. First, the United Kingdom and thirty-seven other nations (or colonies) devalued their currency, thus making U.S. exports less competitive and foreign goods more attractive to U.S. consumers. Second, Europe's productive capacity had largely been rebuilt and the world had shifted from a seller's market to a buyer's market. Foreign aid from the United States was still large but more of it was directed to the less developed nations. Aid in those days was untied, that is, there was no requirement that the products purchased with the dollars had to be products of the United States. Consequently, dollars supplied by the United States could be spent in Europe as well as here. Because economic recovery had been achieved in most European countries by the mid-1950s, additional U.S. aid did not always lead to additional U.S. exports as it had done earlier. However, some aid funds were spent here, and some spent in Europe were subsequently used to purchase U.S. goods.

Not all dollars that flowed abroad were used to purchase U.S. goods. Some were used to increase commercial bank balances and the reserves of developed nations. Gold had been the primary form of reserves until 1949 when gold was about three-fourths of the total for all free-world countries. It declined to 64 percent in 1962 and only 45 percent in 1970. Gold became a smaller share of international liquidity, and dollars a larger share. The increased dollar holdings were welcomed in the early 1950s. Later, the increase was merely accepted, but as time passed, foreign monetary officials became concerned over the increase. This concern was expressed by purchases of gold.

A major problem since the late 1950s in most developed nations abroad is that they have had more dollars than they need for international monetary purposes. Most of these nations have had the foreign exchange needed to finance the purchase of our goods. Our exports are determined more by economic growth rates and trade policies abroad than by the sizes of reserves.

AGRICULTURE'S CONTRIBUTION TO THE BALANCE OF PAYMENTS, 1960–70. Now let us consider in more detail how our agricultural trade has influenced our international balance of payments during the last decade. We need to consider agriculture's gross contribution as well as its net contribution. Also, we need to consider commercial exports and the contribution made by noncommercial exports (those financed by the U.S. government with international grants or credits), both nonagricultural and agricultural.

The United States had a favorable total balance of trade on all products each year from 1960 through 1970. The surplus for these years reached a record high of $6.8 billion in 1960, then declined to a little over $600 million in 1968 and 1969, and increased again to $2.2 billion in 1970 (Fig. 8.7). However, if we subtract noncommercial exports, nonagricultural and agricultural, the commercial merchandise trade balance shows a deficit of $2.7 billion in 1968 and $2.5 billion in 1969 (Fig. 8.8). The total commercial trade balance improved in 1970 but it still showed a deficit of $841 million.[3]

Outstanding progress has been made in enlarging commercial agricultural exports. They increased from $3.5 billion in 1960 to $6.1 billion in 1970. Noncommercial exports of farm products decreased from the record high of $1.6 billion in 1964 to $1.1 in 1970. Total agricultural exports reached a new record high of $7.2 billion in 1970, 50 percent more than in 1960. Agricultural imports also increased but we

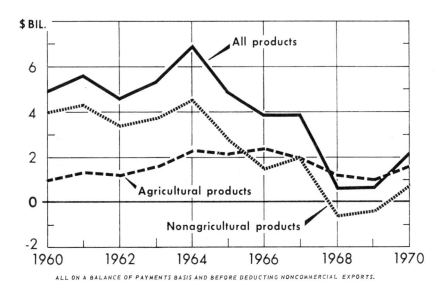

ALL ON A BALANCE OF PAYMENTS BASIS AND BEFORE DEDUCTING NONCOMMERCIAL EXPORTS.

U.S. DEPARTMENT OF AGRICULTURE   NEG. ERS 8358-71 (6)   ECONOMIC RESEARCH SERVICE

FIG. 8.7.   U.S. balance of trade, all on a balance of payments basis and before deducting noncommercial exports.

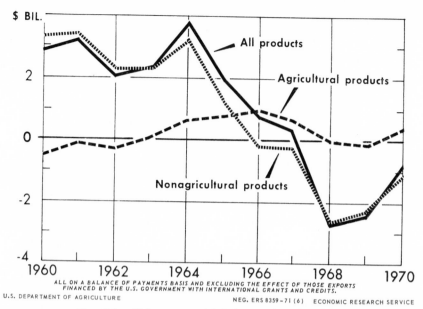

ALL ON A BALANCE OF PAYMENTS BASIS AND EXCLUDING THE EFFECT OF THOSE EXPORTS
FINANCED BY THE U.S. GOVERNMENT WITH INTERNATIONAL GRANTS AND CREDITS.

U.S. DEPARTMENT OF AGRICULTURE   NEG. ERS 8359-71 (6)   ECONOMIC RESEARCH SERVICE

FIG. 8.8.   U.S. commercial balance of trade, all on a balance of
payments basis and excluding the effect of those exports financed
by the U.S. government with international grants and credits.

had a favorable agricultural trade balance each year during the 1960s.
However, if government programs (noncommercial) exports are excluded, the commercial trade balance for agricultural products showed
a deficit in some years. We had a favorable commercial agricultural
trade balance of $386 million in 1970 compared with a negative bal-
ance of $436 million in 1960.

Our trade in nonagricultural products more than doubled during
the 1960s. Exports of these products increased from $15 billion in 1960
to $35 billion in 1970 and imports increased from $11 billion to $34
billion. We had a positive trade balance for nonagricultural products
close to $4 billion in the early 1960s, but it declined after 1964, be-
coming negative in 1968 and 1969, and positive again in 1970. The
trade balance for nonagricultural products looks quite different when
noncommercial exports are subtracted. (Although noncommercial exports are financed by the U.S. government with international grants
and credits, they involve no direct dollar outflow from the United
States. Exports under certain government programs do not involve
international grants and credits and are, from a balance of payments
viewpoint, considered commercial.) Noncommercial exports of industrial or nonagricultural products increased from $669 million in 1960
to around $2 billion annually in the last four years. The trade balance
for nonagricultural products, excluding the noncommercial, declined

from a positive $3.3 billion in 1960 to a negative $2.7 billion in 1968. It was a negative $1.2 billion in 1970.

To observe agriculture's contribution to our balance of international payments we need to consider the dollars saved and dollars received from government program exports. Our food aid programs are far from giveaways in many countries. Some of the foreign currencies received from the sale of farm products under PL 480 and other programs have been used to pay some of the costs of U.S. agencies abroad and thus have reduced the dollar outflow. Also, we have received interest and principal repayment in dollars for credit sales.

Furthermore, some loans of local currencies (which the U.S. government had received as payment for commodities) have been repaid in dollars. The total contribution to the balance of payments from these noncommercial exports increased from $171 million in 1960 to $376 million in 1970. The dollars saved and dollars received in 1970 (from government program exports made mostly in previous years) were equivalent to about a third of the total program exports of agricultural products in 1970.

The financial terms under which we export farm products have hardened since the beginning of food aid programs. Export sales for foreign currencies have decreased and dollar credit sales have increased. As a result of a lag from the time dollar credit sales are made until repayments are made, we will receive in the future dollars from program sales made in the past.

Agriculture's gross contribution to the balance of payments—commercial agricultural exports plus the contribution by noncommercial exports—increased from $3.6 billion in 1960 to a record high of $6.4 billion in 1970 (Fig. 8.9).

It is sometimes considered worthwhile to compute agriculture's net contribution to our international balance of payments by subtracting agricultural imports from the gross contribution. Agriculture's net contribution increased from a negative $265 million in 1960 to a high of $1.2 billion in 1966. It was $762 million in 1970 (Fig. 8.10).

Total agricultural exports may reach a record high of $7.7 billion in fiscal 1971. All the increase will be in commercial sales. Agriculture's gross contribution to the balance of payments probably will be another record high, around $7 billion, in 1971. Its net contribution may be about $1.4 billion.

INTERNATIONAL BALANCE OF PAYMENTS. Now we are ready to look at our international balance of payments. We want to consider two questions: How has agricultural trade influenced our balance-of-payments position? How do other international transactions that cause changes in our balance of payments affect agricultural trade? The first question is quite easy to answer. The second is more difficult.

The favorable agricultural trade balance during the 150 years

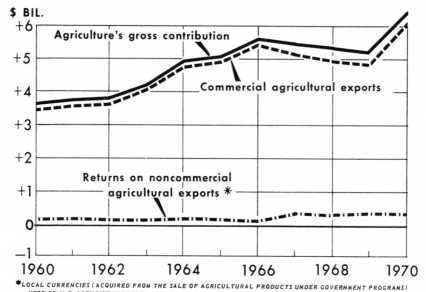

FIG. 8.9. Agriculture's gross contribution to the U.S. balance of payments.

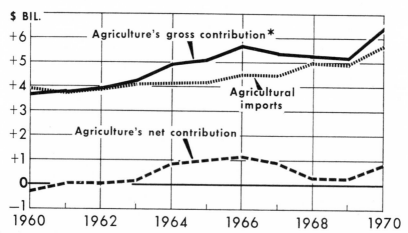

FIG. 8.10. U.S. agriculture's net contribution to the balance of payments.

from 1776 to 1925 helped improve our overall balance-of-payments position. The negative agricultural balance of trade from 1925 to 1940 and in the early 1950s caused our balance of payments position to be less favorable than it otherwise would have been. As explained above, the positive commercial agricultural trade balance in the 1960s caused our balance-of-payments position to be more favorable than it otherwise would have been.

We have had a positive total trade balance on goods and services for many years. It reached a record high of $11.6 billion in 1947 and averaged over $6 billion annually during the 1946–50 period. (See Table 8.1.) It declined to $2.0 annually during 1951–55, then increased to $3.4 billion annually during 1956–60 and to $6.5 billion in 1961–65. It declined again to about $2.9 billion in 1966–70.

But we need to remember that a part of our exports has been financed by government programs. If we subtract U.S. government grants and net capital transactions abroad which financed exports from exports of goods and services, the favorable balance on goods and services would be much less. In fact, it would be negative in 1968 and 1969 and also for several years in the 1950s.

We have had a negative balance on commercial trade of nonagricultural products in the last five years. Income from private investments abroad increased from $3.0 billion in 1960 to $8.7 billion in 1970. Income from transportation and other services increased from $4.2 billion to $9.9 billion. But we also have been spending more abroad. Military expenditures, for example, have averaged nearly $5 billion annually in recent years. Payments for transportation, tourism, and other services increased from $5.5 billion in 1960 to $14.6 billion in 1970.

Much thought has been given to how our balance-of-payments position can best be measured. The Economic Report of the President transmitted to Congress in February 1971 discusses four different measures and presents data for two, which we show in Table 8.1. The balance of payments on a liquidity basis has been negative for most years since 1950. The liquidity balance is measured by the change in dollar holdings by all foreigners, plus changes in our holdings of gold and foreign exchange. We did not have a deficit on this basis in 1968 when net capital investments of foreigners in the United States were $8.7 billion, much more than in earlier years or in 1969 or 1970.

In most other years, U.S. private capital investments abroad exceeded foreign capital investments. United States investments abroad increased to over $140 billion, nearly three times the $49 billion foreigners had invested here. This is one reason for the negative balance of payments reported on a liquidity basis for most years since 1950. Over the years, however, income from investments has more than offset the outward flow of capital. However, in this analysis income from our

TABLE 8.1. U.S. Balance of Payments, Five-Year Averages, 1946–70, and Annual, 1968–70

Items	Five-Year Averages					Annual		
	1946–50	1951–55	1956–60	1961–65	1966–70	1968	1969	1970
	($ bil)							
1. Exports	Goods and services							
Merchandise, total	12.7	13.5	17.9	23.0	34.4	33.6	36.5	42.0
Agricultural	(3.4)	(3.3)	(4.3)	(5.6)	(6.5)	(6.2)	(6.0)	(7.2)
Nonagricultural	(9.3)	(10.2)	(13.6)	(17.4)	(27.9)	(27.4)	(30.5)	(34.9)
Military sales	. . .	. . .	0.3	0.7	1.3	1.4	1.5	1.5
Income on investments, pvt.	1.2	1.8	2.7	4.4	7.1	6.9	7.9	8.7
Income on investments, govt.	0.1	0.2	0.3	0.5	0.8	0.8	0.9	0.9
Other services	2.3	2.7	3.8	5.2	8.1	8.7	8.7	9.9
Total	16.3	18.2	25.0	33.8	51.7	50.6	55.5	63.0
2. Imports								
Merchandise, total	−6.9	−11.0	−13.8	−17.6	−32.9	−33.0	−35.8	−39.9
Agricultural	(−3.0)	(−4.4)	(−3.9)	(−3.9)	(−4.9)	(−5.0)	(−5.0)	(−5.7)
Nonagricultural	(−3.9)	(−6.6)	(−9.9)	(−13.7)	(−28.0)	(−28.0)	(−30.8)	(−34.2)
Military expenditures	−0.6	−2.3	−3.2	−3.0	−4.5	−4.5	−4.9	−4.8
Other services	−1.9	−2.9	−4.6	−6.7	−11.4	−10.6	−12.9	−14.6
Total	−9.4	−16.2	−21.6	−27.3	−48.8	−48.1	−53.6	−59.3
3. Balance (1 minus 2)	6.9	2.0	3.4	6.5	2.9	2.5	1.9	3.7
	Other items							
Remittances and pensions	−0.6	−0.6	−0.7	−0.8	−1.2	−1.1	−1.2	−1.4
U.S. govt. grants and capital, net	−5.1	−2.3	−2.5	−3.3	−3.7	−4.0	−3.8	−3.2
U.S. private capital, net	−0.8	−1.1	−3.1	−4.5	−5.4	−5.4	−5.3	−6.2
Direct investment	(−0.6)	(−0.7)	(−1.7)	(−2.2)	(−3.6)	(−3.2)	(−3.1)	(−4.0)
Other long-term	(−0.1)	(−0.2)	(−0.9)	(−1.4)	(−1.1)	(−1.1)	(−1.6)	(−1.3)
Short-term	(−0.1)	(−0.2)	(−0.5)	(−0.9)	(−0.7)	(−1.1)	(−0.6)	(−0.9)
Foreign capital, net	0.2	0.3	0.5	0.7	4.5	8.7	4.1	3.9
Errors and unrecorded	0.5	0.3	0.2	−0.9	−1.4	−0.5	−2.8	−1.3
4. Total of other items	−6.2	−3.4	−5.6	−8.8	−7.2	−2.3	−9.0	−8.4
	Balance of Payments							
Liquidity basis (3 minus 4)	0.5	−1.2	−2.3	−2.3	−3.2	+0.2	−7.0	−4.7
Official transaction basis	. . .	. . .	. . .	−1.8	−1.5	1.6	2.7	−10.7

SOURCE: Economic Report of the President Transmitted to Congress, February 1971, pp. 298–99.

investments abroad is included in the balance on goods and services which, as stated above, was small and even negative after noncommercial exports were excluded.

When American firms make investments abroad, they put dollars in the hands of foreigners. A large proportion of these investments are in developed countries such as Canada, West Germany, and Japan—nations that today have ample dollars and other forms of international liquidity. The increased holdings of dollars by these and some other nations do not lead to a significant increase in imports from the United States, at least in the short run.

It should be noted too that these dollars can be spent almost anywhere in the world. They may float from country to country for years before being used to purchase goods from us. They can also be used to claim U.S. gold, and this of course has caused the United States some concern over the years. In the long run, a nation that keeps accumulating dollars probably will revalue its currency upward, which will tend to increase imports from the United States.

On the other hand, dollars placed in the hands of less developed nations through the investment procedure are likely to lead immediately to greater U.S. exports. However, when American investors receive dividends from foreign investments, foreigners need dollars to make these payments. They must reduce their imports from us or increase their exports to us in order to have dollars to make interest, dividend, and principal payments to us. Therefore, a secondary effect of our foreign investments in less developed nations may be to reduce the export demand for our products.

During the years when there was a dollar shortage abroad (there was no dollar shortage in the United States and foreigners could, and did, borrow heavily in the New York financial market), it was often stated that the United States could make large loans and grants overseas since we had a strong balance on merchandise trade.

The situation may now be somewhat reversed. The income we received from private investments abroad in 1970 totaled nearly $9 billion, an amount much larger than the total value of our agricultural exports. If we are to receive returns from our large net investments abroad, at some time in the future a negative overall commodity trade balance will probably become necessary. It does not seem likely that foreigners will be able to pay us returns on our large net foreign investments by selling us only tourism, transportation, and other services.

In a timely and farsighted paper on foreign trade and agricultural policy delivered in 1956, Lauren Soth said, "The United States needs more imports. The rest of the world needs more American dollars."[4] He went on to say, "Increased imports are important to the United States to permit balancing our export trade at a higher level and permit returns on our foreign investments." We did greatly step up our merchandise imports in the late 1950s and the 1960s but not for the reasons Lauren Soth said we should. We are importing more from the low-income countries but most of the growth in our imports is in products from Japan and European countries. The developing nations still do not have enough dollars or other foreign currencies to finance the imports they need for economic development. On the other hand, Japan, West Germany, Canada, and several other countries have surplus American dollars, sometimes causing unstable conditions in international money markets.

THE CURRENT ABUNDANCE OF DOLLARS ABROAD. In 1970 we had a balance-of-payments deficit of nearly $11 billion when measured on an official transactions basis (the change in the number of dollars held by foreign central banks or other official monetary organizations plus the change in U.S. holdings of gold and foreign exchange). This deficit mainly reflects a flow of dollars to foreign money markets where short-term interest rates are higher than in the United States. The export demand for our products does not suddenly increase as the result of this kind of increase in dollar holdings abroad.

Recent developments relating to the surplus of dollars in many developed nations abroad can be described briefly.

During 1969, credit conditions in the United States were tight. The interest U.S. banks could charge on loans was high but the interest they could offer to depositors was fixed at a relatively low level by federal reserve regulations. United States banks consequently borrowed dollar deposits from their European branches. These branches hold a large number of accounts denominated in dollars even though they are located in London, Frankfurt, and elsewhere. These accounts are the so-called *Eurodollars*.

In 1970, monetary conditions in the United States eased and U.S. banks repaid their foreign branches. The branches were encouraged to use some of the funds to increase loans to foreign borrowers. Foreign business enterprises faced with relatively tight credit conditions in their own countries, especially in Germany, sharply increased borrowing in the Eurodollar market. As German businessmen converted these dollars into marks, they placed dollars back into the banking systems. German banks consequently found themselves with many dollars which they shifted to their central banks.

As central banks gained dollars, it appeared more and more that the mark was undervalued relative to the dollar. With reserves growing rapidly, it appeared that Germany would have to revalue. Seeing a chance to make a quick profit, speculators rushed to exchange dollars for marks. This sequence of events forced Germany to permit its currency to float upward. Since the Dutch economy is closely tied to Germany's, the Netherlands decided to permit its currency, the gulden, to float also. Since the Swiss and Austrian economies also were in relatively strong positions, these two countries decided to officially revalue their currencies. If they had not done so, a huge rush of dollars into their financial markets from Germany would have taken place. A large influx of dollars into these two small countries would have shaken their monetary stability.

These events may have some effects on U.S. agricultural exports. The revaluations of the Swiss franc and the Austrian schilling will make U.S. exports cheaper in terms of local currencies and may stimulate some additional exports.

For Germany and the Netherlands the situation is somewhat similar but more complicated because rates are flexible (floating) and because the countries are members of the European Economic Community (EEC).

Both the Germans and the Dutch decided to officially maintain the par value of their currencies but to permit the mark and gulden to float in the exchange market for an unspecified period as market forces dictate.

Because Germany and the Netherlands are members of the EEC, special considerations have had to be given to those agricultural commodities for which there are common prices and intervention measures (usually support prices) that have been instituted under the EEC's Common Agricultural Policy (CAP).

For commodities covered by the CAP, the situation is complex because intervention or support prices, levies, and export subsidies are all essentially denominated in U.S. dollars. At the same time, farmers, importers, exporters, and food processors make payments or receive income in their own national currencies.

When an EEC country permits its currency to float but maintains an official par value, two exchange rates come into being for agricultural commodities—the official par value which applies to domestic production through support prices, and the international market value, which applies to imports and exports.

If the appreciation of the German mark and the Netherlands gulden were sufficient, the price of imported CAP commodities could become cheaper in these two countries than domestically produced items. This could lead to an abnormal situation in which food processors obtained all or nearly all their supplies from importers. At the same time Germany and the Netherlands would have to purchase all the domestic production that the food processors did not take.

Furthermore, farm exports from Germany and the Netherlands to other EEC countries would be higher priced than the domestic production of those countries, and German and Dutch commodities would be at a competitive disadvantage within the EEC.

To forestall such difficulties, the EEC Council of Ministers, EEC's legislative body, hammered out a policy which was set forth in Council Regulation 974/71. The articles of the regulation are stated in general terms and are applicable to any EEC country.

In general, the regulation authorizes EEC countries with floating exchange rates to impose compensatory taxes on imports of farm goods covered under the CAP and to grant subsidies on exports of the same commodities. The compensatory import taxes and export subsidies apply to trade both with fellow EEC members and with outside countries.

These events have slowed the progress EEC nations were beginning to make in unifying their fiscal and monetary policies. The Europeans have become experts in patching up the CAP and it is doubtful that the EEC will be destroyed as a result of the heavy inflow of dollars. But these events show how far-reaching international monetary events can be and how important they are relative to our agricultural trade. They also indicate how heavily the world depends upon the dollar as a unit of account for measuring value internationally, as a store of value for maintaining the value of international reserves, and as a medium of exchange for international trade—the three functions money must perform.

NOTES

1. Robert B. Schwenger, "United States Balance of International Payments in Relation to the Problems of Agricultural Exports, Foreign Crops and Markets" (Washington, D.C.: USDA, Bureau of Agricultural Economics, FAS, July 22, 1935).

2. Lawrence Witt, "Our Agricultural and Trade Policies," *Journal of Farm Economics*, no. 2, vol. 32, May 1950.

3. O. Halbert Goolsby, "U.S. Agriculture and the Balance of Payments, Foreign Gold and Exchange Reserves" (Washington, D.C.: USDA, ERS, May 1971).

4. Lauren Soth, "Agricultural Trade and the U.S. Foreign Policy," *Journal of Farm Economics*, no. 5, vol. 39, December 1957, pp. 1109–10.

[9]

Effect of Domestic Political Groups and Forces on U.S. Trade Policy

Ross B. Talbot

POLITICAL INTEREST GROUPS are omnipresent in Western democratic political systems. Although political scientists have developed no precise methods to test comparability, it has been speculated that interest groups in Great Britain and France have more political effectiveness than they do in America.[1]

My comments will be limited to organized interest groups, with particular emphasis on those who produce food and fiber commodities, but with some recognition that those who process and distribute these often transformed commodities are involved in the political process, too.

Both the prevalence and the efficacy of political interest groups are well nigh inevitable in a modern democratic political system, and they are a far-from-recent political phenomenon. James Madison viewed them as pernicious factions, but a certainty and necessity in a free society.[2] Alexis de Tocqueville made mention of their existence. Lord Bryce seemed to overlook them in his fascination with the foundations and intrigues of American political parties.

Arthur Bentley's study in 1908, *The Process of Government,* brought the discipline of political science, really for the first time, to a realistic study of the political interest group in American politics. Unfortunately, it would now seem, Bentley exaggerated their importance. "When the groups are adequately stated [he claimed], everything is stated. When I say everything, I mean everything."[3] Political science was reluctant to shake loose from its philosophical and legalistic underpinnings—and fortunately still is to some extent—but by the late 1920s fairly rigorous empirical studies stressed the structure and function of at least a few of these interest (pressure) groups.[4]

Ross B. Talbot is Professor and Chairman, Department of Political Science, Iowa State University.

141

A literature review would be out of place here, but it is important to observe that during the 1930s and 1940s, and to some considerable extent even today, political scientists viewed interest groups and their legislative representatives (lobbyists) as the prime movers in the process of lawmaking. By the early 1950s, and notably in the publication in 1951 of David Truman's *The Governmental Process,* it was also fairly evident that interest groups were influential in administrative, bureaucratic decision making. Furthermore this model denies the validity of a general public concept, in terms of both its existence and its effectiveness in influencing public decision making. Whirlpools of power, to use Ernest Griffith's expressive phrase, made up of coalitions of private interest groups, government bureaus, and congressional committees or subcommittees were viewed as the primary instruments for policy making.[5] To overgeneralize only modestly from this theoretical position, the lawmaking process was dominated by the demands and strategies of private and public interest groups.

By the end of the 1950s this model was challenged, especially in the area of interest group influence in foreign policy making. Bernard Cohen, in a short but influential monograph, posed this question: "What do we really know about the dimensions of group (and individual) influence on the formulation and execution of foreign policy?" His answer was, ". . . not very much. . . . Despite frequent assumptions to the contrary, . . . interest groups seem to have considerably less effect on foreign policy than they do in the domestic realm."[6]

As a case in point, Cohen noted that ". . . administration bills to renew the Reciprocal Trade Agreements Act have gone through Congress relatively untouched year after year, despite the earnest efforts of commodity groups to influence them in their favor." He agreed that business groups ". . . seem to be the most effective of the various types of interest groups," but they are only ". . . mildly influential and then only with respect to a rather narrow range of economic issues which comprise only a small proportion of the fundamental issues of American foreign policy."[7]

The classic study of this genre is that of Raymond Bauer, Ithiel de Sola Pool, and Lewis Dexter, entitled *American Business and Foreign Policy: The Politics of Foreign Trade.* This study, published in 1963, is difficult to summarize, but its findings are notably important to the theme of our discussions. The Bauer-Pool-Dexter (BPD) thesis is that congressmen have much more freedom to make decisions than political scientists had heretofore recognized, and that interest groups are much inclined to latch onto the coattails of a congressman, particularly members of the House, who already agree with their desires and preferences. The authors reviewed the congressional process relative to the 1953–54–55–58 extensions of the Reciprocal Trade Act during the Eisenhower years, but their principal emphasis was on Kennedy's Trade Expansion

Act of 1962. They held interviews with some 903 corporation executives, as well as with over 500 congressmen, journalists, lobbyists, and others.[8] Perhaps a digest of some of their major findings would be in order:

1. The general public is so uninformed about foreign trade matters that up to half of it can properly be ignored bcause it simply has no knowledge or information about foreign trade issues.
2. Low tariff supporters are usually found to be wealthier, better educated, more politically active and knowledgeable, and more Republican than the protectionists' supporters.
3. Foreign trade is a prominent and noteworthy issue to businessmen primarily (and we can include commercial farmers in business suits here, although this chapter looks only at a few of the state farm bureaus and a scattering of food commodity organizations), and the prospect of loss through imports is a more important motivation to political action than the expectation of economic gain through exports.
4. Political activity in the area of foreign trade policy depends more on the institutional structure of the communication process within the business than on ideology or economic self-interest.
5. Interest groups and other lobbyists are ". . . on the whole poorly financed, ill-managed, out of contact with Congress, and at best only marginally effective. . . ." In consequence, ". . . *the lobbyist becomes in effect a service bureau for those congressmen already agreeing with him rather than an agent of direct persuasion.*"[9]
6. Therefore, a congressman has considerably more freedom of decision making than is generally attributed to him. He determines what kind of representative he wishes to be, what sorts of activities and issues to be involved in, how to schedule his time, and what leadership roles he wishes to assume for himself. He hears few threats, welcomes communications, and ". . . tends to follow the lead, not of any one person, but of a roster of specific [congressional] colleagues sorted by topics."[10]

This BPD concept of interest groups as service agencies to friendly congressmen is enlightening and often persuasive. Nevertheless I think we must be careful when the findings in one case study are applied to a policy area as intricate and complex as foreign trade. A few reservations, at least, seem to be in order.

First, identifying the actors in this area of food and fiber politics is more difficult than it appears at first glance. The food and fiber industry is far from a monolithic or oligopolistic institutional structure. We do have a small number of general farm organizations, although only the American Farm Bureau Federation (AFBF) qualifies in any continental sense of the term. If we use Thomas Hobbes' definition of power (power is the present means to achieve some future apparent good) we have a most difficult time determining whether our several dozen, perhaps hundreds of commodity groups have any effective means of exercising a measurable amount of political power.

Food processors and food distributors are definitely on the political scene, but their capabilities to produce intended political effects are much more a conundrum than are their intentions. The transportation industry—rail, water, air, and motor carrier—are also evident. Labor unions are often involved, and their direct influence will probably be felt increasingly. Importers and exporters have an apparent and active vested interest. Trade associations move into and out of this kind of a political struggle, depending on their estimate of the situation relative to their economic betterment.

Moreover, as noted previously, public interest groups, both legislative and bureaucratic, have developed a powerful political position which is both interdepartmental and intercommittee, and oftentimes intradepartmental and intracommittee. We can, admittedly, carry a typology to the point where it becomes impossible to untangle any political issue, but these actors are often involved, sometimes effective, and therefore need to be identified and evaluated. Only Wesley McCune has done much writing on the infrastructure of food politics, and his research was based on such a pronounced normative bias that a political scientist has to be at least skeptical of the analysis.[11]

Second, natural and biological forces, prevailing market conditions, and the state of the world in terms of war and peace often control the range of possibilities when one views politics as the art of the possible. It is rather commonplace to remark that the reason the food industry groups have become liberal in terms of export trade policies is because the American farmer has developed such an almost incredible capacity to overproduce, that exports are well nigh mandatory. One of every four acres of cropland now produces for the foreign market; export sales comprise around 15 percent of the American farmer's income from marketings.

Typhoons, monsoons, rootworms, leaf blight, drought, and on ad infinitum oftentimes either create the issue or circumscribe its boundaries. Moreover, the so-called Green Revolution is in action throughout this planet, in some degree, for several types of commodities.

Interest groups are far from being masters of their intended desires. On the other hand, it would not seem that they are the victims of some foreordained fate. A realistic understanding of the limits of the playing field called policy making is the art to be cultivated, and to a significant extent each major public issue constitutes a new ball game.

INFLUENCING THE LAWMAKERS. Two major issues in which domestic political groups and forces have had some considerable role in the development and then execution of U.S. trade policies have specific reference to food and fiber policies. Presumably it is obvious now—or, at least, it soon will be—that it would be the utmost in pretension to classify what follows as true case studies. They are simply rough drafts of legislative acts and their administrative aftermaths which are advanced primarily for the purpose of invoking subsequent discussion.

TRADE DEVELOPMENT AND ASSISTANCE ACT OF 1954 (PL 480). Farmer interest groups played a rather important role in enactment of PL 480.[12] Furthermore, PL 480 has been an immensely important, expensive, and influential legislative act. In its original conception and statement of objectives, PL 480 had a certain simplicity: expand international trade; develop and expand U.S. agricultural export markets; combat hunger and malnutrition; and encourage economic development in the less developed countries (LDCs). By November 30, 1970, the act had been amended twenty-three times. Through December 31, 1969, the gross cost of financing PL 480 programs had climbed to a total of nearly $26.5 billion.

Farm groups have consistently, and generally enthusiastically, supported PL 480 programs. The AFBF has on occasion been a critic, primarily because of the fear that PL 480 shipments were cutting into existing dollar markets, or were impeding development of such markets. The criticism of the National Farmers Union (NFU) has usually been that more would surely be better.

Although I certainly have not proved any proposition concerning PL 480 programs, it is my contention that although farm groups were mildly influential in the adoption of the law, their influence in this policy area has probably been on the decline ever since.

The tremendous capacity of U.S. agriculture to overproduce was the principal cause for the creation of PL 480. No doubt altruism and philanthropy were evident as elements of causation, but it quickly became clear—notably in the House Committee on Agriculture—that the primary motivation was to rid ourselves of burdensome surpluses. Apparently the national public (the TV McLuhanesque public, if you will) perceives a kind of transcendental quality in food, as well as a naturalistic belief that hunger and war have a direct cause-and-effect relationship.

In any respect, President Dwight D. Eisenhower and, in a more dramatic manner, President John F. Kennedy popularized the now-named Food for Peace program, and in effect proclaimed it as an executive policy. Viewed in a more "realpolitik" perspective, the Department of State and many if not all other exporting nations were critical of PL 480, primarily because of its avowed market-depressing and ally-alienating effects. A number of the development assistance experts were either concerned, or convinced, that these large shipments of essentially free food were retarding the development of a viable agricultural industry within the recipient LDCs.

Most of the chinks and cracks in the PL 480 program have now been fairly well ironed out, it would appear. The United States Department of Agriculture (USDA) has learned a great deal about the bartering process of which it had been naive and unsophisticated; the Foreign Agricultural Service (FAS) has hand-led and spoon-fed a good number of market development cooperators into existence and then into action; the Department of State has come to realize that food can be used as a helpful tool in advancing U.S. interests abroad, at least when the programs are "properly" administered; the AFBF—with W. E. Hamilton as its spokesman in this instance—has confirmed that PL 480 is "a popular program" but he then observes that ". . . it is a good example of a subject that deserves separate consideration on its own merits."[13]

However, permit me three quick observations which lead to the conjecture that farmer interest groups do not have, or at least have lost, control over the direction and scope of PL 480 programs.

First, strategic and military considerations seem to control the sales for foreign currency and are a dominant influence in the long-term dollar sales. In calendar 1970, of the $266.5 million of Title I, PL 480 sales for foreign currency, over $260 million were sales in Asia to four governments—South Vietnam, India, Korea, and Pakistan. In the long-term dollars sales, under Title I also, the governments of Indonesia, Israel, and Turkey are important recipients.

Second, there is the unique U.S. government–American voluntary relief agency partnership for the use of surplus food to alleviate hunger in the LDCs—what Robert Sullivan recently called "the politics of altruism." This partnership has come to dominate the food donations section of the program (Title II), although their tacit memorandum of understanding now appears to be in some jeopardy.[14] This partnership began with the passage of the Agricultural Act of 1949, then was increased in scope and magnitude by Title II or the original PL 480.

Five agencies—the Cooperative for American Remittance to Everywhere (CARE); the American Jewish Joint Distribution Committee; Catholic Relief Services, National Catholic Welfare Council (NCWC); Church World Service; and Lutheran World Relief—have distributed over 95 percent of these food shipments.[15]

Since the mid-1950s between 2 and 5 percent of all U.S. goods exports (commercial and governmental) have taken place under this arrangement.[16] Through 1968, nearly thirty billion pounds have been shipped at a value of approximately $4 billion. More to the point of our concern are the efforts of voluntary agencies in some of the LDCs, especially through massive feeding programs that have made the continuation of these programs almost mandatory.

"As a consequence," according to Sullivan, "there is a growing threat to the independence of the voluntary agencies. As surplus resources tend to become scarce resources, the [U.S.] government has seen fit to demand a greater political quid pro quo, which in operational terms has meant encouragement to voluntary agency feeding programs in Vietnam, Latin America, and India and discouragement of programs in countries of only peripheral importance to U.S. interests.[17]

In other words, the operations under Title II seem to be increasingly dictated by the perhaps unwitting desires and decisions of the Department of State and AID. "Willingly or not, the U.S. government has in a sense adopted approximately seventy-five million persons simply by virtue of the fact that it allowed the voluntary agencies to set up a permanent massive feeding program abroad."[18]

Third, the continuation of PL 480 appears to be firmly established only if rather large surpluses continue to prevail. A kind of microview of this situation can be derived from a colloquy which took place in March 1970, between Raymond Ioanes, administrator of FAS, and Congressman Whitten, chairman of the House Agricultural Appropriations Subcommittee. The conversation occurred because Mr. Ioanes had requested a one-million-dollar increase in FAS appropriations to be used for market development programs because convertible foreign currencies had become almost depleted.

MR. WHITTEN: You seem to feel that Congress might go for dollar spending for promotion just as readily as we went for foreign currencies which we could not bring home anyway. What makes you believe that your promotion which was easily worth the use of foreign currencies is worth just as much in good hard American dollars?

MR. IOANES: That is a good question.

MR. WHITTEN: Thank you, could you give me an equally good answer?

MR. IOANES: I will try.[19]

The paradox is, or is in the process of becoming, that farm groups may not have the political strength to push through an additional continuation of PL 480 exports under Titles I or II unless they produce substantial and burdensome surpluses. Nor, for that matter, would they necessarily desire to do so under an equilibrium kind of market situation. On the other hand, it may well be in the interests of the U.S. government to have convertible foreign currencies available for use in the pursuit of foreign policy objectives.

A few years ago, Theodore Lowi recommended that in order to survive what he referred to as "interest group liberalism"—of which PL 480 is a type—Congress should ". . . set a Jeffersonian absolute limit of from five to ten years on every enabling act."[20] The act of termination would then compel Congress to review the objectives of the act, as well as its costs and accomplishments. Under the prevailing circumstances, it would seem prudent for Congress to perform its oversight function and to review PL 480 thoroughly. Preferably, the job should be done by either a House or Senate select committee.

THE TRADE EXPANSION ACT OF 1962. Abraham Holtzman emphasizes the importance of this legislative proposal in these words: "For no bill that preceded or followed the trade bill of 1962 did the Kennedy Administration seek in a comparable scale to marshal the unified strength of the White House, the departments, outside groups, and public opinion." Theodore Sorensen concurs to the extent of agreeing that ". . . the 1962 trade bill became the centerpiece of all that year's efforts. . . ."[21] It is not our responsibility to try to explain why President Kennedy concluded that freer trade must continue to be a cornerstone of American foreign policy.[22] The question is, How much influence did the farm groups and to some extent the aforementioned food politics infrastructure have in the passage of the act. Again, the generalized answer seems to be, Not very much. This conclusion needs, however, to be tempered by several qualifications and background statements.

Farmers and farm organizations have historically been viewed as protectionist in their attitudes toward trade policy. Indeed, James Lindeen's content analysis of some three dozen volumes of hearings in the House Ways and Means Committee over the last thirty-five years— from the passage of the Reciprocal Trade Act of 1934 until the adjournment of the Ninetieth Congress in 1968—caused him to conclude that farm lobbyists (he included forestry and fisheries with agriculture) were protectionist on 77 percent of the occasions when they testified during the years 1934–68.[23] This period covered thirteen different revisions to the original Reciprocal Trade Act of 1934, plus that act itself. Only mining interests and manufacturing interests scored higher—95 and 80 percent respectively.

The problem seems to be in part one of definition and classification. Lindeen defined a protectionist strategy as one which sought to "rationalize exceptions" to the basic principles of reciprocal trade. It probably would be more accurate to generalize that post-World War II farm organizations have been fairly consistent advocates of free trade. Every major economic interest group has endeavored to "rationalize exceptions," farmers included. The League of Women Voters was ". . . militantly in favor of liberalizing America's [trade] policy," although the league would not be classified as an economic interest group.[24].

The Meat Imports Act of 1964 is an instance where the American National Cattleman's Association, AFBF, and NFU employed the "exceptions" strategy with a fair measure of success. In 1971 the dairy groups convinced the Tariff Commission and President Nixon that four additional dairy products should be given some protection through an annual import quota.

In the case of the Trade Expansion Act of 1962, the central objectives of President Kennedy fit hand-in-glove with the interests of American agriculture. The BPD study pointedly states this proposition: "The great decision that the United States faced in 1962 was not whether to have higher or lower tariffs. It was whether to react to the competition of the Common Market by isolation and protection of the American market or, on the contrary, by insisting on full U.S. participation in the unified economy of Europe. If the latter, the country would have to pay for it with acceptance of European competition at home."[25] Farm group strategy tended toward the "we would like to have our cake and eat it too" type by developing a hungry desire for access to the European Economic Community (EEC) fused with a much lesser desire to face supplementary (competitive) imports into the U.S. market.

President Kennedy had no cause, in the main, to be concerned about the farm groups in mapping his strategy and tactics for the congressional battle over his Trade Expansion Act of 1962. They were already on his side. Both the BPD and the Holtzman studies provide fascinating and at a few points conflicting accounts of the congressional struggle for the passage of this bill.

In summary, the White House set up an ad hoc unit under the guidance and direction of Howard C. Peterson, a special assistant to President Kennedy, to guide this bill through the labyrinth of congressional politics. At the same time, the regular White House lobbying unit tended to exercise its art of persuasion and accommodation in the same arena. The ad hoc unit made a meticulous intelligence study of the voting patterns and constituency interests of all the congressmen, and they were inclined to compromise only as a matter of last resort.[26] The regular White House liaison unit, and notably Meyer Feldman, deputy special counsel to the president, adopted the tactic of making numerous concessions to interests who opposed the bill, but these concessions were mainly to favor the opposition with desired administrative actions or special bills in other fields.[27]

Secondary sources, at least, provide little evidence that farm groups influenced this congressional struggle in any marked degree. Ernest Preeg does observe that "the reluctant support of the American Farm Bureau Federation was obtained only after the bill was amended to provide a firmer commitment on agriculture. . . ." Also the AFBF's opposition was further assuaged by a concurrent resolution which admonished the U.S. negotiators to retain our access "rights" to EEC domestic food markets.[28]

Once the Kennedy Round negotiations were underway, the U.S. strategy was to tie in progress in the agricultural sphere as evidence that the EEC was willing to engage in a general and comprehensive world trade agreement. The results of the Geneva negotiations, at least in the area of agricultural relations, could hardly be viewed as substantial. On the other hand, one could probably conclude that the U.S.

negotiators faithfully and persistently fought for a liberalization of the Common Agricultural Policy. It might further be argued that we fought valiantly in a battle we were surely destined to lose, and—in John Coppock's judgment, at least—deserved to lose.[29]

My original intention was to review several legislative case studies to see if there were noticeable changes in the patterns of farm interest group efficacy relative to U.S. trade policy legislation in the 1960s. Space and time would not permit such an exercise. Moreover, the empirical evidence is simply not available in many of these situations.[30]

Each legislative issue is confronted with a somewhat different configuration of power. Perhaps this is obvious to any careful observer but the condition is often overlooked. Examples of legislative actions which might have been scrutinized would be the Meat Import Act of 1964, Federal Meat Inspection Act—especially Section 20 relating to U.S. inspection of foreign meat to be shipped to the United States—the Wholesome Meat Act of 1968, the Trade Acts of 1969 and 1970—of which neither passed but the latter measure was approved by the House—and the Sugar Act of 1971.

One generalization stands up quite consistently, and not surprisingly. Farm groups have more effective influence in the foreign trade policies decided on, at least initially, by the House and Senate Agriculture committees. If another committee has jurisdiction of the bill— usually the House Ways and Means Committee or the Senate Finance Committee—the influence of farm groups seems to be lessened an appreciable degree. The cattlemen got a portion of what they desired in the Meat Import Act of 1964.

Most farm groups, including the National Council of Farmer Cooperatives (NCFC), favored the Trade Act of 1969 which renewed the president's power to negotiate certain reciprocal trade agreements and prevent foreign "dumping." This proposal was severely modified by the Trade Act of 1970 and it is probably accurate to conclude that only time prevented its passage in the Senate, despite the concerted efforts of the farm organizations. Technically, the sugar bills are revenue measures and should be sent initially to the House Ways and Means Committee. For historical reasons, the House Agriculture Committee has been granted this authority, much to the delight of the American sugarcane and beet producers.

No encompassing generalization seems to exist that will consistently predict the influence of American farm organizations relative to the enactment of U.S. trade policy legislation. One has to begin anew with each issue, understanding the constants in the power configuration but searching for the variations.[31]

POLICY IMPLICATIONS FOR THE 1970s. What changes might we anticipate in the decade of the seventies relative to the attitudes and policy positions of farm interest groups toward trade policy legislation? We tend to see more continuity than change, but it does seem evident that economic realities have brought at least most farm leaders to the conviction that freer world trade is usually in their best interests. We have a tendency to forget that in order to sell we must also buy. Moreover, the principle of comparative advantage sometimes works economic hardships on unsuspecting producers. The NFU has recently requested import quotas on higher-priced cheeses.[32] The AFB tends to forget that less developed nations can grow quality low cost sugarcane, and instead recommends that a ". . . larger share of future growth in sugar consumption [should be] reserved for domestic producers."[33]

The National Farmers Organization (NFO) is more of an enigma in its attitude toward foreign trade policies. The leadership seems to have assumed the mantle of the old populist movement, both in terms of their defense of the Common Man and their inclinations toward the acceptance of a conspiratorial theory. That is, where there is a good guy presumably there must be his evil counterpart. The conspirators become, in this instance, the Committee for Economic Development, the Council of Economic Advisors—and one of its advisors, in particular, Dr. Hendrick Houthakker. Also, Dr. Kenneth Boulding, the colleges of agriculture, and even the American Agricultural Economics Association are among the suspect.[34]

In all fairness, however, the unrelenting efforts placed by the NFO on farmer bargaining power and marketing controls have not been carefully studied either in terms of methods or results. Also, their inclination to depreciate the importance of foreign trade to the U.S. commercial farmer is a proposition calling for more careful examination than it has been given. On the other hand, the NFO seems to get some of the economic and social realities of farm production and marketing out of focus. One NFO spokesman recently claimed that ". . . the 1 million on relief in New York City alone is a situation manufactured on the farm. The racial strife in this nation, the campus unrest, the growing poverty everywhere—all can be traced to the fact that the farmer has not been getting paid [adequately]."[35]

Kenneth Naden, executive vice-president of the National Council of Farmer Cooperatives (NCFC), placed the production/price/trade dilemma in a clearer and more useful perspective by a recent comment: "The old problem is how to get the price and income benefit of farm programs without suffering loss of trade benefits which such programs usually bring."[36] The "old" problem is still very much with us.

Another question is, How much impact will the seventies have toward revising the strategies of the farm interest groups and the food-fiber infrastructure? If my assumptions regarding their ability and willingness to reorient and readjust their values and attitudes toward the importance of freer world trade are generally accurate, I believe we can assume that strategy, and even tactics, will fall in line with this enlightened realism. Those who need to export must, in the idiom of the day, learn to hang loose, that is, be prepared for both major and minor changes in supply and demand from year to year, and even from one growing season to the next. Natural forces have a violent, sometimes almost subversive, way of altering production estimates and carry-over stocks.

In this regard, the food industry will need to build an even more effective partnership with the institutions of government.

To be competitive, the producer and the processor must strive for even more efficiency; therefore, public funds and expertise in research and education are a necessity.

To be efficient, an attitude of hopeful expectation must be present; a belief that the effort will lead to a better life—therefore, price and income policies will have to be continued.

To be an aggressive and imaginative foreign marketeer, one must be ready to supply both quality and quantity on order, and at the same time understand alien cultures at least to the extent of appreciating that their patterns of taste, color, and texture in food products may vary dramatically from ours.

Again, public support in terms of storage and loan policies, as well as new forms of research and education, appears to be mandatory.

One might commend the FAS for the quality and scope of its intelligence function, and at the same time ponder one of the findings of the BPD study: "The best information source, in the eyes of most businessmen, is to go abroad and to talk there to trusted business colleagues."[37] To be sure, we might query as to where we would find such colleagues. Nevertheless we cannot help but be intrigued by the thought of "Whitten Fellowships" for farm and agribusiness leaders.

We should speculate quickly about the service function to Congress which is so often stressed in the BPD study. The disunity within America seems to lead logically to the conclusion that this service function is dissipated by the presence of a multiple number of farm groups which tend to confuse, if not mislead, a congressman as to both the national interest and his constituency's interests. However, this disunity may be a plus factor in that the divisiveness may accord him the freedom to be more statesmanlike and less driven to a purely political (vote-maximizing) decision.

In conclusion, we should remember that we live in a world system of nation-states. Trade policies tend to follow in the wake of political and military discussions and decisions. The new EEC, the two-China policy, the Arab-Israeli conflict, the United States–Japanese Security Treaty, polycentric communism, a U.S. policy for Southeast Asia, the Strategic Arms Limitation Talks (SALT), and foreign assistance to the Latin American and African nations are cases in point. This condition does not mean that trade policy is less important. Rather we should conclude that trade can no longer follow the flag; this mode of imperialism is not an acceptable or workable strategy.

Trade policies should be founded on the premise that an exchange of foods and services can be mutually advantageous to many diverse interests and can be adjusted to the goals and objectives of many diverse and humane philosophies and religions. The trader can also be a diplomat, and diplomacy in this thermonuclear age means searching for new and better modes of mutual accommodation and human advancement.

NOTES

1. Samuel Eldersveld, "American Interest Groups: A Survey of Research and Some Implications for Theory and Method," in *Interest Groups on Four Continents*, Henry Ehrmann, ed. (Pittsburgh: Univ. of Pittsburgh Press, 1958), pp. 173–97.

2. Alexander Hamilton, James Madison, and John Jay, *The Federalist*, especially no. X, many editions.

3. Arthur F. Bentley, *The Process of Government* (Bloomington, Ind.: Principia, 1935 reissue), p. 208.

4. Betty H. Zisk, ed., *American Political Interest Groups: Readings in Theory and Research* (Belmont, Calif.: Wadsworth, 1969), chap. 1.

5. Ernest S. Griffith, *Congress: Its Contemporary Role*, 3rd ed. (New York: N.Y. Univ. 1961), pp. 50–51.

6. Bernard C. Cohen, *The Influence of Non-Governmental Groups on Foreign Policy-Making*, vol. 2 (New York: World Peace Foundation, 1956), pp. 1, 6.

7. Ibid., pp. 15, 20.

8. Raymond Bauer, Ithiel de Sola Pool, and Lewis Dexter, *American Business and Foreign Policy: The Politics of Foreign Trade* (New York: Atherton, 1963), pp. xi–xii.

9. Ibid., pp. 324, 353 (underlining was included in the text).

10. Ibid., p. 437.

11. Wesley McCune, *Who's Behind Our Farm Policy?* (New York: Frederick A. Praeger, 1956).

12. Ross B. Talbot and Don F. Hadwiger, *The Policy Process in American Agriculture* (San Francisco: Chandler, 1968), pp. 305–6.

13. W. E. Hamilton, "Farm Policy Legislation for the 1970s: The Farm Bureau Position," *American Journal of Agricultural Economics*, 52(December 1970):673.

14. Robert B. Sullivan, "The Politics of Altruism: An Introduction to the Food-for-Peace Partnership Between the U.S. Government and Voluntary Relief Agencies," *Western Political Quarterly*, 23(December 1970):762–68.

15. Ibid., p. 763. There are now 83 voluntary agencies operating in 129 countries. Agency for International Development, *War on Hunger*, 5(May 1971):23–28.

16. Ibid., p. 765.

17. Ibid., p. 767.

18. Ibid., p. 768.

19. U.S. Congress, House, Subcommittee of the Committee on Appropriations, *Hearings—Department of Agriculture Appropriations for 1971*, pt. 4 (Washington, D.C.: USGPO, 1970), p. 510.

20. Theodore Lowi, "The Public Philosophy: Interest-Group Liberalism," *American Political Science Review*, 61(March 1967):23–24.

21. Abraham Holtzman, *Legislative Liaison: Executive Leadership in Congress* (Chicago: Rand McNally, 1970), p. 273; Theodore C. Sorensen, *Kennedy* (New York: Harper and Row, 1965, Bantam Book ed., 1966), p. 460.

22. Ernest H. Preeg, *Traders and Diplomats*, Appendix B (Washington, D.C.: Brookings Institution, 1970), pp. 282–90.

23. James Walter Lindeen, "Interest-Group Attitudes Toward Reciprocal Trade Legislation," *Public Opinion Quarterly*, table 2, 34(Spring 1970):110.

24. Bauer, Pool, and Dexter, p. 388.
25. Ibid., p. 76.
26. Holtzman, pp. 272–83.
27. Bauer, Pool, and Dexter, p. 78.
28. Preeg, p. 144.
29. John Coppock, *Atlantic Agricultural Unity: Is It Possible?* (New York: Mc-Graw-Hill, 1966), p. 222.
30. Roy A. Ballinger, *A History of Sugar Marketing*, Agricultural Economic Report no. 197, February 1971.
31. Lester W. Milbreath, *The Washington Lobbyists* (Chicago: Rand McNally, 1963), pp. 328–58.
32. National Farmers Union, *Washington Newsletter*, 18(April 23, 1971):1.
33. American Farm Bureau Federation, *Official Newsletter*, 50(April 5, 1971):54.
34. National Farmers Organization, *NFO Reporter*, 14(August 1970):8–10, 14; 14(September 1970):6; 14(December 1970):10.
35. Ibid., 14(December 1970):12.
36. National Council of Farmers Cooperatives, *Washington Situation*, September 23, 1970, p. 3.
37. Bauer, Pool, and Dexter, p. 475.

10

The National Need for an Integrated Trade Policy: The Textile Example

R. Buford Brandis

SUNDAY, MAY 30, 1971, the *Washington Post* carried a front page story on lobbying activities relative to current consideration by the House Agriculture Committee of legislation extending the Sugar Act. At stake, as on the occasions of previous renewals since 1934, is allocation of specific quota portions of the U.S. sugar market to American cane growers and beet producers, and to many of the world's less developed countries.

Ten days earlier the Honorable Clarence D. Palmby, Assistant Secretary of Agriculture for International Affairs, testified before the Subcommittee on International Trade of the Senate Finance Committee. He said in part:

> It is thus a matter of very great concern to us that the developed countries of Europe, where we would expect to find our major markets, as well as Japan, are following policies which restrict trade growth. . . .
>
> This is not to say that agricultural trade problems with the UK would disappear were the UK not to join the EC. On the contrary, since 1964 the UK on its own has been moving away from its traditional policies. For a variety of reasons it has been shifting toward an EC type of policy and away from the deficiency payment system. With the recent coming to power of the Conservative Government this shift has been accelerated. Thus, we would in any event be facing unfavorable and restrictive changes in UK agricultural policy.
>
> Agricultural policy problems are not limited to Europe. Japan's agricultural policy has led to a most troublesome rice surplus. High support prices have contributed to increased production far outrunning uses. Japan's rice support price was this year raised to over $390 per ton. By way of contrast, the U.S. rice support price is $107 per ton. Japan's stocks of rice are greater than estimated total world trade in rice in 1970. . . .
>
> Imports of a number of horticultural products from Mexico—fresh and

R. BUFORD BRANDIS is International Trade Director and Chief Economist, American Textile Manufacturers Institute.

frozen strawberries and fresh tomatoes, cucumbers and peppers—have increased sharply in recent years. In 1970, imports were at a record high level for each of these items. Mexico possesses advantages in producing these crops because of lower labor costs and generally more favorable climatic conditions. United States capital and know-how have aided in the expansion of Mexican industry and promise to aid further growth. It is likely that imports of these products from Mexico will continue to increase and the disruptions in the U.S. market from the standpoint of both production and price will become increasingly evident.

U.S. officials have engaged in joint meetings with Mexican officials in an effort to regulate the sharply increasing trends of horticultural imports. We believe the desirable course of action here is to continue to work with Mexican officials to avoid undue market disruption.

Imports of certain chilled or frozen meats, primarily beef and mutton, have been subject to voluntary restraints negotiated with principal exporting countries since the last quarter of 1968. Products included within the restraints are those specified in the Meat Import Law enacted in 1964. . . .

The past year has seen a sharp readjustment in world butter stocks that has removed the burdensome surpluses that demoralized the butter market over the past several years. This was the result of lower production in Western Europe and in New Zealand, which suffered a severe drought. Nevertheless, it has been necessary for the U.S. to take additional steps under the authority of Section 22 of the Agricultural Adjustment Act, as amended, to hold imports of certain dairy products to reasonable levels. The President proclaimed quotas effective January 1, 1971, on four dairy products which were circumventing our import controls and interfering with price support programs: ice cream, animal feeds containing milk (calf replacers), low fat chocolate crumb, and low fat manufacturing cheese. All of these products were relatively new items in international trade and were used mainly by processors. . . .

Our agricultural import system is relatively liberal.[1]

TEXTILE IMPORTS. The American textile industry, like American agriculture, has major import problems. Involved are the developing countries, the European Economic Community (EEC), the United Kingdom, Japan, Mexico—a list very similar to Mr. Palmby's. Over the past decade—in boom and recession, in war and peace—the textile import trend has been relentlessly upward. Future viability of the American fiber-textile-apparel complex is now threatened unless reasonable controls over imports are put in place promptly.

In 1959 the United States imported from all countries the statistical equivalent of one billion square yards of textile products, including yarn, fabric, and apparel, manufactured from cotton, wool, and synthetics. Such imports more than doubled by 1965. Five years later, in 1970, they had redoubled to 4.5 billion yards. First quarter imports in 1971 were up 38 percent over 1970. The present level of imports represents a third of a million jobs.

A decade ago, when the General Agreement on Tariffs and Trade (GATT) cotton textile import controls were first imposed, imports supplied about 5 percent of American consumption of such products. Today some 15 percent of our total textile market is being supplied from abroad. In certain product lines such as worsted fabric for men's suits the import ratio is above 50 percent and rising.

NATIONAL GOALS. Among the national goals of present domestic policy are price stability, full employment, a rising standard of living for all citizens, and the economic development of our country's under-developed areas. In the achievement of each, the domestic textile-apparel industry plays a key role.

Yarn and cloth prices at the mill level are actually lower now than they were in the late 1950s, while wholesale apparel prices have only kept pace with general inflation. Yet textile wages have jumped a dollar an hour over the decade and apparel wages have moved similarly.

The best way to hold the textile price line for American consumers is to encourage healthy competition among our 7,000 textile plants and 27,000 apparel plants. Once the control over the major part of a prod-uct line falls into the hands of foreign interests, provisions of U.S. law for protection of American consumers, such as antitrust regulations pro-hibiting price-fixing conspiracies, go out the window.

A good example of what happens under these circumstances oc-curred when imports killed the American silk textile industry, allowing Japan and Italy to dominate the world's silk textile production. Since the 1957–59 period the wholesale price index of silk textiles in the United States—virtually all imported—has more than doubled. During the same period, with competitive U.S. market influences dominant, the all-fiber textile and apparel index is up less than 10 percent.

We have not yet reached the point where foreign pricing influence dominates most U.S. textile and apparel markets, but unless prompt control action is taken, that point could soon be reached for many dif-ferent textile products, and the U.S. consumer will be the loser.

Taken together as a single industrial complex, textile and apparel manufacturing form a key foundation element in America's economic structure. Not only does this industry make products essential to life and vital to national security, but it fills a primary role in providing economic activity for hundreds of communities large and small, urban and rural, throughout the land.

The industry directly employs 2.5 million men and women in a broad range of occupations. Another million workers are employed in producing the raw cotton and wool, cornstarch, machinery, chemicals, and myriad other materials used by the industry. Of the 20 million manufacturing employees in this country, the industry directly employs one in every eight. It pays them $12 billion yearly.

The industry's impact on the economy of the United States goes even further. It generates major revenues for government—federal, state, and local. It buys $4 billion worth of fiber each year, including two-thirds of the output of this country's 300,000 cotton farms, all the domestically produced wool, and almost all the synthetic fiber produced by the U.S. chemical industry. In addition, it spends $600 million on dyestuffs and other chemicals and several hundred millions annually on new plants and equipment.

Black employment in the textile industry grew from 3.3 percent in 1960 to 14.3 percent in 1970; the present level for all manufacturing is 10.1 percent. Black employment in the textile industry has advanced four times faster than the national average for all manufacturing since 1960, and in some South Carolina areas black workers now account for 40 percent of total "new hires."

In New York City the industry employs one-third of all manufacturing workers. Its payroll, $1.5 billion annually, is second only to that of the welfare department.

Another significant aspect of textile-apparel employment is the number of women involved. Women constitute about 45 percent of the textile labor force and 80 percent of the apparel workers. These figures compare with the all-manufacturing average of 27 percent. Family responsibilities sharply restrict their mobility—a factor blithely ignored by the largely male "adjustment assistance" advocates of the "free trade" theory. In terms then of opportunities for people regardless of race, sex, or education, the textile-apparel industry is remarkably diversified in what it can offer by way of employment opportunity—provided it has a reasonable chance to grow and progress along with the nation's economy as a whole.

These social contributions of the textile industry are important and significant to our national welfare. They are vital to our national commitment to full employment.

Appalachia has the largest population of the underdeveloped regions of the United States. In 1965 Congress passed the Appalachian Regional Development Act "to promote its economic development."

The textile-apparel industry is by far the largest employer of manufacturing labor in Appalachia. As noted earlier, in the United States as a whole the industry provides one of every eight manufacturing jobs. In Appalachia the industry's relative importance doubles: in that region extending from southern New York State to northern Mississippi it provides one job in every four.

In an area encompassing Appalachia and contiguous territory within commuting distance (50 miles) there are more than one million textile-apparel jobs. The federal government has a positive domestic policy involving creation of new manufacturing jobs in Appalachia, yet its foreign trade policy seriously threatens a million textile-apparel jobs already there.

The question is this: Will job opportunities be available in this country to those people and areas where jobs are most needed? Or will they be transferred to low wage nations of the Far East, some of which, like Japan, are already highly developed industrially?

AMERICAN PRODUCTIVITY. This American industry is not suffering import competition as a result of low productivity. Quite the contrary: the American textile industry is the most efficient in the world.

The British Textile Council in 1969 published an exhaustive study of relative productivity in major textile industries around the world. In spinning, American productivity is more than twice that of the Japanese and more than three times that of the British.

When productivity in spinning is combined with productivity in weaving, once again the American industry shows up as by far the most efficient, with Britain second at 37 percent of U.S. productivity and Japan third at 32 percent. We can take pride in the performance of the American textile industry.

However, items made abroad at wages far below the legal U.S. minimum give foreign producers cost advantages that cannot be overcome even by superior American efficiency. American wages are five times higher than those in Japan and eight times greater than in Hong Kong. Korea, Taiwan, and other Asian countries show even wider disparities.

Contrary to claims often heard, the textile wage gap between the United States and its major foreign competitors is not narrowing, but widening. The gap with Japan in 1960, for example, was $1.44 per hour. In 1970 it was $1.98—a 37 percent increase in the gap over the ten-year period. True, Japan's textile wages rose by large percentages, but the actual dollar amount fell far short of the increase in wages that has taken place in the United States. And Japan pays the highest wages of the Asian nations.

The American textile import problem grows out of the fact that as the result of our national trade policy the American market has been opened to overseas production while production cost factors, as the result of our national socioeconomic policy, are highly protected at the border. There is little movement of labor across national boundaries, for example, due to immigration quotas.

Furthermore, currency exchange rates are fixed, rather than flexible, under the present International Monetary Fund system. Hence there is no neutral world monetary system freely reflecting cost differentials among nations.

GENERAL AGREEMENT ON TARIFFS AND TRADE. Since 1961, cotton textile trade has been controlled by a quota system internationally agreed upon and presently overseen by the Cotton Textiles Committee of GATT in Geneva. This control agreement, the Long-Term

Arrangement for Cotton Textile Trade (LTA), has been renewed on several occasions, most recently in September 1970. Its present span extends through September 30, 1973. The United States and thirty other countries are signatories.

Cotton was the dominant fiber ten years ago. This is no longer the case. The U.S. government and industry have proposed, therefore, similar quotas on wool and man-made fiber (synthetic) textiles, hardly the earth-shattering change of policy pictured by some.

Our government under three presidents representing both political parties—John F. Kennedy, Lyndon B. Johnson, and Richard M. Nixon—has administered its cotton textile quota controls so generously and with such a sense of international responsibility both to Japan and to developing countries that our cotton textile imports in 1970 were double the 1961 total. This generous example has not been followed by the Europeans or the Japanese, a statistical fact which opponents of textile quotas neglect to mention while admonishing the United States to set other countries a good example. The Europeans have used fairly visible LTA and other quota regulations in protecting their textile industries, while the Japanese have placed greater reliance on a typically subtle oriental form of mercantilism best translated as "administrative guidance." Yet the results have been similar.

According to United Nations data for 1969, of the total textile and apparel exports of the less developed countries to the developed countries, Japan took 3.5 percent, the EEC 15.9 percent, and the United States 47.1 percent. These ratios are interesting because the combined populations of the EEC countries are about the same as the population of the United States, and that of Japan, half; all three areas are affluent.

THE TRADE BILL. After a year of fruitless attempts to resolve the textile import crisis through international negotiations, the Nixon administration in June 1970 endorsed textile import quota legislation in testimony presented to the House Ways and Means Committee. The president reaffirmed that position during his televised news conference of December 10, 1970, while the legislation was awaiting Senate action. On March 11, 1971, in rejecting the Japanese industry's unilateral program of export control, he called again for textile quota legislation.

That legislation, the textile quota provisions of HR 20, would specifically provide for textile import restraints agreed upon in international negotiations to supersede quota levels provided by law. Furthermore the president is authorized to exempt any imported textile from the prescribed limitation whenever he concludes such action would be in the national interest or necessary to maintain reasonable prices for American consumers. Clearly, legislation is needed to assure the early, successful conclusion of meaningful, long-range, comprehensive agreements with the Japanese and others.

In rejecting the Japanese industry's export control announcement as a solution to our import problem, the president said—

. . . On its face, this unilateral program falls short of the terms essential to the U.S. in the following significant respects:

—Only one overall ceiling for all cotton, wool and manmade fiber fabric and apparel textiles is provided, with only a general undertaking by the Japanese industry "to prevent undue distortions of the present pattern of trade." This allows concentration on specific categories, which could result in these categories growing many times faster than the overall limits.

—The overall ceiling would be based on imports from Japan in the year ending March 31, 1971, plus a growth factor. During the two years that we have been negotiating with the Government of Japan, imports of manmade fiber textile products have greatly increased, and in January 1971 they entered this country at a record breaking level. Moreover, the program magnifies the potential growth of the sensitive categories by including in the base exports of cotton products which are already limited by agreement and which have been declining.[2]

Furthermore, the import growth rate projected in the Japanese industry's proposal is nearly double the actual growth rate of the American textile market since World War II on an annual basis.

Control over product shifts and the coverage and duration of the plan are completely in the hands of the Japanese textile industry. It would encourage a form of economic search-and-destroy strategy which could wreck entire segments of the domestic industry. It would be unconscionable to abandon the responsibility for 2.5 million American textile and apparel workers to the whims of the Japanese textile industry.

A similar Japanese voluntary agreement covering steel imports has not worked as intended because the Japanese have violated the spirit of the agreement by concentrating in certain high priced specialty steel markets. To accept this proposal would mean falling into the same trap.

Since January 1, 1962, Japan's cotton textile exports to the United States have been regulated through bilateral agreements negotiated by the two governments under GATT international cotton textile trade arrangements. During the first five years of this period our cotton textile imports from Japan rose from 243 million square yards in 1961 to 412 million in 1966, an increase of 70 percent. This does not seem excessively restrictive.

In subsequent years, as man-made fibers increasingly supplanted cotton both here and in Japan, cotton textile imports declined. They were 331 million square yards in 1970. The 1971 quota (annual rate) was 432 million. The uncontrolled synthetic textile imports from Japan have more than doubled in just five years: 301 million square yards in 1965; 775 million in 1970. And in the first quarter of 1971 they jumped 77 percent.

Japan accounted for one-third of our textile trade deficit in 1970; or $556 million of our $1.6 billion deficit. The time for responsible and effective governmental action has clearly come.

RETALIATION. Opponents of textile quota legislation have held high the spectre of foreign retaliation against our agricultural and other exports. As painted by the more eloquent of these lobbyists, retaliation becomes a vague horror resembling a brain operation performed under guttering candles on a stormy midnight by Drs. Frankenstein and Fu Manchu.

Actually our textile import policies under the legislation proposed would remain so generous relative to those of other GATT members that retaliation and compensation can surely be avoided by vigorous presentation of the American case to our trading partners.

In view of the subsidies being paid on textile exports to the United States by many of our trading partners, the nontariff trade barriers raised against U.S. textile exports around the world, and the bilateral textile agreements between foreign nations which force additional exports onto our market, the real question is this: Why does not the U.S. government invoke our right of retaliation?

In any event, there is a distinction in practice between violating the rules of GATT and invoking its provisions with respect to retaliation and compensation. Retaliation and compensation enter when the value of the concessions granted a party has been nullified or impaired by the illegal action taken. The GATT has not authorized retaliation nor called for compensation unless the action in question has had an adverse effect on the trade of the complaining country, since as a practical matter, it would be impossible to assess the amount of compensation or retaliation in the absence of trade effects. Only if the import quota has the effect of impairing the value of a tariff concession—if the trade flows involved were adversely affected—would there be a basis for a material grievance.

Since what is contemplated by the legislation is the negotiation of agreements under which some growth in imports would be allowed, if growth occurs in the U.S. market, the U.S. government would have a strong basis, both in GATT law and practice, to defend against any action by the contracting parties calling for compensation and retaliation.

A major retaliation threat often cited as an example of the horrors which lie ahead is that Japan will reduce or eliminate her very large purchases of U.S. soybeans and raw cotton. Yet the truth is that Japan buys our soybeans because she needs them vitally, as the *Progressive Farmer* (May 1971) pointed out in a brilliant editorial in a recent issue. Japan is already buying most of mainland China's soybean exports and except for the United States, there are no major sources in the world.

In 1969 world soybean exports totaled 342 million bushels, of which the United States supplied 311 and China 18.

We have seen our exports of raw cotton to Japan decline steadily during the past ten years—the very years when we experienced such a phenomenal rise in textile imports from Japan. On the other hand, Mexico, which rigidly controls textile imports, sold Japan more raw cotton last season than did the United States.

ECONOMIST NUMBER 4,391. Opponents of the legislation also argue from authority, pointing out that "4,390 economists" signed a statement opposing import controls and comparing this statement to a petition addressed to Congress by economists in 1930 opposing the Smoot-Hawley Tariff Act of that year. A fuller description of the affair of the 4,390 economists, however, would note that the statement was circulated for signature by the Committee for a National Trade Policy, a reputable, long-established, free trade lobbying outfit representing export interests and located on Connecticut Avenue in Washington; that the original endorsers included twenty well-known economists and two lawyers; and that the American Economic Association mailing list was used.

The American Economic Association has approximately 18,000 members and the only qualifications for membership are nomination by a member and payment of an annual fee which, at that time, was ten dollars. Were the remaining 14,000 economists the silent majority? Does their failure to sign the statement indicate that they favor textile quotas?

Perhaps not. Yet, how much more professional a survey of opinion the Committee for a National Trade Policy could have given us had they but provided the addressees an alternate statement favoring quotas, as well as the one circulated. Furthermore, to compare the House-passed Trade Bill of 1970 with the Smoot-Hawley Tariff Act of 1930 requires a peculiar arithmetic. The 1970 bill authorized 20 percent tariff *reductions* of present low rates, while the 1930 act increased already high rates substantially.

Nor do all economists view "the theory of comparative advantage" as being carved in tablets of stone. Of "comparative advantage," wrote Dr. John H. Williams, who served simultaneously as professor of economics at Harvard and as vice-president of the New York Federal Reserve Bank, "the premises are inaccurate in sufficient degree to raise serious question of the soundness of the theory, or at least of the range of its useful application to the trade of the world."[3] Professor Williams served as president of the American Economic Association in 1951.

The noted British economist, Joan Robinson of Cambridge University, writes: ". . . it is not true that no good national arguments can ever be found for protection. . . . The case for Free Trade as a benefit to each nation could not be [proven]." Mrs. Robinson also records, with proper quotations from their works, how those giants of economic theory, Alfred Marshall and Lord Keynes, recognized that free trade theory was peculiarly fitted to the unique circumstances of pre-World War I Britain in which the theory was developed, while Keynes later completely repudiated the theory in the depression of the 1930s. Yet, we are told by the "4,390 economists," through the agency of the Committee for a National Trade Policy, that high tariffs caused the depression.[4]

Where the United States does have an apparent comparative advantage over other producers, a closer look often reveals that the advantage was not derived commercially. American jet passenger planes dominate the skies of the world. Yet our jet technology was developed by Defense Department expenditures for bombers—wholly unrelated to commercial costing.

Our science industry grew large on defense and NASA funding. Surely putting a Polaris submarine down into the ocean or an astronaut up onto the moon has nothing to do with free trade allocation of resources through a competitive pricing system.

A COMMON CONCERN. American agriculture and the textile industry have a strong common interest in establishing and maintaining reasonable restraints on competitive imports produced abroad under cost structures which would be illegal in this country. The raw cotton producers and the raw wool producers, through their organizations, including the National Cotton Council and the National Wool Growers Association, strongly support the pending textile quota legislation, for example.

Agricultural interests can readily appreciate the devastating impact of imports which, in the case of textiles, already amount to 15 percent of U.S. consumption when it has been found necessary to set import quotas for cotton, wheat, and dairy products at around 1 percent of domestic production.

The only real solution to the textile import problem is a system of import quotas negotiated under authority similar to that contained in the Trade Bill passed by the House of Representatives in November 1970, and in the pending HR 20. Such a solution has GATT precedent and need not injure American export industries.

On the contrary, a firm and reasoned U.S. stance on textiles would restore American credibility in the international trade arena—and it is an arena. Such restoration of credibility is the necessary first step in securing proper access for U.S. agricultural and other exports to the highly protected markets of Japan and Europe.

NOTES

1. U.S. Congress, Senate, Subcommittee on International Trade of the Committee on Finance, *Hearing on Foreign Trade,* 92nd Cong., 1st sess., May 20, 1971, pp. 426–49.

2. *New York Times,* March 12, 1971, p. 1.

3. John H. Williams, "The Theory of International Trade Reconsidered," in *Readings in the Theory of International Trade,* American Economic Association (Philadelphia: Blakiston, 1950), p. 255.

4. Joan Robinson, *Economic Philosophy* (New York: Doubleday, 1964), pp. 64, 67, 68.

11

Regional Effects of Alternative Trade Policies

Leo V. Mayer

T RADE in agricultural commodities now employs one of every eight agricultural workers in the United States, requires production inputs of between five and eight billion dollars annually, and uses one-fifth of our cropland resources for the benefit of consumers located halfway around the globe. The importance of agricultural trade provides a background setting from which we may view the many forces attempting to bring about a reversal of the downtrend in tariff levels—a downtrend which has proceeded since well before World War II. If allowed to gain the upper hand, these forces could bring about economic reactions throughout the U.S. economy and undoubtedly would provoke considerable reaction and retaliation throughout the international community.

We must keep this latter entity in mind as we review and attempt to revise the barriers to international trade. No nation stands alone on a planet that can now be circled by man in sixty minutes. If we can act together for the welfare of the few men so circling the planet, can we not act together to plan and conduct our trade affairs on earth for the good of the millions so located? Indeed, while we proceed toward greater cooperation in space, we retrogress toward less resource mobility and greater restrictions on trade in our economic affairs on earth. It may seem trite to repeat what two other authors recently pointed out regarding trade, "If goods don't flow, soldiers often do."[1] The long histories of both war and trade make such a reminder useful, especially now when the United States is already attempting to extricate itself from one calamitous war.

We need no new international actions to further antagonize or raise world tensions and reactions. Instead, we need a period of peace,

LEO V. MAYER is Associate Professor of Economics, Iowa State University.

prosperity, and harmony so the world can adjust to the vast onslaught of new technology which has appeared over the last two decades. That adjustment brings economic pain to many and causes demands for actions to restrict competitive flows of goods and resources. But restrictions only postpone the ultimate adjustment process, as evaluation of the relationships between U.S. farm price support programs and the trend toward fewer farm producers clearly show.

A positive farm program of facilitating resource adjustments to new technology in the 1940s and 1950s would have done more to relieve the economic burden on small, inefficient farm producers than did high, rigid price supports (which incidentally included the use of high tariffs to shut out farm goods from other countries). The small farmer gained little from this policy and ultimately was forced to find other employment with no transfer payments, retraining programs, relocation assistance, or even mustering-out pay. Indeed the benefits went to large, well-financed farmers who, with new technology, could take over and turn the small operation into a profitable enterprise. The potential for repeating the same kind of price support programs through tariff barriers for other sectors of the economy is very real, since a large number of the power points in Congress are still occupied by the same legislators.

LESSONS OF HISTORY ON TRADE RESTRICTIONS. The United States needs, *now*, energetic leadership to explain to the populace where the trends of technology are taking this nation. We need leadership to provide for the populace a telescopic rather than a microscopic view of the aims and goals of the nation. That telescope should reach far enough into the future to provide the population with an idea of the long-range goals and aims of the nation—that is, what it can achieve over the next decade. This kind of focus gives a nation's people hope for the future. Russia, for example, provided an effective set of goals by building so-called economic displays of top quality consumer goods and suggesting to its people, "Work hard and each home will have its quota of these goods within a decade."

This nation also needs a telescopic view of the record of the past. The people in the United States tend to be now-oriented with little appreciation of the past, particularly the mistakes of the past. But the record of history can provide us with substantial guidance for future national policy. In the instance of trade, we need only go back to the 1920s and 1930s—in terms of history, a very short time ago—to find economic pressures similar to those existing in the nation today. The years immediately following World War I saw a slump in demand for a number of goods as the United States attempted to shift from a wartime to a peacetime economy. As European recovery proceeded, many sectors experienced a rise in competition for the consumer's dollar. Imports of watches from Switzerland, lace from France, cork from Spain, olive oil from Italy, and foodstuffs from Canada all brought pressure group activity to raise trade barriers. This pressure, combined with the catastrophic decline in business as the Great Depression began, resulted in passage of the Hawley-Smoot Tariff Act in June 1930.

Discussions on the Hawley-Smoot legislation had proceeded for nearly two years, well before the business slump of October 1929. In fact, the Hawley-Smoot act was not the first tariff act enacted after World War I. The American Tariff Act of 1922 has represented the initial response to the downturn in business after World War I. But the 1922 tariff act had come at the time when economic activity abroad was expanding, as was purchasing power in the United States. As a result other nations did not feel any sizable cutback in their exports to the United States. Consequently the response of other nations to the 1922 tariff act was mild and there was little retaliation.

But the tariff act of 1930 came in a different setting, one in which other nations were experiencing severe strains in their balance of payments. The response to the Hawley-Smoot Tariff Act was immediate and severe. It took several forms: "Indignation of the violation of the equality-of-treatment principle, a general popular demand for retaliation and for cancellation of most-favored-nation treaties with the United States, actual measures of retaliation, new concepts of international responsibility, new practices in commercial relations based upon strict reciprocity—and a growing disrespect of the most favored nation clause."[2]

As nation after nation felt the "open door" policy slam shut, the response was to retaliate against U.S. imports. Spain, for example, cut back imports of U.S. automobiles between 1929 and 1930 from $10.3 million to $334,000 and tripled her imports from Germany. Spain similarly retaliated in 1931 by raising the import duty on Ford automobiles from $350 to $815 per car. Exports of U.S. automobiles to Spain dropped 87 percent between 1930 and 1931. Only 595 American automobiles were sold to Spain in the latter year. By contrast, total registrations of automobiles dropped only 30 percent. The Spanish response to Hawley-Smoot was to shift from importing U.S. automobiles to importing other makes with which tariff negotiations could be reciprocal.

But automobile manufacturers were not alone in feeling the effect as trade doors closed abroad. Between 1929 and 1932, Italian imports of wheat from the United States were cut in half, from 419,000 tons to 198,000 tons; imports of gasoline were reduced to one-fourth their previous level and many other items declined significantly. The effect on American agriculture, which even then faced an inelastic demand for its products, was near-chaos. Low prices led to low incomes; low incomes led to overdue credit accounts; farm foreclosures became common; and in Iowa the "Farmer's Holiday" nearly ended the public (and private) life of many local officials charged with implementing laws society had set up in better times.

These officials bore the brunt of a populous revolt just as today's public officials must face a public complaining of past decisions with which it had little vote and less influence. Indeed, the configuration of similarities between present-day economic conditions and decision making on trade barriers, and that of the 1930s is somewhat alarming. The placing of sharp restrictions on imports and the retaliation which is sure to follow will affect many groups in the United States including ". . . three largely unrepresented and unorganized bodies in the American population—American importing interests, American exporting interests, and the great and unorganized body of American consumers."[3]

PRESENT-DAY INTERDEPENDENCE OF IMPORTS AND EXPORTS. Interrelationships between imports and exports have already been explained in substantial detail by Seevers and Keeton (Chap. 7). My interest is considerably narrower than was that presentation. My objective is to relate the origin of major import items which have raised the ire of present-day competitors in the United States to the destination of two important farm export items, namely corn and soybeans. The import items are textiles, iron and steel, and footwear. The values of these imports and their origins are shown in Table 11.1 by major regions and countries of the world.

Four major areas provide most of the textile imports: the European Economic Community (EEC) countries, the European Free Trade Association (EFTA) countries, Japan, and other Asian countries (including India, Pakistan, Hong Kong, Korea, etc.). For iron and steel, three of these areas again are major suppliers—EEC, EFTA, and Japan. For footwear, all four areas again appear as a major source of imports although other Western European countries (including Ireland, Greece, Turkey, Finland, and Yugoslavia) also provide a significant share. Altogether, Western Europe (EEC, EFTA, and other countries), Japan, and other Asian countries are the major sources for these three categories of imported products.

But the importance of these imports in international trade is demonstrated more clearly in Table 11.2 where the regional destination of two major U.S. agricultural export dollar-earners is given. The EEC countries received 42.8 percent of corn exported in 1968 with 33.4 percent of soybeans going to the same destination. The EFTA countries received 12.0 and 8.4 percent of these respective commodities. Other Western European countries also received a sizable share but Japan, the same nation which shipped 28.0 percent of textiles and 39.7 percent of iron and steel to the United States in 1968, purchased 19.7 percent of U.S. corn exports and 26.9 percent of our soybeans. Truly, the reciprocal nature of international trade is shown clearly in these data. If one

TABLE 11.1. Origin, Value, and Share of Total Textiles, Iron and Steel, and Footwear, Provided by Specified Areas, Calendar Year 1968

Exporting Country or Region	Textiles		Iron and Steel		Footwear	
	Value	Share of value	Value	Share of value	Value	Share of value
	($ thousand)	(%)	($ thousand)	(%)	($ thousand)	(%)
Canada	21,703	3.2	212,189	10.4	6,580	1.7
Latin American republics	34,287	3.6	47,861	2.3	5,688	1.5
EEC	194,257	20.2	708,901	34.6	177,191	45.7
EFTA	103,322	10.7	209,218	10.2	27,810	7.2
Other W. Europe	26,113	2.7	8,880	0.5	50,163	12.9
Eastern Europe	7,633	0.8	11,684	0.6	5,220	1.3
Mideast and Africa	25,984	2.7	25,652	1.3	370	0.1
Japan	269,737	28.0	813,068	39.7	80,009	20.6
Other Asia	278,090	28.9	4,924	0.2	33,976	8.7
Other countries	1,424	0.2	4,050	0.2	1,083	0.3
Total imports	962,551	100.0	2,046,427	100.0	388,135	100.0

SOURCE: United Nations, *Commodity Trade Statistics*, 1968, Statistical Papers, series D, vol. 18, no. 1–23, pp. 5984–6248.

TABLE 11.2. Destination, Quantity, and Share Received of Total Corn and Soybeans Exported from the United States, Calendar Year 1968

Importing Country or Region	Corn			Soybeans		
	Quantity (thousand metric tons)	Value ($ thousand)	Share of value (%)	Quantity (thousand metric tons)	Value ($ thousand)	Share of value (%)
Canada	1,441	66,525	9.0	790	7,735	9.6
Latin American republics	303	16,596	2.3	54	5,774	0.7
EEC	6,423	314,533	42.8	2,702	271,736	33.4
EFTA	1,865	87,639	12.0	675	67,963	8.4
Other W. Europe	863	43,690	6.0	919	93,698	11.6
Eastern Europe	789	38,120	5.2	60	5,997	0.8
Mideast and Africa	175	8,600	1.2	263	27,274	3.4
Japan	2,861	144,804	19.7	2,134	218,005	26.9
Other Asia	158	8,475	1.1	414	42,231	5.2
Other countries	100	5,260	0.7	...	...	...
Total exports	14,959	734,304	100.0	8,022	810,043	100.0

SOURCE: United Nations, *Commodity Trade Statistics*, 1968, Papers, series D, volume 18, no. 1–23, pp. 5981–6248.

171

were to analyze the exports of U.S. wheat, the Asian share of farm exports would increase sizably, again indicating further the importance of imports if we are to export our farm commodities.

REGIONAL IMPORTANCE OF FARM EXPORTS. While agricultural exports are of substantial importance at the national level, their economic importance to certain nonmetropolitan regions of the United States is even greater. For it is in the nonmetropolitan regions of the United States that their influence is heaviest. In these areas, large numbers of farm workers are employed solely for production for the export market. The Corn Belt, for example, provides over one-quarter of total farm exports, exports that are strategic in maintaining employment in farming, in agribusinesses, and in local service industries. In the Plains States farm exports provide a sizable part of the total region's exports, exports which are necessary if the population is to import cars from Detroit, tractors from Moline, and Rice Krispies from Battle Creek. It is sometimes said that Kansas exports two products—wheat and Boeing aircraft—and at the moment wheat is the more certain. Together, the Great Plains and the Corn Belt produce and ship over 50 percent of U.S. farm exports (Table 11.3). With farm exports averaging over $6

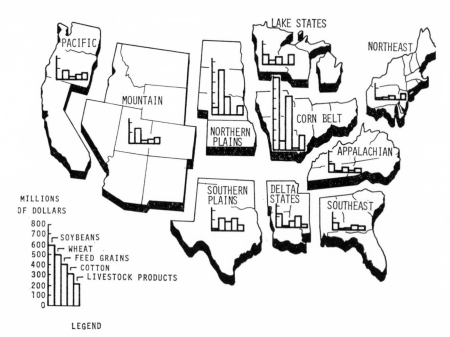

Fig. 11.1. Regional export shares for major crop and livestock products.

Regional Effects of Alternative Trade Policies 173

TABLE 11.3. Regional Shares of Total Agricultural Exports, Selected Years, 1954–70*

| Region | Regional Shares of Total Farm Exports | | | | |
	1954	1960	1966	1968	1970
			(%)		
Northeast	4.5	4.5	4.2	3.5	2.7
Lake States	6.5	6.6	6.6	6.1	6.6
Corn Belt	17.6	20.8	28.1	25.8	28.4
Northern Plains	8.7	10.8	14.0	12.7	13.1
Appalachia	12.1	10.2	8.8	10.0	10.4
Southeast	9.1	7.2	5.9	6.4	6.2
Delta	10.6	8.8	6.8	9.3	9.2
Southern Plains	12.2	12.9	10.3	10.7	8.1
Mountain	6.4	6.4	5.6	5.6	4.7
Pacific	12.3	11.8	9.7	9.9	10.6
U.S. total	100.0	100.0	100.0	100.0	100.0

SOURCE: Data on exports are taken from Isaac E. Lemon and Louise Perkins, "U.S. Agricultural Export Shares by Regions and States, Fiscal Year 1970," *Foreign Agricultural Trade of the United States*, pp. 23–25, October 1970.
* Year ending June 30.

billion annually, the effect on the rural economy of these regions is sizable.

But even in other regions farmers and the rural community have an important stake in maintaining the level of total farm exports. If we look at the share of farm production which is exported by region, the importance of trade for the Delta and Appalachian regions becomes evident. Over one-fourth of the Delta's farm products is now produced for the export market, and 19.0 percent of the Appalachian region's farm products move into international markets (Table 11.4).

TABLE 11.4. Proportion of Regional Exports to Regional Cash Receipts, Selected Years, 1954–70*

| Region | Exports Share of Farm Cash Receipts | | | | |
	1954	1960	1966	1968	1970
			(%)		
Northeast	4.2	6.7	8.3	6.4	7.9
Lake States	6.5	6.6	6.6	6.1	6.6
Corn Belt	6.8	12.5	20.2	15.7	17.6
Northern Plains	8.2	13.1	22.9	16.2	16.1
Appalachia	13.8	17.5	18.4	18.8	19.0
Southeast	13.4	13.4	12.8	12.0	11.3
Delta	18.9	22.5	19.9	23.4	25.1
Southern Plains	14.5	19.7	20.9	19.2	13.9
Mountain	8.7	11.2	12.9	10.9	8.3
Pacific	10.0	12.9	13.2	11.0	12.4
U.S. Total	100.0	100.0	100.0	100.0	100.0

SOURCE: Data on exports are taken from Isaac E. Lemon and Louise Perkins, "U.S. Agricultural Export Shares by Regions and States, Fiscal Year 1970," *Foreign Agricultural Trade of the United States*, pp. 23–35, October 1970.
* Year ending June 30.

In these regions, it is not an average of one in eight farm workers producing for export, but rather one in four or five. These same regions have undergone a technological revolution in farming over the last two decades, a revolution in which capital inputs have replaced huge amounts of labor. The migration of this labor into the expanding industrial communities of Little Rock, Indianapolis, St. Louis, and the metropolises of Chicago and New York attests to the interrelated nature of our advanced economy. A rapid decrease in our level of farm exports would encourage and speed the removal of labor from the agricultural sectors of these regions.

Whereas in the past some offsetting expansion of employment in capital-supplying agribusiness sectors existed as farm labor was replaced, a cutback in export production would also reduce demand for the inputs of agribusiness firms. The reverberations from this kind of multiplier effect would flow throughout these regions, upsetting families, businesses, and political plans. Indeed the political trends in rural regions in 1970 already indicated a dissatisfaction with farm prices and incomes. But that dissatisfaction would be expanded and intensified under a cutback in agricultural exports.

IMPORTANCE OF PARTICULAR FARM PRODUCTS TO PARTICULAR REGIONS. As was pointed out earlier in the conference, certain farm products provide a large part of the total value of farm exports. These farm products are produced in areas where available natural resources, climatic factors, and opportunity cost facilitate their production. This set of conditions causes some regions to gain more from expansion in farm exports, or to lose more, under policies that retard trade. As Figure 1 indicates, the Corn Belt provided over $700 million dollars of soybeans for the export markets in 1969–70. This same region also provided over $500 million of feed grains for shipment in 1969–70.

For the Plains States, the production of wheat depends significantly upon an export market. The expansion of markets abroad as in 1965–66 can bring about a large increase in acreage and production. In the Northern Plains the export of wheat annually provides nearly $550 million in dollar earnings. While a large part of these earnings comes from government subsidized sales, nevertheless the economic effect on the region is the same. Without any government shipments farm income would be lowered, outmigration would be speeded, business declines would be more rapid, and the general economic tenor of the area would be muted. As we have shown elsewhere,[4] the transformation of marginal areas of cropland in this region to its next productive use, grassland, could cut the number of viable towns in half, the number of farms by three-fourths, and reduce business transactions to one-half their previous level. These kinds of changes are posed by policies which retard the flow of trade between the United States and other countries of the world.

EFFECTS OF REDUCED EXPORTS ON REGIONAL CROP ACREAGES. To further demonstrate the importance of exports to farm production and to measure the effects that a cutback in agricultural exports would have on various regions, we completed a parametric programming analysis of regional crop acreages associated with varying levels of exports. The analysis projects to 1975 and focuses on exports of two major commodities—feed grains and oil meals. Exports of these two commodities were varied simultaneously to measure the effect on corn and soybean acreages and production.

The model used included production and demand parameters for the major crops—wheat, corn, other feed grains, soybeans, and cotton— and allowed for transportation of these commodities between major feed-consuming areas of the United States. Export demand for feed grains and oil meals was specified at ocean ports where these commodities have been shipped abroad in the past. As export demand is reduced in the analysis, demand at these points of outshipment is reduced. The associated decrease in acreage may be located within any producing area in the United States, however, since transportation of each commodity is provided between all major producing areas and all major feed-consuming areas. Because we are primarily interested in corn and soybean acreages, regional results are provided for these crops; only national acreages of other crops are reported.

Total corn acreages could rise slightly by 1975 if the probable level of domestic and export demand is forthcoming. With domestic demand for feed grain estimated for a population of 217.5 million persons with a per capita income of $3,000, exports of 25 million tons of feed grains in 1975 are projected to require 58.6 million acres of corn for grain (Table 11.5).

This level of exports is slightly above 1969–70 levels but represents a level consistent with a recent analysis of trends in world demand for feed grains.[5] The programmed acreages show considerable consistency with 1965 and 1970 regional acreages. The Corn Belt remains the major producer with 29.2 million acres compared to 30.9 million acres in 1970. However, should the new "set aside" farm program result in a sharp reduction in individual farm conserving bases in the Corn Belt, an effect not taken into account here, the acreages of corn in the Corn Belt could be larger.

As we move from export level I to possible alternative levels which might result with increased trade barriers, the acreage of corn declines as expected. At level II, with feed grain exports of 20 million tons, total corn acreages decline to 56.0 million acres. This decline continues at each successive export reduction until level VI is reached; feed grain exports are then zero. With exports eliminated, total corn acreage is reduced to 45.3 million acres, a 13.3-million-acre reduction due to the decline in exports. As total corn acreage is reduced, not all regions are affected the same. Corn acreages in the Corn Belt and Northern Plains

TABLE 11.5. Estimated Acreages of Corn for Alternative Levels of Feed Grain Exports in 1975, by Regions of the United States, Assuming Government Programs of Land Diversion are Continued

Region	Actual Acreages		Projected Acreages with Export Level of*					
			Probable level in 1975	Possible levels if U.S. restricts imports of textiles, iron and steel, footwear, or other major import items				
	1965	1970	I	II	III	IV	V	VI
	(thousand acres)							
United States	55,332	57,359	58,632	55,965	52,392	48,987	47,623	45,289
Northeast	1,759	1,956	1,580	1,580	1,580	1,580	1,580	1,580
Lake States	7,367	7,832	8,603	8,622	8,229	8,229	7,500	7,507
Corn Belt	30,406	30,934	29,157	28,771	28,264	25,857	25,589	25,429
Northern Plains	7,172	8,808	8,792	6,805	5,104	4,478	4,478	3,100
Appalachia	3,709	3,412	4,254	3,941	3,868	3,765	3,765	3,733
Southeast	3,045	2,695	3,135	3,135	2,930	2,888	2,546	1,775
Delta States	788	440	1,652	1,652	1,652	1,425	1,425	1,425
Southern Plains	639	592	692	692	656	656	631	631
Mountain	267	424	109	109	63	63	63	63
Pacific	180	266	658	658	46	46	46	46
* Export levels selected were								
Feed grains (mil tons)			25	20	15	10	5	0
Soybeans (mil bu)			640	565	490	415	340	260
Wheat (mil bu)			750	750	750	750	750	750

decline nearly four million acres each. These two regions would suffer two-thirds of the reduction in acreage associated with a sharp reduction in feed grain exports. Other regions are each affected somewhat, including the Southeast which reduces corn production by over a million acres, but the major effect would fall on two regions, the Corn Belt and the Northern Plains.

Of the major farm commodities exported in 1969–70, the value of feed grains exports was exceeded only by one other major commodity, soybeans. For 1969–70, feed grain exports totaled $995.3 million and soybeans $1,069.0 million and together these commodities accounted for nearly one-third of the $6,643.3 million of total agricultural exports.[6] Both corn and soybeans face similar kinds of markets abroad. Each is shipped into markets where competitive conditions largely determine their acceptance. While there is some government subsidy of each commodity, the major portion of these exports move under commercial export conditions. Thus, under a policy of greater trade barriers for major import items from Japan and EEC countries, their purchases of soybeans from the United States would likely be cut back. It is likely that U.S. soybean exports might drop along with corn exports but perhaps not as significantly.

In Table 11.6, acreages of soybeans are reported from the parametric

TABLE 11.6. Estimated Acreages of Soybeans for Alternative Levels of Oilmeal Exports in 1975, by Regions of the United States, Assuming Government Programs of Land Diversion Are Continued

	Actual Acreages		Projected Acreages with Export Level*					
			Probable level in 1975	Possible levels if U.S. restricts imports of textiles, iron and steel, footwear, or other major import items				
Region	1965	1970	I	II	III	IV	V	VI
			(thousand acres)					
United States	34,449	42,447	41,190	37,808	34,948	32,129	29,289	26,562
Northeast	397	459	335	335	335	335	335	7
Lake States	3,766	3,806	3,843	3,830	3,506	2,634	1,662	1,335
Corn Belt	18,837	21,942	20,551	19,524	18,460	18,164	17,514	16,894
Northern Plains	2,113	2,248	2,980	2,444	1,776	1,476	1,068	864
Appalachia	2,148	3,002	1,220	1,044	1,044	1,044	943	923
Southeast	1,321	2,318	3,352	2,222	1,918	1,497	1,497	1,032
Delta States	5,633	8,337	8,132	7,632	7,132	6,687	6,186	5,064
Southern Plains	234	335	777	777	777	292	84	43
* Export levels selected were								
Feed grains (mil tons)			25	20	15	10	5	0
Soybeans (mil bu)			640	565	490	415	340	260
Wheat (mil bu)			750	750	750	750	750	750

programming analysis assuming that exports decline by specified quantities. Level I again represents an estimate of potential exports of soybeans if recent upward trends continue. Under this situation, soybean exports may total 640 million bushels in 1975. This level of exports combined with domestic demand for a larger population with higher per capita incomes would require 41.2 million acres of soybeans. As at present, the Corn Belt would be the major producer with slightly less acreage than actual 1970 acreage. The Southeast indicates some further increase in acreage as does the Northern Plains.

As we shift to the potential levels of oil meal exports which might occur with trade restrictions, acreages of soybeans decline rather sharply even though the assumed rate of export decrease is less for oil meals than it was for feed grains. Lower yields per acre and the fact that such a large proportion of soybeans is exported cause a small reduction in oil meal exports to rapidly reduce soybean acreage. Cutting soybean exports by 60 percent—from 640 to 260 million bushels—reduces acreage by 14.6 million acres.

Three regions feel most of the reduction—the Lake States, the Southeast, and the Northern Plains. But the Corn Belt would also feel a decline which in terms of total acreage exceeds any other region. Total acreage of soybeans would drop from 20.6 million acres to 16.9 million acres. When added to the nearly 4.0-million-acre drop in corn acreage, a reduction in exports of this magnitude would cause the Corn Belt to suffer a significant drop in economic activity in agriculture.

TABLE 11.7. Programmed Price Levels, Projected 1975 Crop Yields, Acres of Land Retirement, and Acres of Other Crops under Alternative Levels of Corn and Soybean Exports

Variable	Actual		Projected 1975 Export Levels*					
	1965	1970	I	II	III	IV	V	VI
	($ per bu)							
Programmed prices								
Corn	1.16	1.36	1.14	1.09	1.05	1.00	0.98	0.96
Soybeans	2.54	2.84	2.14	2.02	1.90	1.78	1.68	1.60
Wheat	1.35	1.34	1.42	1.39	1.31	1.24	1.21	1.19
	(bu per acre)							
Projected crop yields								
Corn	73.8	71.7	88.3	88.7	89.4	89.7	90.3	90.4
Soybeans	24.5	26.8	30.0	30.2	30.5	30.8	31.2	31.7
Wheat	26.5	31.1	32.7	33.8	35.7	35.9	36.3	35.9
	(mil acres)							
Estimated land retirement								
Feed grains	34.8	39.5	34.4	39.4	45.4	48.7	55.2	58.4
Total	57.4	59.7	57.5	63.0	69.7	73.4	80.6	84.2
	(mil acres)							
Other land use								
Wheat	49.6	44.3	45.9	44.3	42.3	42.8	41.9	43.6
Other feed grains	40.7	42.0	34.7	36.1	38.2	38.2	37.7	38.1

* Export levels selected were

Feed gains (mil tons)			25	20	15	10	5	0
Soybeans (mil bu)			640	565	490	415	340	260
Wheat (mil bu)			750	750	750	750	750	750

Fertilizer salesmen, machine dealers, local elevators, the transportation sector, and farm workers would all feel a sharp decline in the demand for their products and services.

A reduction in corn and soybean acreage would not be the only effect of lowered exports. Prices of corn, soybeans, and wheat would decline without a very large increase in land retirement. Even with a 50 percent increase in total acres retired, the corn price was found to decline below a dollar per bushel (Table 11.7).

Of course, these are equilibrium prices derived from a model which assumes instantaneous adjustment in resources, production, and prices. In the real world, the process would be considerably less rapid and involve a succession of production periods in which total output exceeded demand with either sharply depressed price levels or rapidly expanding carry-over stocks. Either possibility would pose a sharp reduction in crop acreage. A rise in carry-over stocks would cause the government to increase the size of land retirement programs to hold down the cost of storage programs. Sharply lower prices for farm commodities would mean that farm operators with high per unit production costs and/or weak capital positions would find it necessary to terminate their farm enterprise. Eventually this process would result in a reduction in crop acreage although the time dimension is considerably longer if we depend on the market mechanism.

The programming analysis provided information of two other facets of the farm economy. One is the effect of acreage cutbacks on crop yields and the other is the crossover effect on other crops of a reduction in demand for particular commodities. As export demand for feed grains and oil meals was reduced, yields of both corn and soybeans rose as production was concentrated in regions with higher yields and lower costs per unit of production. Also, the reduction in demand for feed grains had the effect of cutting back on the use of feed wheat which then caused a reduction in total acreage of wheat, from 45.9 million to 43.6 million. Wheat yields also rose as land in some higher moisture areas was released from corn and soybean production and was shifted into wheat production. These kinds of shifts point up the interrelated nature of the farm economy. Even though wheat exports, with their large level of subsidy, might not be directly affected by raised trade barriers, the crossover effect from changes in other crops could cause considerable economic hardships for wheat growers.

REGIONAL EXPORT SHARES AND PROGRAMMED CHANGES IN EXPORTS. The above analysis indicates that the effect of cutbacks in farm exports would be of two types: one would be a reduction in farm price levels and all producers would experience lowered cash receipts from this effect; a second would be concentrated in regions where major cutbacks in acreage would be necessary. In these regions the combination effect of lowered prices and fewer acres in production would mean a reduction in economic activity similar to the areas hit hardest by the Soil Bank program of the 1950s. That particular program retired large acreages of marginal land, and when combined with low farm exports, caused the agribusiness sectors in rural communities to suffer lowered sales and incomes. The outcries of Main Street agribusiness firms were heard all the way to Washington where the Soil Bank program was terminated after only three years of operation.

A similar situation could easily occur with a significant reduction in present levels of farm exports. The tendency for major reductions in acreage to occur in particular regions means the economic effects would be concentrated in these locations. In these rural communities reduced business transactions would mean an increased rate of structural adjustment. One such region is the Northern Plains, where a reduction in feed grain exports would hit particularly hard.

As shown in Table 11.8 the Northern Plains provided 13.9 percent of feed grain exports in 1969–70, but under a cutback in exports as examined in the programming analysis, total feed grain acreage would drop 14.6 percent and total production by 32.1 percent. The latter change is due mostly to a shift from corn production to lower-cost barley production. Acreages in the Southern Plains and Corn Belt would decline too, but production would drop less due to the tendency for less productive acres to go out of production first.

Reductions in soybean exports would similarly hit the Great Plains areas hard. The Northern Plains would suffer a loss of nearly three-fourths of its acreage and production would decline by over one-half. The Southern Plains, while presently exporting only an estimated one-half of its crop of soybeans, would have acreages of soybeans nearly eliminated as competing regions took over the market. Similarly the Lake States represent an area where a cutback in exports could force a sharp reduction in acreages.

Under the alternative of price supports and storage programs these regions could perhaps postpone the sharp reduction in corn and soybean acreages much the same as cotton acreage has been held in the Southeast by legislative fiat. But just as cotton has lost a large part of its market by high and rigid price supports and ultimately is transferring acreage to more productive and lower per unit cost areas of the Southwest, so would corn and soybeans ultimately tend to concentrate in more efficient production areas. This tendency would spell some sharp economic downturns for areas with large marginal acreages—areas with per unit cost of production near present levels of corn and soybean prices. A cutback in demand for these commodities could mean lower prices, less production, and lowered farm incomes.

A POSITIVE APPROACH TO IMPORT COMPETITION. The above analysis has argued that any attempts to sharply limit imports into the United States might bring a sharp reduction in farm exports. If true, it can be demonstrated that the agricultural sector would be economically depressed by such an outcome unless government farm programs are greatly expanded. The present capacity of grain-producing subsectors is large relative to domestic demands for agricultural commodities. Even with considerable increases in export levels over the last decade, there has been a continual need to hold nearly one-sixth of our cropland resources out of production. Any reduction in aggregate demand would start with a supply capacity which is already held down by land retirement programs. Any reduction in demand has the potential to depress farm prices and incomes. Thus international policies that could provoke retaliation among countries which import our farm products should be closely examined, with particular emphasis on their potential effects on our farm exports.

In the process of considering the levels of tariffs to be established, the national leadership must look not only at the immediate future but rather toward the more distant goals and objectives of a world interdependent upon each other for their very survival. Perhaps it is worth noting what another analyst wrote in the early 1930s—that there is always an ongoing battle in the United States over trade barriers. The participants, ". . . fall into two classes—one group interested in higher tariff generally or upon specific products, and the other group interested in either the maintenance of the status quo or in lower tariffs generally or upon specific products. The government in power at any given moment represents . . . the temporary compromise between these forces."[7]

During the last forty years in the United States the battle over tariff legislation has been one of continuous ebb and flow. The debacle of the 1930 Hawley-Smoot act was sufficient to place freer-trade forces in the forefront after 1934. This group held the upper hand through World War II and the period immediately thereafter. But as European recovery proceeded after 1950, forces favoring higher tariffs and other nontariff trade restrictions began to slowly regain their former positions of influence. By 1962, a current historian could suggest that, "Although the record is mixed, close observers are substantially agreed that over the last ten years there has been a distinct erosion of American trade policy. Legal restrictions on the President's power to reduce tariffs, political obstacles to the full use of the power he had, and positive action to impose new import restrictions have all contributed to this process."[8]

The power to affect trade barriers, however, was once again shifted when the Kennedy administration came into power in 1961. As with the increasing influence of trade restriction forces in the Eisenhower era of the 1950s, the forces favoring freer trade began an ascendency after 1960. By 1962, the new Kennedy administration was able to pass legislation to expand trade through reductions in trade barriers. This legislation, known as the Trade Expansion Act of 1962, brought forth a new approach to offsetting the negative effects of larger imports. As described in the *Department of State Bulletin* in 1962, the new act,

. . . accepts the premise that action in the national interest to reduce trade barriers entails a national responsibility to assist those who may be adversely affected. It does not expect individual groups to bear the burden of a policy felt to be in the interest of the nation as a whole. It seeks, however, to meet this burden in a positive rather than a negative way, consistent with a dynamic rather than static economy. It seeks to facilitate their adjustment to other fields where they can be competitive. In these ways it attempts to provide for a more efficient use of our resources, for a higher level of national growth, and, in the last analysis, for a better livelihood for our people.[9]

The concepts embodied in the 1962 act provide a broad set of alternative ways to approach trade problems. The act allows for negotiations for orderly marketing agreements to limit imports, and government assistance to firms or groups of workers who are negatively affected by larger imports. The act represents a major step toward

TABLE 11.8. Percentage Changes in Corn and Soybean Acreages by Regions Compared to Regional Shares of Corn and Soybean Exports in 1967–70

Region	Feed Grains			Soybeans		
	Share of total production exported in 1969–70*	Change in regional average—level I–VI	Change in regional production—level I–VI	Share of total production exported in 1969–70*	Change in regional acreage—level I–VI	Change in regional production—level I–VI
				(%)		
United States	14.7	−15.8	−14.6	49.3	−35.5	−31.6
Northeast	12.8	0	0	46.8	−97.1	−98.0
Lake States	9.5	−5.7	−7.8	47.4	−65.3	−55.7
Corn Belt	16.7	−15.3	−11.5	45.7	−17.8	−15.5
Northern Plains	13.9	−14.6	−32.1	49.9	−71.0	−57.4
Appalachia	12.9	−0.7	−0.5	47.1	−24.4	−13.0
Southeast	13.0	0	0	46.1	−69.2	−48.8
Delta States	6.6	−9.8	−9.5	45.2	−37.7	−27.0
Southern Plains	19.4	−16.9	−13.9	50.0	−94.5	−75.5
Mountain	9.8	0	0	...	...	...
Pacific	11.1	0	0	...	...	...

* SOURCE: Isaac E. Lemon and M. Louise Perkins, "U.S. Agricultural Exports Shares by Regions and States, Fiscal Year 1970," *Foreign Agricultural Trade of the United States*, October 1970.

development of a positive national policy to facilitate sectoral adjustment of labor and capital resources to the development of new technology abroad. As specified, the act provided some indication that the nation was past the point of attempting to maintain the status quo in production sectors at the same time that it encourages development of new technology through taxation and subsidy policies. It was a new philosophy of structural adjustment—one greatly needed in this nation where almost revolutionary change in technological innovation has become commonplace.

In summary, the concept of a positive policy of structural adjustment is the essence of what is needed for trade policy in the United States. Had we had a policy of facilitating adjustment in the agricultural sector over the last three decades, many of the problems still with us today could have been solved long ago. Similarly if trade policy legislation can be focused in this positive direction for the future rather than in a backward, negative pattern of the past, the nation will be far better off in 1980. Consumers will gain, taxpayers will gain, and the goodwill created in other countries may allow the world to be in one whole piece in the year 2000. These gains represent a positive, forward-looking set of national goals for the last third of the twentieth century.

NOTES

1. E. Howard Hill, "What Farmers Want to Know about Trade," and Joseph W. Barr, "National Economy and Trade," *Farm Prosperity—Imports and Exports* (Ames: Iowa State Univ. Press, 1965), pp. 7, 15.

2. Joseph M. Jones, Jr., *Tariff Retaliation: Repercussions of the Hawley-Smoot Bill* (Philadelphia: Univ. of Pennsylvania Press, 1934), pp. 18–19. Chapters one through three provide an excellent description of the vast and intense reaction of other nations to the Hawley-Smoot Act of 1930. Several of the data cited come from this source.

3. Ibid., p. 27.

4. Leo V. Mayer, Earl O. Heady, and Howard C. Madsen, "Farm Programs for the 1970s," *CAED Report No. 32* (Ames: Iowa State Univ., Center for Agricultural and Economic Development, November 1968), pp. 43–46.

5. Donald W. Regier and O. Halbert Goolsby, "Growth in World Demand for Feed Grains," *Foreign Agricultural Economic Report*, no. 63 (Washington, D.C.: USDA, ERS, July 1970).

6. Isaac E. Lemon and M. Louise Perkins, "U.S. Agricultural Export Shares by Regions and States, Fiscal Year 1970," *Foreign Agricultural Trade of the United States* (Washington, D.C.: USDA, ERS, October 1970).

7. Jones, p. 7.

8. William Diebold, Jr., "Trade Policies Since World War II," in *Foreign Agricultural Trade*, Robert L. Tontz, ed. (Ames: Iowa State Univ. Press, 1966), p. 35.

9. Leonard Weiss, "Trade Expansion Act of 1962," reprinted from the *Department of State Bulletin*, December 3, 1962, in Robert L. Tontz, ed., p. 42.

12

Contradictions in U.S. Trade Policy

Vernon L. Sorenson

ACCORDING to conventional wisdom the only consistent approach to trade policy is one that leads to elimination of all government intervention. Under a regime of "free trade" all production would move to areas of lowest cost and the world would in some sense be best off. But over time a wide range of theoretical arguments has risen to dispute this well-known logic of the classical economists and in general these theories lead to the call for a policy other than completely free trade.

One of these has been formalized in deriving conditions for optimal tariffs. This analysis demonstrates that under certain conditions individual countries can increase their gross national product by interfering with the free flow of trade. Another major deviation, or addition to the free trade doctrine, is imbedded in the infant industry argument. The objective is to accelerate the process of development by protection of industries where the basic conditions for efficient production exist, but where achieving comparative advantage would involve training workers, accumulating capital, and otherwise developing internally. Another important theoretical argument is that under certain circumstances free trade tends to reduce real income of labor, and a deviation from free trade can change income distribution in a desirable way.

The most devastating theoretical argument of all, however, is that any departure from the ideal conditions of perfect competition provides justification for interfering with the free flow of trade. These deviations take many forms and are built into most economies. Wage and price rigidities due to large-scale business organization and the existence of labor unions are of particular importance. Internal government policies that interfere with free price adjustments, the existence of externalities,

VERNON L. SORENSON is Professor, Agricultural Economics, Michigan State University.

underemployment, and a range of other conditions lead to what has become known as the theorem of second best. This theorem was originally developed as a part of international trade theory and has been summarized by Meade as follows:

> There are strong theoretical reasons why in many cases any tariff or trade control should not be removed so long as some other particular tariff or trade control or domestic duty or other divergence between marginal values and costs remain in operation. The maintenance of one particular divergence between marginal values and costs may help to offset the evil effects of another divergence. Welfare might be improved if both were removed; but if one is going to be kept it may be better that both should be kept.[1]

The overall result of this flow of theory is that we are left in something of an intellectual jungle when it comes to assessing trade policy on economic or welfare grounds. Economic theory leaves room for justification of almost any form of protection called for by individual groups and by governments. No common denominator is available to define what is an optimum set of objectives to be sought in trade policy nor what is right or wrong in terms of political action to implement trade policy. Despite this limitation, I think it is clear to most reasonable people that our house has not been in very good order with respect to trade and agricultural policy.

This disorder has its roots in divergent developments in domestic agricultural policy and international trade policy that began in the early 1930s. Each took on its own set of objectives and program dimensions. The new focus in trade policy was developed in the Reciprocal Trade Agreements legislation, and this was followed by the Trade Expansion Act of 1962.

The rationale for our liberal trade program has changed over time. The program "initially was fostered as an emergency recovery measure designed to restore or increase foreign markets for the export of American products, and particularly agricultural products."[2] During the war and postwar period the role of the program shifted to emphasizing the benefits that expanded trade would have in complementing economic recovery and in building an economic and political foundation against the threat of communism. This rationale remained in force until the mid-1950s when again the question of finding markets for U.S. products with a view toward sustained prosperity and improved balance of payments became important. In the postwar period the United States has provided leadership in undertaking six rounds of trade negotiations which have had a major effect on the level of trade restrictions for the bulk of industrial commodities entering world trade.

The story of agriculture for much of this period is, of course, quite different. Both import protection and export disposal programs have been important complements to domestic U.S. price supports. Section

22 of the Agricultural Act of 1935 provided for import quota restrictions on commodities subject to price support. Section 32 provided for the use of customs receipts for disposal of surplus farm commodities. Our export programs increased greatly during the postwar period through Public Law (PL) 480 and expanded subsidy payments. These actions, along with specific commodity legislation to establish import quotas, voluntary agreements, customs administration procedures, overseas procurement requirements, and national security provisions, provide a formidable array of import protection for agriculture if implemented to the full degree.

INTERNATIONAL PROBLEMS AND U.S. TRADE POLICY. The inconsistencies of these two lines of development began to show almost immediately when the United States took international leadership in implementing its drive for liberalized trade. Our efforts led to the general agreement on tariffs and trade and establishment of a set of basic principles for international commercial policy. Among other things, the General Agreement on Tariffs and Trade (GATT) principles provided for—

1. Tariffs as the only acceptable means of protection; no quantitative or other forms of restrictions were allowable;
2. Elimination of direct subsidies including income or price supports that would prejudice international trade relationships;
3. Consultation between countries to avoid injury through unilateral action by individual countries; and
4. Compensation to cover the damages involved if unilaterial action were undertaken that created injury to another country.

Shortly after these principles were established a series of exceptions began to develop. Some of these exceptions were initiated by European countries to protect the balance of payments, to stimulate food production, and in other ways to accelerate postwar recovery. Probably, however, it is correct to say that the real breakdown in effectiveness of GATT in agriculture came with U.S. actions in the late 1940s and early 1950s. In 1948 Congress extended Section 22 import restrictions to make it mandatory for the president of the United States to impose quotas or fees to restrict imports on price support commodities irrespective of preexisting international agreements. In 1951 we insisted that the escape clause be added to the general agreement and if injury were proven to domestic interest as a result of action taken in GATT, our GATT obligations were automatically suspended; we passed legislation requiring quotas or even embargoes on certain dairy products.

These actions built largely around protection for agriculture greatly damaged our bargaining position. We presented a confused picture in the relationship between our principles and our actions. This became particularly important during the Kennedy Round, when one of our major motivations was to achieve a reduction in European Economic Community (EEC) price levels and liberalization of their agricultural import policy. We asserted, possibly somewhat with tongue in cheek, that we wanted inclusion of agriculture in trade negotiations and that we would be willing to discuss our domestic policies as a part of these negotiations. It probably is somewhat fortunate that our hand was not called. Our prior actions such as passing the meat import quota bill at the time negotiations were underway indicated that we probably were not ready to make substantial concessions on our own agricultural protection.

Another philosophical dilemma arose when we argued that the variable levy system of import control was not an acceptable and sanctioned system in GATT. This we did in the face of our own quota controls established through unilateral U.S. action and which were clearly inconsistent with the initial principles of GATT.

These kinds of contradictions are difficult to face up to in international discussions and serve to damage negotiating positions. This burden was with the United States in the background discussions on agricultural trade policy that took place in the Organization of Economic Cooperation and Development (OECD) during the Kennedy Round negotiations, and probably also in Geneva for those who were attempting to negotiate.

Another form of inconsistency in U.S. policy has been brought about by the methods we have used to expand commercial sales. Export subsidies have been used heavily by the United States over time, and despite recent changes in domestic programs on major export commodities, we are still in the export subsidy business. More recently the EEC has taken over the dominant role in subsidizing exports. We complained heavily about this and with some justification. European dumping has a substantial impact on world markets, particularly in dairy products and grain, and their actions are detrimental to our export interests. Yet because we have refused to establish a two-way agricultural trading relationship, particularly by importing their dairy products, there is no direct leverage to deal with it even through anti-dumping regulations.

Another form of contradiction generated by our search for agricultural exports is the action we have taken regarding specialized trading arrangements and access agreements largely in the grain markets.

During the 1950s and early 1960s, the United States held a price umbrella over world grain markets and accumulated large grain stocks. Our initial participation in an international grains arrangement was based primarily on complementing our domestic price supports through establishing international trading prices reasonably consistent with our support levels. There is also evidence that price collusion existed between the United States and Canada on wheat.[3] By definition, price maintenance agreements and price collusion at the national level contradict a policy of free trade.

Following the change in U.S. programs that allowed domestic prices to seek world market levels, another criterion entered the picture. We began a search for market access. We entered into the United Kingdom (U.K.) grains agreement with the apparent belief that an important step had been taken to further the U.S. goal of export expansion. This agreement called for stabilized participation by exporters in the British import market. As it turned out, the British, largely for balance-of-payments reasons, set about to minimize the total size of the British market by expanding domestic production, and it became clear that guaranteed access was not a meaningful concept.

Our search for guaranteed trading arrangements carried over into the Kennedy Round negotiations. The only concrete result was negotiation of the grains arrangement, but with no guaranteed access provisions and a compromise price which seems to have little relationship to an objective of permitting international markets to work or of fulfilling what we seem to view as the need for income protection in agriculture.

Finally, our search for export outlets combined with protection for agriculture has led to a degree of inconsistency in our objective of assisting less developed countries. Overall, encouraging progress has been made within the program in moving from a concept of surplus disposal to one where PL 480 has become a more important tool for economic development. Even if well handled, however, the contradiction between the objectives of this program and the negative effect of our import protection program on items that can be produced cheaper in developing countries is of concern.

Shipments under PL 480, if appropriately handled, can represent a net addition to the capital resources available for development purposes. These would be obtained with little or no expenditure of foreign exchange. Exports, on the other hand, represent a use of resources to exchange commodities which can be produced efficiently for commodities that can be produced more efficiently elsewhere. The net resource gain depends upon the extent to which production efficiency is improved by specialization among countries. In one sense it can be argued that since there is less net resource gain by trade than by transfer of commodities as aid, the less developed countries (LDCs) should be content to push for aid even at the cost of some trade.

The trade-off between trade and aid, however, is not that simple. In part this becomes a question of how LDCs can effectively allocate aid if they are severely restricted on trade. It seems logical to argue that aid should at least in part be allocated to the most efficient industries, that would be expected to enter world markets as exporters. Trade and aid thus are complementary, and for aid to be most effective, trade must exist.

Over time, LDCs will have to rely primarily on exports to pay for their import needs, but our import policies tend to inhibit growth of new export industries. For the most part we do not restrict noncompetitive agricultural products or raw materials, but for commodities that are competitive with American farmers we generally maintain a combination of quotas and tariffs that are significant barriers. More important from the viewpoint of development is the structure of our tariff system. Our tariff rates normally are higher against processed and semiprocessed products. Even small differences in nominal rates can be highly discriminatory when viewed in terms of the effective rate applied to the value added in processing. This kind of tariff structure can be a major force in preventing logical export diversification based on available raw materials, and it inhibits the process of developing efficient patterns of industrialization.

DOMESTIC PROBLEMS AND U.S. TRADE POLICY. An assessment of U.S. agriculture and trade programs would not be complete without some mention of their domestic implications. One key issue is the differential impact of trade policy on consumer and producer interests. Import protection penalizes consumers and they have a right to expect that over time they will not be required to support inefficient industry unless this is clearly justified on some national interest grounds. This is not the case for what remains of protected domestic U.S. agricultural industries.

Another domestic issue centers around the windfall gains and losses created and the effect of protection on income transfer. Choosing quotas as a means of restricting imports creates windfall gains that could be avoided or shifted by tariff protection. Importers buy goods at world market prices and sell in domestic markets at protected prices. The gains from this price differential are private. If import protection were achieved through tariffs, the difference between domestic and foreign value would be collected by government and would represent a consumer tax available for public sector use and not for private use.

Any form of protection raises prices to domestic producers and creates an internal income transfer. This protection can have varying consequences. Depending on production conditions and the level of protection, high levels of income for given individuals can be created. This is certainly true for the large efficient rice producer, the large efficient sugar producer, and some farmers in all protected lines of production. On the other hand, income protection can succeed largely in prepetuating poverty. To some extent this has been true in tobacco, and would probably be the case if import protection were achieved on textiles at the present time.

Finally, there is the question of the effect of protection on output patterns and efficiency of resource use. Price supports for our major agricultural export commodities have been reduced to world market levels and the acreage control provisions in the 1970 act permit regional shifts in production that could help reduce production costs. This will improve internal resource use efficiency and help our competitive position on world markets.

For products on which we do not have a comparative advantage we seem to have retrogressed during the 1960s. We have maintained rigid protection on such items as sugar, peanuts, and rice and have increased protection on beef and manufactured dairy products. Our policy in dairy products has been particularly bad in that it has sought to reverse a desirable adjustment process that was well underway.

In the early 1960s dairy cow numbers were declining, dairy farm size was increasing, and total imports of manufactured products were on the way up. An economically desirable course would have been to permit this kind of adjustment to continue until a market balance between domestic production and imports was reached. All fluid milk and cream sales, which represent approximately 65 percent of total output, would have been retained by American farmers. The primary inroad would have been in certain kinds of cheese and smaller amounts of butter.

If we assume that an equilibrium point was represented by, for example, 15 percent of U.S. dairy consumption being imported, the ratio of fluid milk to manufactured milk products by domestic producers would have increased substantially. Programs to stabilize fluid milk prices would have become of dominant importance in the incomes of American dairy farmers. Rather than permit this adjustment to occur, a reverse course was taken. Severe import quotas were imposed. This action generated one of the more sensitive issues we face in attempting to deal with other countries on restrictions they place on American agricultural exports. Our dairy policy thus has succeeded in reversing an adjustment process that was underway, and at the same time it increased consumer costs and created international ill will.

CONCLUSIONS. It is clear that over time a wide range of inconsistencies has developed in U.S. trade programs. This has resulted from a basic inconsistency in objectives, which have included efforts to liberalize world trade while at the same time providing a measure of protection to prevent serious harm to any domestic industry. In agriculture the inconsistencies are particularly apparent both because of a concentrated effort to expand exports and the maintenance of income protection programs. United States trade policy is now in a state of flux. Protection is being sought by many industries. The question that seems to present itself is whether any kind of consistent trade policy can be generated.

One of the major problems of achieving consistency is that the process of trade policy formulation is politically weighted. Despite the pervasiveness of international trade policy in terms of its effects on groups within an economy, it is not an area of interest to a large number of people. Primarily the formulation of trade policy has been left to government and a limited number of pressure groups who have a direct commercial interest. Because the effect of trade policy on consumers and export industries often is indirect and delayed, these groups tend to be inactive in policy formulation. Pressure arises in those industries seeking protection and is not offset by those who will be damaged by protection. These positions in turn are reflected directly in negotiations between countries. Bargaining becomes a process of trading off special interests. The result to this point has been a laborious process of commodity-by-commodity negotiation which has not succeeded in reducing import barriers on agricultural commodities.

To change this process and achieve progress at least three kinds of concepts should be introduced into trade policy formulation.

1. We must define policy objectives that emphasize national rather than group interest. This means that trade policy should reflect our national foreign policy objectives and such domestic objectives as balance of payments, as well as the composite interest of groups including, among others, consumers, producers of export goods, and producers whose products compete with imports.

   Most individuals would agree that U.S. national interest would best be served by continued progress toward more liberalization of agricultural trade. Policy changes that expand exports create little conflict with group interest, and policies to serve export objectives are not difficult to implement. Since the mid-1960s our agricultural policies have been pretty well adjusted to this end, but even before that there was little domestic political objection to the methods we used for export expansion.

   Our national interest would also be served by increased imports of agricultural products and raw materials both through its impact on consumer prices and raw material costs, and through its effect on less developed countries. Agricultural and other raw material exporters would increase their foreign exchange earnings and thereby make it possible for them to increase imports of items needed for development. But change in our trade policies to serve this kind of national interest is inevitably damaging to the interest of individual producer groups. This leads directly to the second concept that should be introduced into trade policy.

2. We should not expect individual groups to bear the cost of change in trade policy. Adjustments made to serve the national interests should be paid for by society. To do this, compensation and mean-

ingful public assistance are needed as a part of the package in trade negotiations.

The principle of adjustment assistance has broad application both within and outside agriculture. It should come into play if trade barriers are reduced and serious market disruption and injury occur. The Trade Expansion Act provides the basis for assistance in such cases but has been used only sparingly in connection with the Kennedy Round.

Our trade policy could be further improved if the basis for use of adjustment assistance were expanded to industries that for various reasons can no longer compete. The U.S. textile industry is seeking protection because it cannot compete with Japan and other countries whose labor-intensive factor endowment provides a comparative advantage. Economists have long recognized the infant industry concept and accepted it as justification for protection to achieve faster economic growth. We should also recognize that economic development in other countries and basic differences in factor endowment along with the international transfer of technology can shift comparative advantage and create conditions under which industries should contract, or at best be maintained only with continuous protection. Where this is the case and the basic ingredients for survival do not exist, assistance in their demise makes fully as much sense as protection for infant industries.

3. The third concept that should be introduced into improved trade policy is that interaction among governments must be based on a new process that seeks to identify national interest and develop trade policy in this light. Clearly the format of confrontation implicit in GATT has not worked in agriculture or for reducing a wide range of nontariff barriers in nonagricultural industries. The general problem involved in bargaining as a technique for international policy development has recently been stated as follows:

> The logic of the bargaining technique does not run to the public interest; therefore, bargaining is not very effective in reducing an unneeded trade barrier if there is vigorous protest from a domestic interest involved. The rationale of the bargaining program is that the barrier must be reduced for the good of a foreign country; the foreign government will, in turn, reduce one or more of its barriers in order to try to help U.S. exporters. The bargaining format dramatizes a distorted and oversimplified conflict of interest: On the one side, domestic producers keenly conscious of current foreign competition; on the other, a loose alliance of foreign sellers, international traders, and domestic producers vaguely hopeful of expanding foreign markets.
>
> Other considerations, the consumer interest, alternative profitable use of the domestic producing resources, expected market expansion to offset the alleged injury, the effect of the barrier on dynamic competition and growth in the national economy, even the facts proving the alleged danger from foreign competition tend to be neglected in the emotions generated in the bargaining con-

flict. In the moment of negotiation decision, a government will rarely decide to risk injuring a going concern, however undesirably protected. Due deliberation of the general national public interest in the matter, not to mention the world public interest, is hardly to be expected.[4]

John Schnittker has recently expressed the need for a refocusing of negotiation in terms of the need for "a new rationale, constituency and rhetoric."[5] Other agricultural economists have argued that the dilemma in trade policy formulation for agriculture can be overcome only through broadly based international discussion to deal with issues of price support level, import protection, export subsidization, orientation of domestic farm policy, and agreement by individual countries, both exporters and importers, to cooperate in programs of supply adjustments and production reorganization.

How all this is to be brought about and what mechanisms of negotiation can replace the concept of confrontation that has grown up in GATT is not clear. I think, however, that we have had enough experience to recognize that a philosophy of trade-off with commodity-by-commodity negotiation will lead to little progress in agriculture. Achieving progress on any other basis will be difficult, but I see only one alternative to trying, and that is to accede to conditions as they exist or as they develop without meaningful influence by the United States.

NOTES

1. J. E. Meade, "The Theory of International Economic Policy," *Trade and Welfare*, vol. 2 (London: Oxford Univ. Press, 1955).

2. Joe R. Wilkinson, *Politics and Trade Policy* (Washington, D.C.: Public Affairs, 1960).

3. Alex F. McCalla, "A Duopoly Model of World Wheat Pricing," *Journal of Farm Economics*, vol. 48, no. 3, pt. 1, August 1966.

4. Robert B. Schwenger, "The Restructuring of Foreign Trade Negotiations," *Issues and Objectives of the U.S. Foreign Trade Policy, a Compendium of Statements Submitted to the Subcommittee on Foreign Economic Policy* (Washington, D.C.: USGPO, September 22, 1967), p. 79.

5. John A. Schnittker, "New Conditions of Debate on Agricultural Policy," address to the Trade Policy Research Center, London, July 14, 1970.

13

Agricultural and Trade Developments
in the Less Developed Countries

Willard W. Cochrane

Resource ENDOWMENTS of the less developed countries (LDCs) vary tremendously, and as a consequence, their agricultural development processes and trade potentials must differ markedly.

The LDCs fall into two major groups: those for which the pressure of population on land and water resources is great—hence, the land-to-man ratio is low; and those for which the pressure of population on land and water resources is considerably less and land-to-man ratio is relatively high.

The countries of Asia uniformly have a low land-to-man ratio. "Land" in this case is defined as the available cultivated land and potentially arable land; and "man" in this case is the total population of the country or region. As of 1965, the number of acres of cultivated land and potentially arable land per person was 1.5 acres for the continent of Asia.[1] Important increases in agricultural production for the countries of Asia cannot take place through extensive developments. They must occur through intensive developments on the existing cultivated land and the very limited potentially arable land. Increased agricultural production in the LDCs of Asia must occur through improved water control and management, increased application of nonfarm-produced inputs, and transformation of farming operations from a traditional state to a modern, scientific state, all of which operate to increase output per cultivated acre. And this is what is happening over wide reaches of the Asian subcontinent and in limited enclaves in southeast and east Asia. Now we are calling it the *Green Revolution*. This term is perhaps a bad one, since it implies that more is happening over a

Willard W. Cochrane is Professor of Agricultural Economics, University of Minnesota. This chapter benefits and builds on the paper he presented to the President's Commission on International Trade and Investment Policy, titled "Agricultural Aspects of the U.S. Economic Relations with Developing Countries."

wider area than really is the case. But it is important to recognize that the principal components of the Green Revolution—high yielding plant varieties, water, fertilizer, and plant protection—which had their origin in Mexico, are now finding their greatest application in south and east Asia.

The dramatic production developments in Asian agriculture seemed to burst across the developing world in 1967–68, but they had really been in the research and development pipeline for a decade. Now these developments may be broken into three categories:

1. The new dwarf varieties of wheat, in combination with water, fertilizer, and pesticides have enabled farmers adopting the new wheats in Pakistan, India, and a few other countries to double their production of wheat in areas with ready access to water.

2. The new dwarf varieties of rice have been adopted by farmers more slowly than wheat, hence they have had less dramatic impact on total output for several reasons: they are more demanding with regard to water management than the new wheats; for numerous reasons (e.g., lack of water management, disease problems) the yield increases have been less dramatic than for wheat; and consumer acceptance of the new rices has not been good in many cases. Nonetheless, solid and steady gains in research, development, and adoption of the new rice varieties have been made. We can expect continued and significant increases in rice production in the hot, wet regions of the world.

3. A wide variety of production developments are occurring throughout the developing world in such diverse commodity areas as maize, mushrooms, potatoes, grapes, and dairying. These production developments are so varied that it is difficult to find a good term to describe them, but they are based on the spirit of science and modernization sweeping across the agricultural economies of Asia, and they often reflect a spirit of enterprise lacking in the LDCs in the past.

There is no reason to believe that the dramatic production developments in Asian agriculture of the past five years are likely to phase out in the 1970s. On the contrary, continuous breeding programs in rice and continued efforts to improve management of water on paddy fields suggest to me that paddy yields will increase throughout the 1970s, with significant increases occurring in rice production in many Asian countries.

The search for and development of new crops are playing an important role too. Ten years ago potatoes were rarely produced in India; now potatoes are grown widely across northern India in the winter season. Similarly, grapes, apples, maize, and soybeans are being produced more widely in India, and often with spectacular success. These and other crops in conjunction with the high yielding wheats and rices are contributing importantly to increases in aggregate farm output through the practice of multiple cropping.

Lester Brown makes the following important point about the practice of multiple cropping:

> The genetic characteristics of the new varieties—high yields, early maturity, and reduced sensitivity to day-length—are opening new vistas for multiple cropping. Farming around the calendar with two, three, and occasionally even four crops per year is becoming feasible in the tropics and subtropics, wherever water is available for irrigation. Historically tied to the monsoon or rainy season, agriculture in these regions is developing a new rhythm; farmers are beginning to discover the potential for expanding food production during the dry, sunny season. Data from both Indonesia and the Philippines show higher yields in the dry season than in the rainy season for four high-yielding varieties grown at several different sites; dry-season yields were consistently higher, averaging 52 percent above those obtained during the rainy season. The potential of multiple cropping is suggested by the performance of Taiwanese farmers, who expanded the area producing multiple crops from 18 percent in 1946 to 89 percent in 1966. By 1969, they were harvesting an average of two crops per year on all cropland in Taiwan.[2]

From these production developments briefly described by Brown, most LDCs in Asia are experiencing a growth rate in agricultural production of 2.5 percent per year or more. Several have growth rates exceeding 4 percent per year—for example, Thailand and Taiwan.[3] By U.S. or any standards, this is an outstanding record. But the LDCs in Asia are not yet flooding the world market with agricultural surpluses, as are the developed countries of the West. They are not, because in most of those countries the demand for agricultural products is increasing more rapidly than production.

Let us explore this relationship in more detail. In a number of LDCs in Asia, mostly in west Asia, population growth is equal to or exceeds the rate of increase in agricultural production. These countries are growing both in terms of population and agricultural production, but they are not developing economically because the per capita availability of agricultural products is holding constant, or declining. Happily, most LDCs in Asia are experiencing a rate of increase in agricultural production that exceeds population growth; but because of rising incomes and the resultant increase in the per capita demand for agricultural products, the rate of increase in total demand exceeds the rate of increase in production.

Although these countries are making good progress in the development and modernization of their agricultural plants and are having some success in increasing the per capita availability of food supplies, they continue to experience food problems because total demand exceeds supplies, and incomes are extremely unequal—a fourth to a half of the population cannot afford a diet adequate even in calories. India is a case in point. Finally, a few Asian countries are on the brink of a production surplus for food grains (Pakistan, for example), or have achieved such a satisfactory state of overall economic development that they have become important exporters of certain specialty products (mushrooms from Taiwan, for example).

Now we face these questions: As agricultural development continues to occur in the 1970s along the intensification route outlined above, how are the production fruits of that development likely to be distributed? Will more Asian LDCs become intermittent grain exporters as now is the case with Pakistan? Or will some countries follow the Taiwanese example and seek to export high income elasticity agricultural products? Or will most Asian countries look inward and try to improve the economic lot of the masses of people living in extreme poverty in those countries? Or will something else occur?

First, we should recognize that if LDCs in Asia become involved in civil wars and internal strife such as we have witnessed in Cambodia, Laos, Vietnam, and Pakistan over the past decade, those countries are not going to enjoy rapid and sustained agricultural development. In this connection, the Green Revolution could itself lead to social and political revolution in those countries, where the production gains from that production revolution are distributed in a highly inequitable manner. In a sense, this is what has occurred in Pakistan: the agricultural sector of western Pakistan developed in a spectacular fashion, whereas agricultural development in what was East Pakistan lagged badly.

This threat, added to certain other grievances including racial differences, touched off a civil war. We can expect more of this in the LDCs where one region or one social class benefits directly and significantly from the agricultural development process, and other regions or social classes fail to prosper. This kind of uneven development and unequal distribution of the fruits of development could easily choke off and destroy the development process in certain Asian countries over the next decade.

But assuming that the political and social processes support and facilitate the adoption of new and improved production technologies in agriculture and further speed the rate of output increase, how will the surplus product be distributed? Given the existing and physical marketing machinery including transport facilities in these countries, and the need to earn foreign exchange through increased merchandise exports, a powerful tendency exists to move grain surpluses over and above absolute minimum needs into export. Hence, countries like India and Pakistan would become intermittent grain exporters as quickly as possible and to the greatest extent possible in the 1970s.

Countering the drive for commercial grain export is the urgent need to improve the lot of many millions of the poorest of the poor in these countries by increasing their consumption of food. Professors Dandekar and Rath in their path-breaking study of poverty in India estimate, for example, that 40 percent of the rural population and 50 percent of the urban population in India in 1960–61 lived in such poverty that they could not afford to purchase sufficient food to provide them with a diet adequate in calories.[4] And poverty amongst the urban population has deepened and widened since 1960–61, with the extent of poverty holding about constant in the rural population.

If public works programs or special food programs were designed and placed in operation to reach the nearly 50 percent of the Indian population living in poverty, and to raise their consumption of food to a level of adequacy, the prospective grain surpluses of the next several decades would melt like snow on a May day on the dusty plains of northern India.

But public works programs designed to raise the daily incomes of more than 200 million people or special food programs designed to reach that number would be terribly costly and place a huge drain on the treasury of the government of India. India and other Asian countries with great masses living in poverty are likely to move cautiously into such programs. In my judgment, governments of Asian LDCs will nibble on their poverty problems during the coming decade, and take such actions as are required to maintain social tranquility and political stability, but little more. And they will seek wherever possible to move short-run market surpluses of grain into the export market. By such a policy they improve their budget position rather than make necessary the imposition of a sharply progressive income tax.

Asian LDCs are not, however, tied to food grains or to such traditional exports as tea, oil seeds, and hard fibers. Agricultural development in the past two decades has opened up numerous opportunities for Asian LDCs to move into the production and export of nontraditional products.

Thailand, a leading rice exporter for decades, has watched the spread of the Green Revolution with fear and trepidation and has felt its first harsh consequences in the form of a decline in rice export prices of some 25 to 30 percent. Fortunately for Thailand, some farmers, businessmen, and research workers began to experiment with maize production in the early 1950s. The production of maize increased rapidly in the upland areas of Thailand, enabling maize exports to increase by 30 percent per year (compared with a 1.4 percent increase for rice, for example) from the middle 1950s to the middle 1960s. By 1965 maize had become Thailand's fourth largest export commodity.

Thailand discovered a nontraditional agricultural commodity—maize—which it could produce efficiently and for which the foreign demand was increasing rapidly (particularly in Japan), and Thailand has come to enjoy an expanding export trade in maize.

Currently the government of Thailand is attempting to develop a swine industry, which at this infant stage is making modest progress. Promoters of hog production expect first to export live animals to Singapore and Hong Kong, and second to develop a meat packing industry. And there is considerable talk among research workers and economic planners of producing vegetables as a second crop after rice, process some or all these vegetables, and export canned vegetables to markets such as Japan and Hong Kong.

Similarly, Taiwan has deemphasized sugarcane production, held the acreage devoted to rice about constant, and diversified its agriculture. Acreages devoted to vegetables, peanuts, soybeans, tobacco, and fruits have increased importantly in the past two decades. Three nontraditional export commodities have become important foreign exchange earners in recent years: mushrooms, canned asparagus, and plywood. It could be said that Taiwan became the mushroom capital of the world in the 1960s.

True, every developing country cannot turn to mushrooms. But every LDC can look for commodities with a high income elasticity, which it can produce efficiently and then can explore the possibilities of exporting to rapidly developing areas like Japan, Western Europe, and North America. As long as the economies of the developed countries continue to grow, there will be a strong demand for maize and soybeans out of which to produce meat, for meat products themselves, and for specialty items like canned vegetables, fruits, and nuts. The best hope for many an LDC to increase its export earnings from agriculturally related industries in the decades ahead is to turn to the nontraditional commodities with high income elasticities.

In sum, through research and development, increased application of nonfarm purchased inputs, and more intensive farm operations, a revolution in the production of food grains and many other commodities is occurring throughout south and east Asia. Research developments, technologies currently available, and investment plans suggest that this production revolution in agriculture will continue throughout the next decade or two. In this event, a rate of output expansion in agriculture of 3 or 4 percent per year could be the norm.

Whether these rates of output expansion will be achieved in fact will depend upon the success of these countries in achieving internal political and social stability. Assuming sufficient internal peace and tranquility to permit and facilitate the achievement of rates of agricultural output expansion of 3 or 4 percent per year, we can expect the LDCs from Asia to become more active exporters of food grains and a variety of nontraditional agricultural exports (e.g., feed grains, swine, canned fruits). These new exports of wheat and rice will tend to be of low commercial quality, and come onto the market in a rush. Thus, these exports will have a destabilizing influence on the world grain market—perhaps at times a chaotic effect.

Such adverse effects on the world grain market would be reduced, perhaps even eliminated, if the countries involved would make a serious effort to achieve a more equitable distribution of agricultural production gains within their own populations. And we can hope that this will occur; perhaps even help to make it occur. But poverty is so ubiquitous in these countries that extraordinary measures involving significant re-distribution of income will be required to effect a tangible improvement in the lot of the masses living in poverty, including a discrete jump in their food consumption. It could be done. And it may be done to avert political chaos and civil war. But it is doubtful that it will be done with less than violent internal strife. A choice may have to be made between great production gains and exportable surpluses on the one hand, and internal political strife and social upheavals on the other hand, which will choke off the agricultural production developments that are tech-nically possible.

The LDCs of Latin America and Africa are typically high land-to-man ratio countries. The number of acres of cultivated and potentially arable land per person in Latin America is 9.5; the number of acres of cultivated and potentially arable land per person in Africa is 7.1. The LDCs of Latin America are poor and economically backward, but the masses do not suffer grinding poverty as they do in the LDCs of south and east Asia. Further, the LDCs of Latin America and Africa typically have an option open to them that is not open to Asian LDCs, namely, increasing aggregate agricultural output through bringing new land into cultivation. In other words, extensive agricultural development has been and will continue to be for an indefinite period an important, if not the dominant, source of production increases in Latin America and Africa.

It is important for use to recognize that there are extreme differences in the wealth, or income, position of countries falling in this high land-to-man ratio category. For example, the per capita gross domestic product (GDP) for the period 1955–67 for countries in Latin America ranged from $935 per year in Venezuela and $758 per year in Argentina to $176 in Bolivia and $79 in Haiti. The same extreme differences in wealth, or income, position are to be found in Africa. For example, per capita GDP for the period 1955–67 for LDCs in Africa ranged from $1,062 for Libya to $50 for Malawi and $44 for Upper Volta. But there may be a question of whether Argentina is really an LDC; in my opinion it is a developed country suffering from a prolonged period of economic stagnation. And the white settlements in Kenya and Rhodesia and the French in Algeria, with ready access to European capital and technology, certainly placed those countries, at one time at least, in a different posi-tion from that of most LDCs in the same areas (Fig. 13.1).

The LDCs in Latin America and Africa also exhibit a wider range in the average annual growth of agricultural production than do the LDCs of the Far East (see the range in production growth rates in Fig.

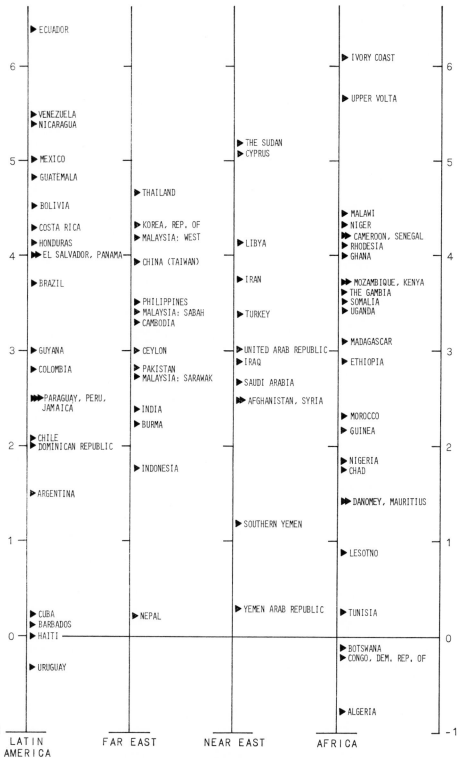

FIG. 13.1. Average annual growth of agricultural production in 75 developing countries, 1952–54 to 1967–69.

13.1).[5] For the period 1952–69 four LDCs in Latin America had growth rates in agricultural production that exceeded 5 percent per year (Ecuador, Venezuela, Nicaragua, and Mexico). And the growth rates of five Latin American countries exceeded that LDC with the highest growth rate in the Far East, Thailand.

At the other end of the scale, four LDCs in Latin America had growth rates in agricultural production of less than 1 percent per year (Cuba, Barbados, Haiti, Uruguay), and Argentina could muster a growth rate in agricultural production of only 1.5 percent per year. Similarly we find the same extreme range in the rate of growth in agricultural production in Africa. Two countries, Ivory Coast and Upper Volta, had growth rates for the period 1952–69 that exceeded 5.5 percent per year; three countries, Algeria, the Congo, and Botswana, had negative growth rates, and Tunisia limped along with a rate of 0.2 percent per year.

Given the fact that most LDCs in this category could increase agricultural output by intensifying farming operations on existing cultivated areas and by bringing new land under cultivation, *why* are some of these countries able to develop their agricultural economies at a fantastically rapid pace, while others fail completely? Obviously there is no easy, general answer to this question of how to speed up development in the lagging LDCs.

But some observations are helpful in thinking about the problem. Most countries that achieved high rates of increase in agricultural production in this high land-to-man ratio category of countries did so through an expansion in their agricultural plants—by bringing new land under cultivation. Brazil, for example, which achieved a rate of increase in agricultural production of 3.7 percent per year over the period 1952–69 did so almost exclusively through extensification. Louis Herrmann writes about Brazil. ". . . Less than 1 percent of the 6 million hectares in the frontier states was in crops in 1960, compared with 10 percent of the 2.5 million hectares in the settled states. It is not surprising, then, that Brazil's agricultural growth from 1947 to 1965 came mainly from increases in cropland."[6]

A few other countries such as Mexico were able to marshal a total development effort involving (1) increased area under crops; (2) increased fixed and working capital invested per acre; (3) new and improved technologies adapted to the area; and (4) a favorable economic climate and stable government. This development package is exceedingly difficult to put together, and only a few LDCs have succeeded in doing so, but when they do, agricultural production soars.

There is another route to successful agricultural development which a few LDCs have discovered; it is to seek out and find a high-income-elasticity agricultural product which complements the agricultural economy of certain developed nations, hence does not encounter formidable import barriers and many be produced efficiently in the LDC in question. Ecuador has found such a commodity in bananas; it has achieved a growth rate in its agricultural production of 6.3 percent per year based primarily on one commodity, bananas. So it can be done, but to borrow a phrase, "It ain't easy."

The LDCs in this category with the poorest production records have ready, almost easy explanations. Almost without exception they have suffered from wars of independence, civil wars, serious internal strife, and highly unstable governments. In this political climate significant and sustained agricultural development was and in some cases continues to be impossible. Countries such as Argentina and Chile, Dahomey, Chad, and Guinea, besides suffering from poor and arbitrary governmental management, have been handicapped by various other factors.

In some cases governmental pricing policies have operated as a disincentive to agricultural production (Argentina being the classic case in point). In more cases, inadequately financed policies, poorly administered policies, or no policies at all have resulted in the failure to develop a necessary transport system, to develop the necessary new and improved technologies adapted to the area, to provide the necessary production inputs (e.g., fertilizer and pesticides), to provide the necessary production credit, to begin to control and efficiently manage water supplies, and on and on. Without these components a modern, productive agriculture cannot be established, even where new land is available to be brought under cultivation. Hence, when and where they are not provided, or are provided in minimal amounts, agricultural development proceeds at a slow pace.

Are forces at work that will operate to reduce the extreme range in rates of growth in agricultural production, and tend to concentrate LDCs from Latin America and Africa in a high level band of, say, from 3 to 5 percent increase per year? I think not. I see no reason to believe that governments in this category of LDCs will be more stable and less arbitrary in the next twenty years than in the last. Revolution, internal strife, and the coming and going of military dictators will be the norm for many, if not most, of these countries for a long time to come, none of which is conducive to economic development.

Improvements in transport, electric power, and water management will come slowly because of the large investment costs involved. The payoff from research and development in the form of new and improved technologies in agriculture, we have learned over and over again, takes time, often a very long time. I would expect that rates of growth in agricultural production, as a general pattern, will continue much as they have in the past. But this in itself does not represent failure. The model countries in this category of LDCs are increasing their total output from agriculture by 2 to 4 percent per year, and as we have already noted, a few exceptional countries are exceeding 5 percent per year.

We should, however, expect some shift in the country pattern of growth rates. I do not believe, for example, that Ecuador can maintain a growth rate of 5.3 percent per year on bananas alone; limits to the size of the market and external competition are likely to place some brakes on this growth rate. On the other hand the sleeping giant, Argentina, must awaken someday and start producing agricultural products more nearly in line with its resource endowments. And Brazil could well be the next country to make it big in terms of total economic development.

In Africa anything can happen. But in the long run Algeria could not be expected to have a negative rate of growth in agriculture production, and Upper Volta to sustain a rate of 5.7 percent per year, however it may have achieved that rate between 1952 and 1969.

Bearing in mind the agricultural development facts and relationships discussed above, what are the agricultural trade prospects for this category of LDCs over the next decade or two? There is no reason to expect any diminution in the rate of increase in the production and export of tropical products from these countries. They have experience with these products and know how to produce them; they have new lands that can be devoted to their production; they need the foreign exchange earnings; and tropical products typically do not encounter prohibitive import restrictions in developed countries.

We can expect this group of countries to continue to expand production of tropical products—probably to the point where total supplies are pressing against world market demand and chronically depressing world prices. Perhaps these countries will have some success in regulating world supplies through international commodity arrangements, as they seem to be having now with respect to coffee, but it would seem doubtful.

In the area of competitive agricultural products—the grains, livestock, oil seeds, and nontropical fruits and vegetables—almost anything may happen to exports from the LDCs of Latin America and Africa. Both Mexico and Brazil, for example, increased their production of feed grains (primarily maize) sufficiently in the 1960s to become exporters of feed grains by the end of the decade. And we should expect feed grains from these two countries to increase further in the 1970s, since both countries have put together a highly successful development package for agriculture. But the world market for feed grains is expected by some to expand so greatly during the decade of the 1970s that exports of feed grains from Mexico and Brazil will be dwarfed by the larger developments.

The authors of the publication *Growth in World Demand for Feed Grains* argue, for example, that—

From a net export position of 5 million tons in 1965, the less developed countries as a group appear destined to become net importers of at least this amount [of feed grain], if present per capita levels of meat consumption are not to be reduced. They would import even larger amounts if expected relationships to income growth hold and no change is made in present production policies in some less developed countries. Exports of some less developed countries (LDC's) are projected to increase, and the United States should continue through 1980 to lead the world in net exports of coarse grain.

Less developed countries are expected to feed their livestock 65 million tons of grain in 1980; central plan countries, 150 million tons; and developed countries, over 300 million tons. These figures imply more than doubling the use of feed grain in less developed countries, 65 percent expansion in central plan countries, and 51 percent growth in developed countries.[7]

I would argue as follows then with regard to the export trade of LDCs from Latin America and Africa in the competitive product category. Some startling developments may occur in certain LDCs in this category, but it is difficult to predict when and where. Such agricultural developments may be large relative to the production capacity of the LDCs in question, and lead to high rates of growth in the production of competitive products, *but such developments and such rates of growth will be small relative to the world demand for the products involved.* With one or two possible exceptions, we would not expect increases in the production and export of competitive products from these LDCs to play an important role in the world trade picture. And if they play an important role, it will be principally in denying the developed countries an increasing role in supplying the market for grains and livestock products in those LDCs, as the demand for meat and animal products increases with increased general economic development.

Two countries in Latin America, Argentina and Brazil, could prove to be the exception to the above generalization. Both these countries have the potential of greatly increasing their domestic production and export of food grains, feed grains, and livestock products. The production potential is there; the potential volume of grain and livestock exports from these countries could significantly influence world trade in these commodities in the 1970s and 1980s. But whether these two countries will formulate the policies and organize their productive resources in a manner that will enable them to realize their potential remains to be seen.

What are the implications of the foregoing developments for the United States?

1. As a direct result of the Green Revolution, PL 480 exports of wheat have been cut just about in half over the past four years.
2. Wheat production developments in the LDCs are likely to reduce PL 480 exports of wheat to a trickle by the end of the 1970s.
3. Wheat production developments in certain LDCs are likely to result in those LDCs becoming intermittent exporters of wheat in the 1970s. Such exports will come onto the market with a rush when

they come, and be of such low commercial quality that they will cause prices to fall sharply when they hit a thin world commercial market.

4. In Asian LDCs, developments in the production of rice have progressed more slowly than in the production of wheat. Nonetheless, there is reason to believe that paddy yields per acre and rice production in the aggregate will increase importantly in the 1970s and 1980s. In this event, we can expect PL 480 shipments of rice to Asian LDCs to wither away in the 1970s.

5. Given the expected increase in the demand for meat, and the feed grains to produce that meat, in the less developed world in the 1970s, it seems improbable that the LDCs in the aggregate will become a net exporter of livestock products and feed grains in the 1970s and 1980s. There is always the possibility, however, that countries such as Argentina and Brazil will produce and export sufficient meats and feed grains to become formidable trading competitors of the United States.

There is a high probability that the loss of export markets for wheat and rice and low, chaotic prices in world markets will force U.S. wheat and rice producers to undergo some significant production adjustments. In the first instance, producers of those commodities may wish to consider further reductions in production through control programs. But in the intermediate run there will be a strong pressure to shift wheat-producing resources into feed grains, and rice-producing resources into soybeans, cotton, feed grains, and vegetable crops.

Through the process of substitution the impact of the loss of export markets for wheat and rice will be transferred through the farm economy. In the long run, lower grain prices generally may force some wheat-producing areas into grass and extensive cow-calf operations. Finally, although not probably, it is possible that American farmers may face stiffer competition in feed grain markets abroad from certain African and Latin American LDCs in the 1970s and 1980s.

The fifteen-year-long period of foreign surplus disposal of food grains seems to be coming to an end, and the competition for commercial export markets for food grains seems certain to become more intense. The feed grain export picture is generally bright, with only a dark cloud or two on the distant horizon.

But it is important for us to recognize that agricultural development in the LDCs will bring new export opportunities to the United States and other industrial nations. Sustained agricultural developments in those countries will require a large and continued inflow of all kinds of agriculturally related capital inputs: electric motors, well tube and water pipe, construction steel, trucks, railway cars, fertilizer, fertilizer factory construction materials, tin plate, copper wire, road building equipment, machine tools, and on and on. As an economically advanced country, the United States has a technical superiority in the production of many of the above products, and it should expect to increase its exports to the LDCs in those high-valued product lines.

This is what development is all about—the adjustment in each country (DC and LDC) wherein resources shift out of low productivity lines and into higher productivity lines. In India this may mean shifting away from single-crop monsoon paddy production to multi-crop production involving high yielding varieties; in the United States this may mean shifting from rice and wheat production into soybean and beef carcass production, or into assembly line housing construction and wood products. In this context, we trade where it is mutually advantageous to do so. Then we adjust some more—in a never ending process that brings both gains and losses, joy and sorrow. But if development is occurring for the countries involved, the real income gains will outweigh the losses.

How will the farmers of the United States, their spokesmen, and concerned government agencies react to the foregoing developments? Without strong and wise leadership they (the farmers and the concerned government agencies) are likely to react in a highly negative way. Wheat and rice farmers will resent the loss of their PL 480 markets, and they will seek to avoid the production adjustments that follow as a consequence.

Given the history of agrarian discontent in the United States and the response of government to it, it is logical to expect that wheat and rice farmers will petition the government for increased income support, temporary production controls, and subsidized export measures designed to expand sales in the international commercial market. It is also possible that farmers will use their political influence to further curtail foreign economic and technical assistance. The wheat and rice farmers hit by the loss of PL 480 markets are likely to cry out "to hell with our downtrodden neighbors."

But strong and wise leadership at the national level should have made itself felt before we reach the special interest panic point. Clearly our national interest in satisfactory development and stable governments in the less developed world transcends the possible adverse repercussions of the Green Revolution on American grain producers.

1. As noted earlier, successful economic development in the less developed world means an expansion in foreign markets for high-valued fabricated products in the United States.
2. Maintenance of stable governments and avoidance of internal strife and civil wars in the LDCs is vital to the international political interests of the United States. Internal strife and civil wars invite political adventuring by third countries and lead to international con-

frontations. It is in the economic and political interests of the United States to assist and support sustained economic development and stable nonaggressive governments in as many LDCs as possible; certainly not to take actions that are intended to weaken them.

What actions, then, should the United States take to assist and reinforce the important agricultural developments, as a part of total economic development, that are underway in the less developed world?

1. The United States must be prepared to make some permanent downward adjustments in the production of wheat and rice—commodities that have lived on foreign surplus disposal for nearly two decades; most certainly it should not succumb to new and more aggressive export subsidy schemes for these commodities.
2. We must not weaken our foreign aid program. On the contrary, our foreign aid program should be expanded in terms of total assistance and be improved in quality. In this connection our aid program might well be concerned with assisting LDCs to use the fruits of the Green Revolution internally to improve food consumption levels in those countries.
3. The United States should take steps to reduce tariff barriers on processed and semiprocessed primary products from the LDCs. The effective tariff rates on processed primary products in almost all developed countries, including the United States, is stifling industrial development in the LDCs. Perhaps the United States could take the initiative in convening a United Nations Conference on Trade and Development (UNCTAD), which would concern itself with lowering the very high effective tariff rates on processed primary products in the developed countries in return for improved conditions and less arbitrary rules governing the investment of private capital in the LDCs.
4. The United States should consider extending trade preferences to LDCs on a general basis, if possible (i.e., in concert with all other developed countries). But if that fails, which seems likely at present, then it should consider extending trade preferences to all nonaligned LDCs on a unilateral basis. The product coverage of such a preference scheme cannot be detailed here, but it must be sufficiently wide to assist in a significant way with the industrial development of the LDCs.

The United States can do much in furthering its self-interest in the less developed world, *if it will.* The four courses of action I have outlined indicate some important things this country could do. Some pain is involved in those courses of action. But if they were pursued vigorously under strong and wise national leadership, they could have some wonderfully beneficial results for the United States and the LDCs.

NOTES

1. Computed from data in *The World Food Problem,* vol. 2, tables 7–9, a report of the President's Science Advisory Committee, the White House, May 1967, p. 434. The ratio of 1.5 for Asia compares with 30.0 for Australia and New Zealand, 6.8 for North America, 9.5 for Latin America, and 7.1 for Africa.

2. Lester R. Brown, *The Social Impact of the Green Revolution* (New York: Carnegie Endowment for International Peace, January 1971), p. 11.

3. "Economic Progress of Agriculture in Developing Nations, 1950–68," *Foreign Agricultural Economic Report,* no. 59 (Washington, D.C.: USDA, ERS, May 1970), p. 11. The production data in this report differs in some degree from production data presented in *The State of Food and Agriculture, 1970* (Rome: FAO, 1970). In the FAO report, for example, production increases for Taiwan fall to 3.9 percent per year, but the central point is not changed.

4. *Poverty in India,* Indian School of Political Economy, Poona, January 1971. Available through the Ford Foundation, New Delhi, India.

5. This figure is taken from *The State of Food and Agriculture, 1970* (Rome: FAO, 1970), p. 129.

6. "Economic Progress in Agriculture in Developing Nations, 1950–68," *Foreign Agricultural Economic Report,* no. 59 (Washington, D.C.: USDA, ERS, May 1970), p. 126.

7. Donald W. Regier and O. Halbert Goolsby, "Growth in World Demand for Feed Grains," *Foreign Agricultural Economic Report,* no. 63 (Washington, D.C.: USDA, ERS, July 1970), pp. x, xi.

14

Exports of U.S. Capital and
Technology and International Political Conflicts

Kenneth E. Ogren

S CORES of articles as well as numerous books have been and are being written on the subject of the U.S.-based multinational firm, which is the major vehicle for exports of U.S. capital and technology. The ever increasing mobility of capital and technology is propelling the world, and especially the more highly industrialized countries, into a more interdependent economic world. How can policies of the United States and other countries be framed within their own needs, aspirations, and goals and still be consistent with external forces to an increasing degree beyond their control?

MULTINATIONAL CORPORATIONS IN A NATIONALISTIC WORLD. The multinational enterprise is by no means the only channel for the export of U.S. capital and technology. Foreign producers often can (and do) obtain access to U.S. technology through licensing arrangements with U.S. firms or through direct purchase of U.S. capital goods. They can obtain funds from the U.S. economy, either directly through loans and grants or indirectly through U.S.-financed international agencies.[1] These various means are all used but the U.S.-based multinational enterprise is the most important single source of transfers of U.S. capital and technology through direct foreign investment and establishment of foreign subsidiaries.

American private investments abroad include two broad types— *direct,* in which a business is controlled from abroad, and *portfolio,* in

KENNETH E. OGREN is Deputy Assistant Administrator, Commodity Programs, Foreign Agricultural Service, United States Department of Agriculture, and formerly Staff Economist, President's Commission on International Trade and Investment Policy. The author is indebted for helpful comments and suggestions on the first draft of this chapter to Scott Pearson, a colleague on the Commission staff who was on leave from the Food Research Institute, Stanford University.

which foreigners hold debt claims or equity interest (stock) in a business, but are not involved in management. Direct foreign investment is the only one treated in this chapter. It is not only the more important in total dollars and in economic impact but it is a reason for political tensions in the United States and in foreign countries.

THE FACTS BEHIND THE TENSIONS. What are the facts and statistics on this phenomenon? Here lies the basis of many problems and lack of agreement on the implications. No consistent set of statistics with a common set of definitions exists, even with respect to what companies should be classified as multinational.

Several things are clear, however. Production by U.S.-owned foreign affiliates exceeds by several times the volume of U.S. exports. The volume of total world production that comes from foreign-financed sources is growing at a faster rate than total production. World exports are also growing faster than total production but more slowly than international production, and international trade in goods is likely to consist more and more of goods produced by multinational companies.

It is estimated that at least 25 percent of U.S. exports are now intraenterprise transactions between U.S.-based multinationals and their subsidiaries. Another 25 percent of U.S. exports may be between U.S.-based multinationals and firms in foreign countries with whom they have license, patent, or other joint venture affiliations.[2]

United States direct investment abroad more than doubled in the 1960s, increasing from $30 billion to $71 billion (Table 14.1). But even more significant was the increase in manufacturing investments, which tripled during the decade—thereby increasing from 30 percent of total direct investments to over 40 percent. Foreign investments in natural resources such as petroleum and mining are a declining part of the total and are growing at a more modest rate.

In the manufacturing area the multinational firm can exercise its greatest flexibility and mobility and behave more like a supranational enterprise. Furthermore, the investments of U.S. companies abroad in natural resources are generally not competitive with domestic output. Direct investments in manufacturing, therefore, arouse the greater apprehensions on the part of U.S. interest groups and on the part of foreign host governments to U.S.-based company affiliates.

Another relevant part of the statistical picture is the changing geographical distribution of direct investments (Table 14.1). Overall, about 30 percent of the total is now in Canada and another 30 percent in Europe. The pattern is different with respect to both kind of activity and trends. At the beginning of the 1960s almost two-thirds of all U.S. direct foreign investment was in the western hemisphere; by the end of the decade this proportion had dropped to slightly less than half. The big increase was in Europe, and especially in manufacturing. The

TABLE 14.1. Direct Investments Abroad, by Major Areas, 1959 and 1969 (Book Value at Year-end)

Geographical Area and Year	Type of Activity			Total
	Manufacturing	Petroleum and mining	Other*	
		($ bil)		
Europe				
1959	2.9	1.5	0.9	5.3
1969	12.2	4.9	4.5	21.6
Canada				
1959	4.6	3.5	2.2	10.3
1969	9.4	7.1	4.6	21.1
Japan				
1959†	0.1	0.1	...‡	0.2
1969	0.6	0.5	0.1	1.2
Latin America				
1959	1.4	4.2	2.6	8.2
1969	4.4	5.6	3.8	13.8
Other areas				
1959	0.7	3.9	1.2	5.8
1969	2.8	7.5	2.8	13.1
Total				
1959	9.7	13.2	6.9	29.8
1969	29.4	25.6	15.8	70.8

SOURCES: *Survey of Current Business,* October 1970; *Statistical Abstract of the United States,* 1961.
  * Includes public utilities, transportation, trade, and other industries.
  † Estimated on basis of data for 1960.
  ‡ Less than 50 million.

relative importance of the less developed countries (LDCs) as places for investments by U.S. multinationals has declined with the increased importance of investments in manufacturing activities in Europe.

Japan is the anomaly in this picture. It is the fastest growing industrial country; it now has the second largest gross national product (GNP) in the free world. More than 10 percent of our trade is with Japan—and of course, agriculturally it is number one and the fastest growing. But foreign direct investment in Japan is a minuscule 1.4 percent of the U.S. total (Table 14.1). This is not an accident but a result of deliberate Japanese policy to restrict foreign investment. The Japanese, however, have not been without the benefits of American based and developed technologies; they have obtained it through means other than U.S. direct investment, such as licensing arrangements.

The statistics in Table 14.1 give no breakdown on what proportion of investments is related to production of agricultural goods. While likely a small part of the total, there are several cases of concern to certain U.S. agricultural producing groups. Mexico, for example, has increased sharply its exports of fresh tomatoes to U.S. markets. Some

U.S. capital, skills, and techniques in tomato production have moved to Mexico although no specific statistics are available to measure the exact involvement of U.S. capital and management. Portugal has captured an increasing share of the U.S.-processed tomato market with the establishment of modernized tomato production made possible by foreign capital and know-how.[3] Likewise, with the importation of capital and know-how, Taiwan has become a strong competitor for the U.S. producer in our domestic markets for mushrooms.

SOURCES OF TENSIONS IN THE UNITED STATES AND ABROAD. Capital is mobile and investments can be moved with relative ease. The labor resource in production is relatively immobile. Herein lies an important source of disenchantment of American labor with the liberal trading policies generally followed by the United States in recent decades. Their views are summarized in a Statement of International Trade and Investment by the AFL-CIO Executive Council, Bel Harbour, Florida, February 19, 1971.

In labor's view, "jobs and employment opportunities have been exported . . . U.S. policies that were designed for the world of the 1930s and 1940s have become outmoded. They now contribute to undermining the U.S. economy at home and abroad. . . . The United States government must now make economic conditions at home a starting point for U.S. policy and posture in international economic relations. Policies should be based on the premise that trade is a complex network of international relationships and measures are needed to deal with the foreign investments of U.S. companies and banks."[4]

Among the policy actions called for by this council were government measures "to stop helping and subsidizing U.S. companies in setting up and operating foreign subsidiaries" and "to supervise and curb the substantial outflows of American capital for the investments of U.S. companies in foreign operations." These actions and others (including quantitative restraints on imports to the United States) were urged on Congress and the administration by this same council in a statement of May 13, 1971.[5]

This mobility factor is also a source of tension among host governments to U.S.-based multinational enterprises. If the French government, for example, is hostile to the interests of a potential U.S. investing firm, this firm may choose to invest in another European Economic Community (EEC) country and thus compete with a French-owned and -based firm for the markets of the community as effectively as if it were located in France.

The initial decision of plant location is only a part of the increased mobility and flexibility of the decision making of the multinational firm. Once established with subsidiaries in several countries, the multinational firm can shift the rates of expansion among its affiliates, change product mixes, alter sources of supply, or even phase out of a market without going out of business. More and more decisions can be centralized in the parent company, including the location of different stages of manufacturing parts for and assembly of the final product. For example, the director of research of the AFL-CIO in a paper prepared for the Williams Commission stated that "Ford's Pinto has been heralded as the U.S. answer to imported small cars. But major parts of the Pinto are imported from England and Germany, and some of the Pintos sold in the United States may be assembled in Canada."[6]

Pricing decisions can be centralized not only in intraenterprise sales but also for retail and export sales. Research and development programs, financial management, and long-range planning can be under the prime control of the U.S.-based parent company. All these factors add to the bargaining strength of the multinational enterprise when it confronts the host government.

The multinational firm is often viewed as a challenge to national sovereignty. Many countries have adopted a type of capitalism through which the government plays a significant role in guiding the development of the economy in certain directions. This type of capitalism may involve the encouragement of certain key industries that are considered vital to national defense and/or prestige. Government leaders fear that if they allow U.S.-based firms to take a dominant role in these industries, their countries will become too technologically dependent on U.S.-owned affiliates. The technological advancement, size, and efficiency of U.S.-based enterprises together with the availability of funds for scientific research sponsored by the U.S. government is the major source of concern emphasized by the French journalist-politician Jean-Jacques Servan-Schreiber in his well-known book "le Defi Americain."[7]

In no foreign country is U.S. capital as pervasive as in Canada. The Canadians generally welcome the economic benefits to their economy from the infusion of U.S. technology and management into their country. But many worry about the dependent position in which this places their economy on the fortunes of the U.S. economy, and they fear the increasing political dependence on the United States that this may bring. (During his trip to the Soviet Union in May 1971, Canadian Prime Minister Trudeau stated that his visit was motivated by concern that the "over-powering presence" of the United States posed dangers "to our national identity from a cultural, economic, and perhaps even military point of view.")[8]

As noted earlier, there is an insignificant amount of U.S. direct investment in Japan, which also leads to political tensions in our foreign economic relations with that country. If the Japanese refuse to allow us to invest in their expanding economy and thus foreclose opportunities for gains to our stockholders, say some U.S. business executives, why should the United States allow unrestricted entry to Japanese products? Labor representatives, however, voice a different point of view. They would like to shut off (or at least slow down) Japanese access to U.S.-developed technology whatever the means of transfer.

Another aspect of tensions is the controls that the U.S. government exercises or attempts to exercise with respect to multinational firms or plants with U.S. parent companies.

In the 1960s, because of its balance-of-payments concerns, the U.S. government imposed a series of controls on direct foreign investments. National controls of international movements of capital are by no means unique to the United States—or to the 1960s. But the potential impact of these controls is much greater in today's highly interdependent economic world and especially when imposed by the country which is the major source of international investment capital.

The United States has long had the authority to prevent private transactions with "enemy countries." Many conflicts have arisen in recent years, especially with Canada and France, when controls by other governments differ from ours and when the U.S. government attempted to extend this control to foreign affiliates or licensees of the multinational enterprise.

Antitrust extraterritoriality is another source of tensions—in applying U.S. antitrust laws to operations of foreign-owned affiliates in the United States as well as to those of U.S.-based affiliates in foreign countries. Here is an example of a different philosophy towards competition. While U.S. law is founded on the philosophy that competition is a per se good, in European law concern is more directed on misuse of a dominant position, not the absence of competition per se. In fact, Europeans generally believe that competition often leads to undesirable results.

PERSPECTIVES FROM THE WILLIAMS COMMISSION: OPPOSING VIEWPOINTS. The Presidential Trade and Investment Policy, referred to as the Williams Commission in this chapter,[9] completed in June 1971 its year-long task of charting a suggested course for U.S. foreign trade and investment policies for the 1970s. Its assignment was to "produce a set of recommendations for future policy which will take full account of the great changes that have taken place on the world economic scene since the end of World War II."

Among the principal issues included in the charter of this commission was "the rapid expansion of the role of the multinational firm, which has greatly increased the mobility of productive resources across national frontiers."[10]

In the course of its deliberations, the Williams Commission heard views expressed by experts from U.S. academic, government, and business circles and from foreign countries and international organizations. It became clear early in the commission's study that the stepped-up pace of exports of U.S. capital, skills, and technology has introduced new issues and new sources of political tensions both at home and abroad.

The commission was in general agreement on the nature and impact of much that is happening. Capital, technology, and management skills do flow more easily and more rapidly across international borders than ever before. In direction, the flow is largely outward from U.S. shores, but it is by no means a one-way flow. The multinational firm, and especially the U.S.-based company, has become a major vehicle for accelerating these exports of U.S. capital and technology.

A consensus emerged from commission discussions that the mobility of technology and management more than likely will accelerate in the 1970s. Investments in manufacturing subsidiaries will continue to increase, as they did in the 1960s, as a proportion of total U.S. foreign investment. And in many LDCs, manufacturing will become of greater importance in their output of goods.

The commission generally agreed that this stepped-up flow of U.S. capital and technology has promoted to an important degree a growing interdependent economic community, especially among the more industrialized countries of the free world—the United States, Canada, Western Europe, and Japan. There was a general (but not unanimous) consensus among the various U.S. and international experts that this increased mobility of some productive resources contributes to a more efficient use of the world's goods and hence greater global welfare when measured in economic terms. But there was also a general consensus that it is difficult to identify the distribution of these benefits among various interest groups at home and abroad. As stated by Raymond Vernon:

> . . . who shares [in these benefits] and how much is a little more obscure. Stockholders probably gain something . . . ; management almost certainly does; the economy of the host country almost certainly does, as well. Labor in the United States, on the other hand, must count on getting its benefits by a relatively indirect route; from the stimulus that goes with the increased prosperity of the trading partners of the United States; and from the stimulus that derives through shifts in the comparative advantage of the United States, leading to higher grade jobs.[11]

The Williams Commission in its report concluded "that in most cases international investment benefits both the United States and other countries. It increases the global mobility of resources, thereby improving overall economic efficiency throughout the world. The benefits for the United States include contributions to overall productivity, stimulation of exports and substantial, growing return flows of income." But, the report warns that "These benefits are impaired or induced by special factors." Therefore, the commission recommends: (1) neutral tax systems that provide neither an incentive nor deterrent to foreign over domestic investment; (2) lowering trade barriers to reduce incentives to invest abroad; and (3) phasing out U.S. balance-of-payments controls on direct investment.

With respect to the U.S. consumer it was argued that he "reaps real benefits directly and indirectly from lower cost products, increased research and development, and the improved access to raw materials which may accompany foreign direct investment."

The commission in its report acknowledged the fears among "many individuals and organizations" that U.S. direct investment in foreign manufacturing causes our domestic economy serious losses of production, jobs, and exports. But the commission stated "that freedom of U.S. enterprises to establish foreign facilities should be maintained even if it is occasionally associated with shifts in production and jobs," stating, "In most cases, if American firms had not invested abroad, foreign firms would have, and U.S. jobs and exports would have been lost in any event, albeit with a lag." Further, "To attempt to control foreign investment is both undesirable and ineffective. It is undesirable because the United States would fail to take full advantage of its technological potential; and more U.S. workers would tend to be employed in lower paying jobs, causing relative losses of income to the present and future generations."[12]

The two commissioners from organized labor, however, filed a minority report in which they took sharp exception to much of the commission's report. In their view, "the report fails to deal realistically with the choices before the nation and thereby fails to present a series of realistic proposals for a U.S. Government policy to meet the nation's needs in international trade and investment."

This minority report concludes:

Sharply rising foreign investments of U.S. companies—as well as advances in transportation and communications and the increase in patent and license arrangements with firms in other countries—have caused the rapid transfer of American technology, production and enlargement to foreign operations. . . . The impact of managed national economies in other industrial nations, the internationalization of technology and the emergence of the multinational corporations and the international banks have made obsolete old theories of free trade and protection.[13]

Their minority report calls for immediate and specific recommendations to safeguard the jobs of American workers and the well-being of the American economy. Those related to exports of capital and technology include: (1) new tax measures for global runaways (the multinational firms) to eliminate incentives for foreign investment; (2) the curbing, supervision, and regulation of capital outflows by the U.S. government; (3) similar controls over export of U.S. technology; and (4) the U.S. government pressure for adoption of international fair labor standards.

Another far-reaching recommendation in the minority report is that "Quotas are necessary as a matter of U.S. policy to maintain a productive and varied U.S. economy. Because of the swift changes in imports, quotas by product and component are needed."

POLICY IMPLICATIONS FOR U.S. AGRICULTURE. The first section of this chapter reviewed some of the international tensions that accompany the increasing mobility of U.S. capital and technology. In the second section I used the opposing viewpoints represented in the report of the Williams Commission to illustrate the conflicts among U.S. political groups that this mobility has brought to the determination of U.S. international economic policy for the 1970s.

Several chapters in this book have emphasized the critical importance of agricultural trade to the income of U.S. agriculture. As pointed out in the report of the Williams Commission, the United States is endowed with plentiful good land and highly efficient technology and organization and has a productive capacity far in excess of its domestic needs. "Only on the basis of large and growing exports can we [the U.S.] use our resources efficiently and thereby exploit our comparative advantages in agriculture." The cornerstone of the commission's recommendation on agricultural trade policy is "that the United States actively seek policies worldwide that will promote a more rational use of the world's agricultural resources."[14]

This goal is not an easy one to achieve or even move toward in a world of highly protected agricultures; domestic and international political conflicts on issues such as the role and benefits of the multinational firms will make the goal that much more difficult to attain. It is essential that U.S. agricultural interests be aware of the policy conflicts that surround the increased mobility of capital, management, and technology, and if possible, reach judgments on the issues implicit in these conflicts.

THE "REAL" ISSUES. What are the "real" issues? As is so often the case, the real or fundamental issues are often obfuscated by the rhetoric of opposing factions.

One set of issues includes the economic vs. the political effects of the increased mobility of U.S. capital and technology. What are the consequences on the growth and development of the economies of the United States and other countries? If the economic benefits are in the aggregate beneficial to the U.S. economy, there is still the question of the distribution of any economic benefits among the factors of production. Who shares in the gains—management and the owners of capital, stockholders, and/or U.S. labor? (Similar questions can of course be raised with respect to owners of productive factors in foreign countries.)

Whatever the answers are to the economic questions, the political questions cannot be ignored. If nations are unwilling to surrender areas of sovereignty to the multinational firm or join with other nations in exercising joint control over the multinational firm, then potential economic benefits arising from the multinational firm may in part be prescribed by political factors. Economic and political factors are likely to be so highly interdependent that separation of these factors will be extremely difficult.

Another set of issues covers the short-term vs. the longer-term effects of increased mobility of U.S. capital and technology. United States labor leaders believe that investment of U.S. capital abroad loses jobs for U.S. labor now and also in the future; others argue (as did the majority of the Williams Commission) that the answer, at least in the longer run, is different. They say that foreign investments in the electronics industry, for example, are essential if U.S.-owned firms are to maintain a share of the growing foreign markets for the products of this industry. Further, some components or electronic parts likely will still be manufactured in U.S. plants for the U.S.-owned foreign subsidiaries. Also the U.S. multinationals will maintain a larger research base in the United States to develop high-technology products for production in U.S. plants (with above average wage rates) than would be true if the U.S. electronics firms were prevented from establishing production facilities in foreign countries.

A third set of issues relates to the basic economic assumptions for devising rules under which international trade and investment should be conducted. One view can be stated as the conventional view of economic theory as represented by "classical" economists such as Ricardo and Adam Smith who expounded the theory of comparative advantage based on an international division of labor. In this view controls on trade and capital flows should be minimized. This view is the one generally taken by the multinational executives as well as the academics represented on the Williams Commission. Others argue that the realities of managed national economies have changed these underlying premises.

For example, a recent congressional staff report states that the theory of comparative advantage breaks down because labor is not mobile internationally, markets are not free from government interference, and exchange rates are relatively fixed. Large firms (but not small firms) can often adjust to import competition because of the mobility of capital and management.[15]

The present state of knowledge does not give satisfactory answers to these issues. On this conclusion, there is some measure of agreement. In their minority viewpoint the Labor commissioners stated that "Federal standards of reporting by U.S.-based firms of their international accounting is needed." In its report, the commission majority acknowledged that no sound statistical base exists to permit firm conclusions to the "important question" of whether direct investment abroad in manufacturing causes serious losses of U.S. production, jobs, and exports. And therefore "we strongly recommend increased efforts to gather and analyze such information." In fact, one of the commission majority in a supplementary statement pointed out that the commission does not —and indeed could not—support with convincing evidence their conclusion that the rapid growth of U.S. foreign direct investment benefits rather than burdens the U.S. domestic economy.[16]

Indeed, Raymond Vernon in one of his two papers presented to the Williams Commission stated that—

There are no economic models as yet sufficiently subtle and dynamic to capture the medium term and long term consequences of creating an overseas subsidiary. In the end the decision on whether to support or retard this kind of development must be made by what amounts to an intuitive leap.[17]

THE ISSUES AND U.S. AGRICULTURE. As can be seen from the preceding discussion, a familiar dilemma is posed. We know that adequate statistical evidence and economic analyses are not available for determining the "right" policy decisions. So "intuitive leaps" may continue to be necessary although it is surely in the national interest to improve the state of knowledge on the consequences of increased mobility of U.S. capital and technology.

United States agriculture is of course not a homogeneous sector within the economy. The mix of land, labor, and other productive factors varies by both product and geographical area. Any conclusions for U.S. agriculture as a whole may well not apply for individual farmers, products, or areas.

The increased mobility of factors of production such as capital, technology, and know-how has limitations in application to production of agricultural products. For example, we grow soybeans and feed grains and export large quantities because that valuable piece of real estate called the Corn Belt lies within our borders, and we don't grow bananas because we don't have the required tropical climatic conditions. These soil and climatic resources are not mobile (at least not yet) even though the technology, know-how, and capital required for growing soybeans and bananas could be quite mobile.

It would appear that in those cases where U.S. agriculture has an underlying comparative advantage (such as soybeans, feed grains, and other crops) the increased world mobility of productive factors would be beneficial to U.S. agricultural interests—at least no direct harmful consequences appear likely. But some so-called agricultural production requires little if any land base. For example, consider a manufactured product such as broiler meat. In the 1950s the United States pioneered in the development of a highly efficient production-marketing system that resulted in marked gains in efficiency, a higher quality and more available product, and an expansion of consumption and production.

Other countries have now developed similar factory-type production of broiler meat. The greater the mobility of the new technology and know-how, the more short-lived is the likely advantage to the U.S. broiler producer from added markets created overseas as a result of these developments.

Domestic agricultural and trade policies no doubt accelerated factory-type production of broiler meat in some countries, but the transfer of technology was almost sure to occur. It is interesting to note the successive increases and declines in U.S. exports to West Germany of first broilers, then turkeys, and later processed poultry products as our poultry production and processing technology passed through various stages.

On the other hand, expansion of broiler production in foreign countries could in the longer run (although not necessarily) expand the markets for U.S. producers of the feed ingredients for which the U.S. has a more enduring comparative advantage.

Measurement of *direct* economic consequences to various groups of U.S. agricultural producers from increased mobility of capital and technology in the longer run as well as now is, if anything, likely to be a complex matter. One conclusion seems certain, however. For all farmers, both crop and livestock, greater mobility of productive factors means greater pressures for change in the nature and composition of their foreign markets and in their competitive position compared with foreign producers. In short, more rapid economic adjustments.

The *indirect* consequences of increasing U.S. exports of capital and technology may be the more significant ones for U.S. agriculture. In this respect, I refer mainly to political factors.

If the increased apprehensions among U.S. interest groups such as organized labor lead to political pressures and enactment of more restrictive trade and investment policies, then I would conclude that there would be harmful consequences for specific agricultural producers and indirectly for agriculture as a whole. Agricultural trade policies cannot be separated from trade and investment policies for the nonagricultural economy.

Our trade flows in agricultural goods are three-cornered, as pointed out in earlier chapters of this book. Our major customers are not major suppliers of our agricultural imports. If restrictive trade policies on industrial goods in the United States lead to retaliation by major trading partners such as the EEC, then our agricultural products are a likely target. Soybeans are a prime example; they enter the community duty-free and are a competitor for the increasing grain production in the community which has been stimulated by high price supports and highly protective variable import levies.

Trade Policy Solutions for the Future. During the 1960s international trade negotiations such as the Dillon Round and the Kennedy

Round achieved little in the way of liberalization of agricultural trade policies. The barrier to progress lay in domestic agricultural programs, especially high price supports which stimulated major expansions of uneconomic production in many industrialized countries. These price supports were determined with too little regard to market changes or to changes in agriculture itself: rapid technological progress, increases in labor production, and sharp reductions in the number of farms and farm workers required to produce the needed food and fiber. Instead of finding solutions for the economic adjustments required, countries increasingly curtailed foreign access to their home markets, and disposed of surpluses by export subsidization. These actions raised prices to consumers and restricted markets for farmers in the United States and other countries.

Now, at the beginning of the 1970s, domestic economic adjustments are pressing on such U.S. industries as textiles, shoes, and steel, in part caused by increased import competition for these industries. As in agriculture, protective measures are being sought to isolate domestic policies from international trade policies. As in the case of protective measures for agriculture, they would raise prices to consumers and in their indirect consequences restrict markets for farmers, as illustrated in the soybeans example referred to earlier.

In the Trade Expansion Act of 1962 an attempt was made to link the process of domestic adjustment and competition from imports. Adjustment assistance to workers who lost jobs because of import competition was intended to assist them in transition to new jobs through allowances covering a limited period of retraining or relocation, and through direct assistance in meeting costs of retraining or relocation. Provisions were also included to assist firms injured by import competition. These programs proved to be ineffective because of overly restrictive criteria for eligibility, time-consuming procedures, delays in processing petitions for assistance, and too little emphasis on anticipating the need for adjustment.

It is easier to suggest the directions that policy solutions for the future must take than to outline the specific content of the solutions. My principal premise is that social, economic, and political adjustments to change cannot be divided into domestic and international segments that can be considered separate and independent policy issues. The United States and other advanced industrial countries in their international negotiations on trade, investment, and monetary issues must find ways to successfully include the relevant domestic policy issues.

For this approach to be successful, domestic adjustment programs must be devised that are accepted as fair and equitable to those most directly concerned and affected by the need for adjustment, and at the same time be acceptable as a basis in international negotiations without preventing accrual of the benefits of technological progress and economic growth associated with this change. No firm or individual (or for that matter, country) should bear a disproportionate share of the costs associated with change and economic progress.

I accept as a basic assumption that pressures will continue to mount for increased interdependence of national economics, both economically and politically. Whatever policy actions may be taken regarding the curbing and supervision of the activities of international firms, it is difficult to foresee any other result if technology continues its rapid pace of development along with continued expansion in communications, transportation, travel, and the interchange of ideas. The pace of modernization and economic growth may be speeded up or slowed down by national policies but not the direction unless there should be a general outbreak of war or worldwide depression.

In this context, I also accept as a basic assumption (or intuitive leap), that the increasing mobility of capital and technology in general enhances economic growth and brings benefits to all countries. To match this mobility, we need programs to enhance the quality and mobility of all productive resources including labor. This is the foundation of any successful adjustment program. The inadequate adjustment assistance programs of the 1960s need to be strengthened so they will anticipate the need for adjustment, for example, providing retraining before rather than after the worker has lost his job.

Integrated development programs are needed for regions to combine their national resources with the available human resources and institutions so that adjustments can be made to changing markets, demands, and input-output relationships without forcing undesirable social changes. The Williams Commission recommended "an industrial and manpower policy which would coordinate and augment programs for anticipating and assisting adjustments to economic change arising from international trade and investment."[18]

To be successful, however, it would appear that a national industrial policy should not be limited only to assisting adjustments to economic change that can be directly attributed to that arising from international trade and investment.

Critics of U.S. agricultural policy have long maintained that more attention should be given to the human resource. Price policies have not met the economic and social needs of those rural people who cannot earn adequate incomes in farming. As stated by the National Advisory Commission on Food and Fiber "the most important (and most neglected) aspect of policy for agricultural adjustment is the task of finding better opportunities for those whose economic prospects are limited by the onset of technology."[19]

A challenge for the 1970s is for U.S. agriculture and nonagricultural interest groups to work together to find better opportunities for those whose economic prospects are altered by the consequences of increasing mobility of capital and technology in an interdependent world.

NOTES

1. R. Vernon, "The Economic Consequences of U.S. Foreign Direct Investment," in Williams Commission, *United States International Economic Policy in an Interdependent World,* 2 vols., vol. 1 (Washington, D.C.: USGPO, July 1971).

2. Nat Goldfinger, "A Labor View of Foreign Investment and Trade Issues," *United States International Economic Policy,* vol. 1.

3. *Portugal's Tomato Processing Industry* (Washington, D.C.: USDA, FAS M-196, January 1968).

4. Jack N. Behrman, *National Interests and the Multinational Enterprise* (Englewood Cliffs, N.J.: Prentice-Hall, 1970).

5. *New York Times,* May 13, 1971.

6. Goldfinger.

7. Jean-Jacques Servan-Schreiber, *The American Challenge* (New York: Atheneum, 1968).

8. Pierre Trudeau, "Trudeau Seeks Soviet Ties to Counter U.S. Influence," *Washington Post,* May 5, 1971.

9. Williams Commission, *United States International Economic Policy.*

10. Press release, Commission on International Trade and Investment Policy (Washington, D.C.: Office of the White House Press Secretary, May 21, 1970).

11. Vernon.

12. Summary, Chap. 8, "Investment and Production on a Global Scale; Import on U.S. Economy," *United States International Economic Policy.*

13. "Minority Statement of I. W. Abel and Floyd E. Smith," Annex 2, *United States International Economic Policy.*

14. Summary chap. 7, "Agriculture: The Need for a New Approach," *United States International Economic Policy.*

15. *Foreign Trade: A Survey of Current Issues to be Studied by the Subcommittee of International Trade of the Committee on Finance, United States Senate* (Washington, D.C.: USGPO, 1971), p. 2.

16. William R. Pearce, "Statements and Dissents of Individual Commissioners," *United States International Economic Policy,* no. 3 in Annex 1.

17. Vernon.

18. "Governmental Responses to Competition from Imports," *United States International Economic Policy,* chap. 3.

19. *Food and Fiber for the Future,* report of the National Advisory Commission on Food and Fiber (Washington, D.C.: USGPO, 1967), p. 115.

INDEX